WORKING WITH DEAF PEOPLE

ABOUT THE AUTHOR

Susan Foster obtained her Ph.D. in 1983 from Syracuse University in the area of special education. Since 1984, she has worked as a Research Associate in the Center for Postsecondary Career Studies in Deafness at Rochester Institute of Technology's National Technical Institute for the Deaf. Using qualitative research methods, Dr. Foster has studied topics related to the educational and occupational attainments of deaf people. She has numerous publications on these topics, including a recently completed book entitled *Deaf Students in Postsecondary Education* (1992, co-edited with Gerard Walter).

WORKING WITH DEAF PEOPLE

Accessibility and Accommodation in the Workplace

By

SUSAN B. FOSTER, PH.D.

Rochester Institute of Technology
National Technical Institute for the Deaf
Center for Postsecondary Career Studies in Deafness

CHARLES C THOMAS • PUBLISHER
Springfield • Illinois • U.S.A.

Published and Distributed Throughout the World by

CHARLES C THOMAS • PUBLISHER
2600 South First Street
Springfield, Illinois 62794-9265

© *1992 by* CHARLES C THOMAS • PUBLISHER
ISBN 0-398-05808-3
Library of Congress Catalog Card Number: 92-12533

With **THOMAS BOOKS** *careful attention is given to all details of manufacturing
and design. It is the Publisher's desire to present books that are satisfactory as to
their physical qualities and artistic possibilities and appropriate for their particular
use.* **THOMAS BOOKS** *will be true to those laws of quality that assure a good
name and good will.*

Printed in the United States of America
SC-R-3

Library of Congress Cataloging-in-Publication Data

Foster, Susan Bannerman.
    Working with deaf people : accessibility and accommodation in the
workplace / by Susan B. Foster.
        p.   cm.
    Includes bibliographical references (p.   ) and index.
    ISBN 0-398-05808-3 (cloth)
    1. Deaf—Employment. 2. Communication in personnel management.
3. Supervision of employees. 4. Deaf—Employment—United States.
I. Title.
HV2504.F67 1992
658.3'045—dc20   92-12533
                                                                                          CIP

FOREWORD

The quality of life for deaf citizens in the United States has improved markedly over the last quarter of a century. Certainly one relevant factor in how well deaf people live is their status in the world of work. We know that levels of educational attainment and levels of economic achievement in the workplace are related. Access to higher education, and, in particular, to technical education, has widely opened up business and industrial positions for deaf people. We no longer think in terms of "good positions for deaf people" because of the diverse employment accomplishments they have already attained.

This employment success does not necessarily mean that all is always well, or that being a deaf person is an insignificant problem once one has a job. In fact, we know too little about the daily adaptations that are required to achieve access and accommodation for deaf people in the workplace. Susan Foster addresses this void in our knowledge in depth. In this regard alone, the book is an important work.

This book probes beyond the tendency of supervisors to gloss over problems that might exist and to generally report that deaf employees are doing well. While the body of this work describes deaf people as competent and contributing workers, sometimes even at levels of excellence, it also reveals the kinds and patterns of work adjustment problems that occasionally surface among deaf employees. The information is valuable, because it can directly benefit the preparation of deaf students in higher education for the world of work, particularly through seminar sessions. It also can begin to prepare deaf persons to consider barriers to advancement on the job that they may confront.

Working with Deaf People: Accessibility And Accommodation in the Workplace includes points of view of both supervisors and deaf people. The perspectives of each group are often different. Together they are insightful. As one reads this book, the specific coping mechanisms that deaf people use become evident. Relatedly, the book examines how supervisors become aware, over time, of the types of accommodations that are required to attain maximum productivity from deaf employees. We see how the relationship and roles between the supervisor and the deaf employee, and also among other employees, often need to be directly addressed to foster a positive work environment.

Some of the adaptations that occur in the workplace emerge naturally over time. As noted throughout this book, quite often changes made are appropriate. Occasionally, other modifications on either the part of the supervisor or the deaf person would have been more beneficial. Thus, another important use of this book is as a basis for consultation between professionals providing orientation to future employers and supervisors of deaf workers. Use of this information by supervisors could shorten the adjustment period for new deaf employees and thus enhance their productivity and integration in the workplace.

Counselors, instructors, and rehabilitation personnel will find this book helpful in preparing deaf youth for successful adjustment to the workplace. Young deaf adults, particularly those completing programs of study or preparing for a cooperative work experience, will directly benefit from information in this book.

In a different vein, students of deaf culture will find that the book provides an additional slice of life, depicting how people who are deaf cope and function in the process of earning their daily living. Moreover, the detailed stories of supervisors offer an often overlooked perspective on interaction between deaf and hearing people in employment settings.

In conclusion, I found this book to be an important contribution to the literature on employment of deaf people. As a deaf professional working in the field of higher education, I am very familiar with many of the issues raised in this book from the perspectives of *both* supervisor *and* employee. Time and time again, the themes raised in the various chapters struck home, striking chords within my own experience. I believe this book will be a valuable resource for both deaf and hearing people as they strive to make the workplace fully accessible for deaf employees, and I encourage all who work towards this goal to make it a part of their professional library.

ALBERT T. PIMENTEL *Director*
Career Education for the Deaf
Northwestern Connecticut Community College
Winsted, Connecticut

PREFACE

I came to work as a researcher at the National Technical Institute for the Deaf (NTID), a college of Rochester Institute of Technology (RIT), in 1984. My first assignment was with the National Center on Employment of the Deaf (NCED), an area that is responsible for helping students find cooperative work and permanent job placements. One day when I was talking casually with a colleague in this department, he said, "You know, we always ask supervisors to fill out evaluation forms on our co-op students, but we know that they don't write down the problems they encounter. They say everything's going just fine. But when we call them about something or have a chance to talk with them one-to-one, they tell us about the difficulties they face in working with deaf people. I wish we could do some research that would help us learn what supervisors really think."

Later, I learned that survey research had been done with supervisors of deaf RIT graduates. The responses had seemed unrealistically favorable to the researchers, which led them to conclude that many supervisors were unwilling to put in writing their most serious concerns about working with deaf people.

As a qualitative researcher, my work often requires that I broach difficult or sensitive topics with people. I have talked with parents about raising a child with disabilities, conducted observations in residential institutions for developmentally disabled people, and interviewed nurses who worked in a neonatal (newborn) intensive care unit. My experience has been that people often share perspectives, feelings, and opinions in conversation which they would not express on a written survey.

Could qualitative interview techniques be used to learn supervisors' perspectives about working with deaf people? I felt certain they could and set about developing a project with this goal in mind. The result is this book.

I wrote this book with several audiences in mind. First, I hope the book will be useful for employers of deaf people. The Americans with

Disabilities Act of 1990 (ADA) clearly mandates that employers provide access and reasonable accommodations for employees with disabilities. By learning how other supervisors have dealt with issues such as hiring, communication, and promotion of deaf workers, employers may find answers to their own questions and the challenges they face in similar situations. A second audience is deaf employees, who may find it helpful to know the perspectives of supervisors on working with deaf people. Lastly, professionals who work with deaf people (for example, teachers, vocational rehabilitation specialists, and counselors) may find the book useful in preparing their students/clients for successful employment.

I have many people to thank for their assistance and support in preparing this manuscript. I am grateful to RIT for creating an educational and scholarly environment within which a task such as this could be developed and brought to maturity. A special thanks to the deaf people who gave me permission to interview their supervisors. Without them, the project would never have gotten off the ground. I'd like to express my deep appreciation to the twenty supervisors who shared their time and experiences with me. Their ideas form the core of this book.

David Johnston, Gary Meyer, and Janice Smith contributed greatly to this project by reflecting on supervisors' comments and sharing their own experiences as deaf employees. Their discussions appear at the end of chapters 2 through 6 and provide the book with a critical balance of perspectives. Interpreters Patricia Mudgett-DeCaro and Richard Smith facilitated communication and recording of these discussions; their skills were central to the smooth flow of communication and the production of high quality transcripts.

The resource sections at the end of Chapters 2 through 7 were prepared by Gail Kovalik, Staff Resource Center Specialist at NTID, with the assistance of Melanie Norton, NTID Librarian/Bibliographer in RIT's Wallace Memorial Library, and Mary Ellen Tait, NTID Employment Information Center Specialist. These sections provide readers with additional sources of information and are a special feature of this book.

Many others shared their time and expertise with me. Thanks to Gerry Buckley, Harry Lang, Marcia Scherer, Paul Seidel, and Bill Welsh, who read portions of early drafts and gave valuable suggestions for improvement. Rosemarie Seewagen and Cynthia Wiegand provided superb technical support. Gerard Walter, Director of the Center for Postsecondary Career Studies in Deafness and my supervisor, gave encouragement, support, and valuable feedback at all stages of the project. Last, but not least, thanks to my husband, Tom, and children, Brenna and Colin, who put up with a wife and mom who often spent long hours at the computer!

SUSAN FOSTER

CONTENTS

	Page
Foreword	v
Preface	vii
Chapter 1	
BACKGROUND AND HISTORY	3
Chapter 2	
HIRING, TRAINING, AND EVALUATING	
WORK PERFORMANCE	21
Chapter 3	
COMMUNICATION	57
Chapter 4	
RELATIONSHIPS WITH HEARING PEOPLE AT WORK	107
Chapter 5	
EVALUATIONS OF THE DEAF EMPLOYEE'S	
POTENTIAL FOR MANAGEMENT	141
Chapter 6	
ROLES AND RESPONSIBILITIES	171
Chapter 7	
PUTTING IT ALL TOGETHER	201
Bibliography	229
Index	231

WORKING WITH DEAF PEOPLE

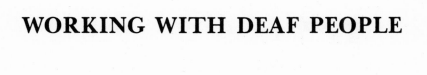

Chapter 1

BACKGROUND AND HISTORY

A supervisor's job is seldom simple and often challenging. Usually, it involves assuming responsibility for the amount and quality of work produced by others, allocation of resources, management of a wide range of operations, and resolution of conflicts and problems. One of the most difficult tasks a supervisor must face is the evaluation of others, since these decisions often have serious repercussions, including whether a person is hired, retained, or promoted. Underlying all these responsibilities is the notion that people should be treated fairly and afforded equal opportunities to succeed and move ahead in their work. Some people thrive under these pressures, while others come to dread them.

Given these challenges, it is understandable when supervisors have special concerns about working with a deaf person. How will they communicate with the person? What if the person gets hurt because they can't hear the warning alarms in areas where hazardous chemicals or machinery are used? Can the person use the telephone? If a customer comes in and wants information, will the deaf person be able to help?

In addition, there is a legal imperative to treat deaf people fairly. For example, Section 504, Title V of the Rehabilitation Act of 1973 prohibits discrimination "on the basis of handicap" in services and employment offered by federal grantees. More recently, the Americans with Disabilities Act (ADA) of 1990 prohibits discrimination against individuals with disabilities in a range of settings, including employment, public services, public accommodations, transportation, and telecommunications. Laws such as these also raise many questions in the minds of employers about how they should respond. For example, the ADA calls for employers to make "reasonable accommodations" for employees with disabilities, unless they can demonstrate that to do so will cause them "undue hardship." What is a reasonable accommodation? How difficult or costly must an accommodation be before it is considered an undue hardship? The regulations which spell out these concepts were published in July, 1991. But even with this level of detail, the full impact of the ADA will not be known for some time. Only as the regulations are played out through countless negotiations, debates—and, in some cases, court battles—will the real definitions of these concepts become clear. This will almost certainly take years.

In the meantime, supervisors must continue to work with all the people in their employ, including those who are deaf. Most would agree that everyone should be treated with equal consideration, even when to do so is stressful or somewhat difficult. Supervisors strive to make the work environment accessible to every worker and conducive to successful completion of work tasks. In the case of a deaf employee, this may mean adopting a range of communication strategies, such as writing or learning to face the deaf person when speaking. It might require purchase of a TDD (Telecommunication Device for the Deaf, which enables deaf people to use the telephone). It may involve hiring an interpreter for staff meetings, or asking someone to take written notes for the deaf person. Most importantly, it requires that supervisors form partnerships with deaf employees to solve communication difficulties and to find ways of insuring the deaf person's inclusion in the activities of the workplace.

However, there is often a wide gap between the ideal and the real. For example, knowing what needs to happen and making it happen are two very different things. Moreover, supervisors may have good intentions, but be unaware of how to proceed. They may have never met a deaf person before, let alone worked with a deaf person. If they are to develop a positive and productive working relationship with deaf employees, they need information and support in several areas. First, they need to know they are not alone and that most people have the same concerns and anxieties in situations like this. Second, they need ideas and strategies for overcoming communication barriers and insuring the deaf person equal access to the work environment. Third, they need to understand the perspective of the deaf person and view him or her as a partner and resource in overcoming barriers and solving problems, in addition to being a valued employee. Fourth, they need specific information about the kinds of resources available to them.

The goal of this book is to present readers with opportunities to learn about all four of these areas. Through interviews with supervisors, group discussions with deaf people, and lists of specific resources, both deaf and hearing readers can acquire information and strategies that will enable them to work well together.

The primary focus of this book is the perspectives of supervisors of deaf workers. Interviews were conducted with twenty such people. In *Chapters 2-6* supervisors describe their decisions to hire deaf people and their experiences as they train, evaluate, and develop working relationships. Much of what they say will strike the reader as common to supervising *any* person. Closer analysis shows that communication emerges as a constant theme, a context within which routine habits, traditions, and expectations are challenged. Supervisors' stories shed light on the everyday experience of working with a deaf person, as well as specific strategies which both deaf and hearing people can use to insure a productive and enjoyable working relationship.

Supervisors' experiences are only one part of the employment "equation." In order for there to be a balance of views, the experiences of deaf employees must be understood. Consequently, a discussion group consisting of three deaf people was formed for the purpose of reflecting on supervisors' comments and describing the employee-supervisor relationship from the perspective of the deaf person. The group's reflections, opinions, and suggestions follow the presentation and discussion of supervisors' experiences within each chapter.

Providing an accessible and supportive work environment for deaf people requires more than an open mind and appreciation of the perspectives and experiences of others. Moreover, the strategies and suggestions offered by the twenty supervisors and three deaf discussants are not exhaustive, nor do they always include specific guidance on how to operationalize an idea. For example, a supervisor/reader may recognize the need for purchasing a TDD, but have no idea about how to get information on the range of models available or the cost of this equipment. A deaf employee/reader may decide to offer co-workers a short workshop on sign language, but be unaware of the wide range of products (some of which are free) which can be used in making such a presentation. Therefore, a resource list is included at the end of each chapter. These lists put readers in touch with a wide range of resources, including further reading, information about national referral centers, instructional videotapes, and technical support.

The remainder of this chapter includes several kinds of background information, each of which is useful for interpreting and using the material presented in subsequent chapters. First, the interview study with supervisors is described. Readers will learn about the types of companies visited, the supervisors interviewed, and the methods used to collect and analyze interview data. Second, the discussion group process is explained, including brief biographies of each of the three deaf participants. Third, the categories of information provided in the resource lists are given, in order to help readers make full use of these lists. Fourth, readers are offered a preview of what is to come through a synopsis of *Chapters 2–7.* The chapter is concluded with a brief history of the employment circumstances of deaf people. This history provides readers with a context for thinking about current employment opportunities and challenges.

DESCRIPTION OF THE INTERVIEW STUDY

The design of the study involved the collection of detailed descriptive data through open-ended, in depth interviews with hearing people who supervise a deaf employee. In this section the methods used to conduct the interviews and organize the data are reviewed, and the organizations, deaf employees, and supervisors described.

How Were the Interviews Done?

Names of potential supervisor/interviewees were generated through two strategies. First, a presentation was made to the local alumni chapter of the National Technical Institute of the Deaf (NTID), a college of Rochester Institute of Technology (RIT). Research related to the employment circumstances of deaf people was presented, the proposed study introduced, and an invitation to participate extended. Second, letters were mailed to approximately one hundred alumni of NTID/RIT. The letter included a description of the research project and a request for permission to contact and interview the person's supervisor. As a result of these efforts, twenty-four people granted the researcher permission to interview their supervisor. Two people listed the same supervisor, which reduced the number of potential interviewees to twenty-three.

After this permission had been received, supervisors were asked whether they would be willing to meet to discuss their experiences working with a deaf person. In total, twenty interviews were completed (three supervisors declined to meet with the researcher).

Interviews were conducted using qualitative research methods (Bogdan and Biklen, 1983; Spradley, 1979). This approach places the researcher in the role of learner, and the person being interviewed in the role of expert. The interview proceeds more like a relaxed conversation than a structured dialogue, with the researcher asking open-ended questions around a set of general topics and the pace and direction of the interview unfolding according to the responses of the interviewee. The interview is also in depth, in that respondents are asked to elaborate on their statements and to give examples whenever possible.

Interviews were conducted at the convenience of the supervisors. Most often, the researcher went to the supervisor's place of work. One person preferred to meet at a local restaurant. Interview topics included the decision to hire the deaf employee, communication and interaction between the supervisor and the deaf worker, evaluation of work performance and management potential, and strategies for working effectively with a deaf person.

Interviews lasted between one and two hours and were sometimes preceded or followed by a brief tour of the department or facility. Nineteen interviews were recorded on audio tape and later transcribed. One interview was recorded in written notes. Interview transcripts and notes provided the basis for data analysis, a process through which information is sorted and reviewed for recurring themes (Bogdan and Biklen, 1983). The results of the analysis were then organized within the broad topics that became the chapters of this book. While the chapters draw heavily on direct quotations from interviews, privacy considerations dictated that neither names of individuals nor companies be used.

Description of Organizations, Deaf Employees, and Supervisors

The organizations represented in this study varied in size, structure, and mission. Although some organizations were quite large (i.e., over one thousand employees), a few employed less than one hundred. Even in the largest organizations, however, the department or team within which the deaf person worked was usually relatively small, and over half were in departments of fewer than ten people. In the smaller companies there were predictably simpler management structures, while in large corporations there were many departments and the organizational structures were complex.

Several kinds of organizations were represented in the interview group. They can be categorized through the Industrial Classification System (US Bureau of the Census, 1980) as *Professional and Related Services* (9), *Manufacturing* (6), *Personal Services* (2), *Business and Repair Services* (1), *Financial/Insurance Services* (1), and *Retail Trade* (1).

All the deaf employees who were the focus of discussion within interviews are graduates of RIT. Collectively, they hold positions in a wide
range of fields, including social work, medical lab technology, accounting,
drafting, data entry, optical finishing, and product assembly. Ten of the
twenty-one[1] deaf employees are male. At the time of the interview,
seventeen were employed full time. (Of the remaining four, three worked
part time and one had left the job.) Two deaf people were in supervisory
positions; in both cases, the work involved the provision of direct services to deaf clients.

Of the twenty supervisors interviewed, half are male and nineteen
have normal hearing. (One supervisor had recently begun using a hearing aid upon diagnosis of a mild hearing loss.) All but one supervisor
worked directly with the deaf person. Supervisory responsibilities included
hiring, assigning work, conducting evaluations, promoting, firing, as
well as general responsibility for the work produced by the staff.

DISCUSSION GROUP

The perspectives of supervisors are, of course, only one part of the
story. What are the perspectives of deaf employees towards working with
hearing people? It was not feasible to interview the deaf people who had
given permission to contact a supervisor. To pair the comments of
supervisors with those of the person they supervised would seriously
compromise everyone's anonymity. Given this, presentation of conflicting
viewpoints in interview data might harm working relationships between
supervisors and employees.

Instead, a group of three deaf people was formed for the purpose of
reflecting on supervisors' comments and sharing experiences. Like the
deaf people who consented to having their supervisor contacted, the
discussion group members are graduates of postsecondary educational
programs. They had each worked in environments in which they were
the only (or one of a very few) deaf employees.

A series of meetings was scheduled, each of which focused on a single
chapter (*Chapters 2 through 6*). Discussants were asked to read each chapter before the group convened and to record notes regarding their
reactions to supervisors' comments, connections with their own experience,
and advice they would give to supervisors and deaf employees.

Two interpreters were used in each meeting. Interpreter services were
used in two ways. First, the interpreters facilitated communication within

the group, which was critical to a smooth flow of conversation. Second, they made possible the recording of the discussion on audio tapes. One interpreter signed for the researcher (who, while skilled in general sign communication, was not fluent in American Sign Language (ASL)—the language of choice in the group) and the other voiced for the deaf discussants (the researcher voiced for herself). Audio tapes of the discussions were transcribed in full, and condensed. Discussants reviewed the condensed version for accuracy, making changes as necessary. Revised discussions follow the presentation of supervisors' perceptions in *Chapters 2 through 6*. A brief autobiography of each discussant is included below.

David Johnston

I was born in Washington, D.C. in 1960. At that time, my mother (who is deaf) was a student at Gallaudet. My father (also deaf) was a printer. I have three sisters, two deaf and one hearing. My family made several moves while I was very young, but by the time I was five we had settled in a suburb of Washington, D.C., in the state of Maryland.

I attended Maryland School for the Deaf (MSD) from kindergarten through high school. That school was what I would call a "total deaf world." We had deaf teachers, deaf house parents, and of course, deaf peers. I had many positive role models there. Although the formal policy of the school required the use of Total Communication, we really used ASL most of the time. I was involved in many school activities, especially sports, including football, wrestling, and track. I lived at the school all week, going home to my family on the weekends. I feel very positive about my years at MSD. That school gave me many things. It gave me self esteem. It made me proud to be deaf and proud to be a part of Deaf culture.

In 1979, I graduated from MSD and went off to college at NTID. After a year of college, I decided to take a leave of absence and go to work. However, I found the world of work pretty frustrating and difficult and eventually decided that I needed a college degree in order to get a good job. So I returned to NTID in 1981 and in 1984 I completed an associates degree in electromechanical technology. I didn't join many extracurricular activities during those college years, because I wanted to concentrate full time on my studies.

After graduation in 1984, I went to work for Burleigh Instruments, Inc., as an electronics technician. My job responsibilities involved testing electronically driven micro-positioning products that are used in research and high technology applications. It was a small company, and I worked there for five years.

In 1989 I left that job to accept a position as electro-mechanical technician in the Department of Electro-Mechanical Technology (EMT) at NTID. In that job, I have many different responsibilities. For example, I service the different pieces of equipment which EMT students use in lab work, and I teach a course to first year EMT students entitled "Tool Skills."

At the present time, I live in the Rochester area with my wife and son. I continue to work at NTID.

Gary Meyer

I was born in Cleveland, Ohio, in 1957. But then we moved to Wilmette, a town north of Chicago. That's where I was raised. My parents are hearing. I have one older sister, who's also deaf.

I attended Evanston High School. I was one of about ten deaf students in a system of approximately six thousand total. It was a very big school. Not surprisingly, I was always the only deaf person in my classes. During my earlier education days, there was a person who visited the school to make sure we deaf students were doing OK, but I didn't have notetakers or interpreters in class. I remember I had to sit in the front of the room and remind the teacher to face me when speaking. I was a good athlete, so my social life after school was related to sports.

I graduated from high school in 1975 and went to the National Technical Institute for the Deaf (NTID), one of eight colleges of Rochester Institute of Technology (RIT) in Rochester, New York. That was my first real exposure to deaf culture and sign language. I did have support services for classes at RIT, including interpreters and notetakers. In 1980 I graduated from RIT with a bachelor's degree in accounting.

My first job was with Allstate Insurance. I worked at their home office in Chicago, which employed about three thousand people. I worked in the Accounting Department, where my job was to keep track of monthly losses for the insurance claims. My title was Statistics Accountant.

In 1983 I moved back to Rochester. I worked for a local bank for a short time as an accountant, preparing monthly statements for the mortgage department. During that period, I went back to school to get my sales license for life and health insurance.

In 1984 I changed my career and went to work for Prudential Insurance in full-time sales. During my first year there, I was the "Top Rookie Agent" in my office. Our office was in the top five agencies in the company, which placed me in the top 25% of the company for sales for the next four years, out of thirteen thousand agents in the United States.

I was in the insurance business until 1988, when I changed careers again to accept a position as a Career Opportunities Advisor at the National Center on Employment of the Deaf at RIT. In this job I help students find both co-op and permanent jobs. I also do a lot of consulting with employers of deaf RIT graduates, advising them how to deal with a deaf person on the job, helping them deal with problems they encounter during the interview process, and so forth.

Today, I'm married with two children, ages five and two. I'm living in

Rochester and continue to work at the National Center on Employment of the Deaf. I also am enrolled in the MBA program at RIT.

Janice Smith

I was born in 1964 in Baltimore, Maryland. I have deaf parents and one older deaf sister. When I was five years old, my family and I moved to Columbia, South Carolina. I went to the public schools, where I attended most classes with hearing students. But I and the other four deaf students in the school system were also pulled out for special classes, like for English. My special teacher did sign, but she was very slow and she signed straight English, not American Sign Language. I had no special services when I was in classes with hearing students. It's funny, because looking back now, I wonder how I did it without interpreters.

I was involved in a lot of different kinds of sports during high school, and really enjoyed it. I was the only deaf student on the teams, but I could lipread pretty well. I also had a hearing friend who learned a few signs from me. During a game, when the coach would speak very fast, my friend would help me out by interpreting what the coach was saying. You know, I didn't really get the full point like the hearing players did, but I followed enough of what was going on.

I graduated in 1981 and went to the University of South Carolina. I did have interpreters and notetakers there, but some interpreters were not certified or very fluent in sign language. In 1986 I graduated with a bachelor of science degree in Management Information Systems.

From 1987 through 1989 I worked for the Computer Company of Richmond, Virginia. I started as a programmer trainee and moved up to the position of programmer. Responsibilities included claims processing modifications and implementation of report programs, using COBOL.

In 1989 I went to work for the Medical College of Virginia. in their Hospital Information Systems. I started out as a programmer, where I developed and maintained application systems in association with affected users and senior programming staff. I also assisted in evaluating system performance and recommending plans of action to resolve system deficiencies. Then, six months later, I was promoted to programmer/analyst. In that position, I was responsible for analyzing, designing, developing and implementing projects and systems for financial applications.

In January, 1991, I came to RIT's National Technical Institute for the Deaf, where I was an adjunct instructor in the School of Business Careers. Responsibilities in this job included teaching courses in COBOL I and COBOL II, Beginning Computer Operations, Data Processing for Business Occupations, and Data Processing Technical Communications.

In September, 1991, I was hired for the position of Instructional Materials Specialist in the Department of Instructional Television and Media Services at NTID. My responsibilities in this job include serving as a liaison between

NTID and educational media production companies, in order to facilitate the captioning of selected materials for use with NTID students and faculty.

Today, I continue to live in Rochester and work at NTID. I am engaged to be married in June, 1992, to Farley Warshaw.

RESOURCE LISTS

The resource lists at the end of *Chapters 2 through 7* provide readers with specific information which they may find helpful in working with deaf (and/or hearing) people. Information presented in the Resource Lists is organized within four categories: (1) library resources, (2) pamphlets and brochures, (3) media, and (4) contacts.

Library Resources

The selections in this category will be of interest to those who want to pursue ideas raised within a chapter through further reading. Examples of library resources include popular journals, autobiographical accounts by deaf people, general topics of interest to the deaf community, and research which describes the experience of being deaf.

Pamphlets and Brochures

Resources which provide information on a variety of deafness-related topics in a summary, review, or checklist fashion are listed within this category. Examples include a set of cards that show the twenty-six handshapes for the letters of the manual alphabet and a four-page brochure in which commonly asked questions about the employment of deaf people are answered.

Media

This category covers videotapes and captioned films. Some of these materials are available on loan, while others must be purchased. Examples include instructional videotapes for learning sign language and a video in which a lawyer and an IBM manager describe the attitudes and barriers that hindered them in education and employment, as well as factors related to their success as deaf professionals.

Contacts

Many disability, policy, and service organizations are valuable sources of information, referrals, or "on the spot" assistance. For example, the Job Accommodation Network is a computerized information service which stores accommodation experiences submitted by employers for employers, job placement personnel, and people with disabilities. The Tele-Consumer Hotline is a free consumer information service for all consumers in need of assistance in dealing with telephone shopping requirements.

SYNOPSIS OF CHAPTERS 2 THROUGH 7

Chapter 2 begins with an analysis of supervisors' descriptions of the decision to hire a deaf person. Five factors emerged as significant to this decision: (1) characteristics of the applicant, (2) urgency and difficulty in filling the position, (3) personal recommendations and connections, (4) the perspective of the hiring supervisor towards deafness, and (5) organizational policy or mission.

Sometimes the deaf person came into the new job with experience in a similar position, which facilitated the learning process greatly. However, even experienced people need to learn the daily routines and standard operating procedures which are specific to individual work environments. Supervisors' descriptions of how they handled this period of introduction, training, and adjustment, as well as their approach to informing deaf employees about new procedures and changes in policy, are described. Lastly, supervisors' evaluations of deaf employees' work performances are presented.

Communication between deaf employees and others in the work environment is the focus of *Chapter 3.* Specific topics include communication at meetings, one to one, and over the telephone. The chapter concludes with a discussion of issues and challenges related to communication, such as the impact of different environmental conditions on communication in the workplace, strategies used by supervisors and deaf employees to facilitate communication in a variety of settings, and the role of time and familiarity in improving communication.

Supervisors were asked to describe their perceptions of how the deaf employee related to co-workers. Their responses form the basis for discussion in *Chapter 4.* While several supervisors said the deaf employee got along well with others, most qualified their response by noting that there were constraints on full interaction between the deaf person and hearing colleagues. Supervisors' descriptions of interactions between deaf and hearing employees cover a wide range of relationships, including incidents of open hostility as well as close friendships. Analysis of their comments suggests that several factors contribute to the range and quality of these relationships. These are (1) environmental conditions, (2) the personality, attitude, and interpersonal skills of the deaf person, (3) the attitude, awareness about deafness, and sensitivity/maturity of hearing colleagues, (4) the skill of the supervisor in providing appropriate intervention and support, and (5) the length of time within the environment.

In *Chapter 5* we turn to supervisors' evaluations of their deaf employees' chances for promotion, with a focus on movement into supervisory or management positions. Ten supervisors did not think the employee had the potential for management. Of the ten who thought the employee could enter a management position, six qualified their response with a discussion of the barriers to mobility which would have to be overcome before promotion could be considered. The conditions most often associated with decisions regarding promotion include (1) technical job skills of the employee, (2) personal qualities of the employee (i.e., interpersonal skills, assertiveness, ability to work under pressure), (3) communication skills, constraints, and/or accommodations, and (4) attitudes of others.

In discussing their experiences working with a deaf person, supervisors offered suggestions about those strategies, conditions, and individual qualities that facilitate accommodation and assimilation. Many of their suggestions are covered in early chapters. In *Chapter 6* they are organized within the categories of (1) roles adopted by deaf employees (teacher, mediator, super-employee, and entrepreneur), and (2) roles adopted by supervisors (learner, mediator, advocate, and mentor).

In *Chapter 7* information presented in the preceding chapters is synthesized into a set of concepts relative to supervising a deaf person and the development of successful working relationships between deaf and hearing workers. In particular, the need for an ecological model of the workplace is discussed. An ecological model is then used as a framework for analyzing barriers to access and as a framework for creating work settings in which the participation, productivity, and potential of deaf employees can be more fully realized.

HISTORY OF EMPLOYMENT CIRCUMSTANCES
OF DEAF PEOPLE

Historically, deaf people have *not* enjoyed the same employment opportunities as their hearing peers. However, their employment history has been better at some times than at others. In the following pages, some of the factors that have had the greatest impact on the employment of deaf people are reviewed. The section concludes with a discussion of current and future trends in the American work force and the ways in which these trends may influence deaf workers and their employers.

Prior to the urbanization and industrialization of the economy, deaf people were on more of a par with hearing people. Van Cleve and Crouch (1989) suggest that this was due in large part to the fact that the major occupations of that time, handicrafts and farm labor, could be learned through "visual observation, long practice, and an intimate acquaintance with their teacher or coworkers" (page 156). The shift to factory work, in combination with large numbers of people immigrating to America during the last decades of the nineteenth century and early decades of the twentieth century, presented deaf people with new challenges regarding access to educational and training programs and increased competition for jobs.

World War I influenced the employment circumstances of deaf people positively. As with women, deaf men found themselves in demand to fill gaps left open by men who left their jobs to serve in the armed forces. Companies which had previously turned down deaf men seeking employment now hired them more readily. While this emergency was temporary, it improved the perspectives of some employers regarding the employability of deaf people.

Perhaps the greatest factor in explaining the history of employment of deaf people is educational opportunity. At the turn of the century, many deaf people received their elementary and secondary educations in separate state institutions, usually referred to as "schools for the deaf." Instruction in these institutions included vocational training in a variety of fields. The most common occupations for deaf boys were printing and shoemaking; dressmaking and sewing were the girls' most common occupations. While printing may seem today to be a career choice reserved for students who are not academically talented, Van Cleve and Crouch (1989) note that for the deaf community, exactly the opposite was true, i.e., the most gifted students learned printing. In explaining this phenomenon, they describe the power of printing in the formation of the deaf community (newsletters and other written formats being a major form of communication among deaf people) and good wages associated with printing jobs. However, limited access to other careers was probably also a factor.

Since the turn of the century, changes in the structure of the American work force have presented deaf workers with new challenges. Rapid changes in technology have altered the employment circumstances of many older workers, including those who are deaf. Printing is an area that has experienced particularly radical change, resulting in displacement of deaf printers and requiring their adjustment to very different operations and organizational structures (Emerton, Foster, and Royer, 1987).

Technological advances also resulted in increased requirements for advanced training for many technical and professional jobs. As a result, there has been tremendous growth in postsecondary education during this period, especially during the post World War II era. Initially, requirements for advanced training presented serious problems for many deaf people.

Until quite recently, the main (some might say only) postsecondary institution accessible to many deaf students has been Gallaudet College (changed to Gallaudet University in 1986). The only liberal arts university in the world specifically for deaf students, Gallaudet has graduated more than seven thousand students since its establishment in 1864 (Gallaudet University Factbook, 1989).

Historically, mainstream institutions of higher education (that is, those serving primarily hearing students) have been largely inaccessible to deaf students. Many deaf students were not academically prepared for continued education. Those attending mainstream elementary and high schools often struggled to learn without support services, and thus missed much of the instruction. Those attending separate schools sometimes found the academic curriculum wanting, or focused more on the development of speech or vocational skills. Moreover, those who were academically prepared to enter colleges and universities were confronted with communication and attitudinal barriers in interactions with hearing faculty, staff, and students, which made it difficult or impossible for them to fully participate in the instructional and extracurricular activities of the school.

The increasing need for higher levels of education in workers, coupled with growth of postsecondary programs, led to concerns regarding access to higher education for those who had traditionally been excluded, including students from low income families, members of minority groups, and people with disabilities. These concerns eventually led to passage of a series of laws which were designed to insure the rights of people with disabilities to equal opportunities in a range of environments and activities, including those which are educational in nature. In 1965, Congress passed Public Law 89-36, also known as the National Technical Institute for the Deaf Act, through which a second national postsecondary institution for the deaf was established. The National Technical Institute for the Deaf, a college of Rochester Institute of Technology, offers students a range of technical careers in science, business, visual communication, and engineering. To date, 2,725 deaf students have graduated from NTID/RIT (*NTID Annual Report,* 1991).

Other legislation has focused more on increasing direct access to mainstream educational programs. For example, the passage in 1973 of Section 504 of the Education of the Handicapped Act prohibits discrimination against people with disabilities in any agency or institution receiving federal financial assistance (which includes many colleges and universities). This law has required many mainstream postsecondary educational institutions to offer interpreters, notetakers, and other support services that make their programs more accessible to deaf students.

In combination, changes in social attitudes and public policy since 1960 have promoted tremendous growth in postsecondary educational opportunities for deaf students. Correspondingly, the numbers of deaf students attending college has increased. The most recent edition of the *College and Career Programs for Deaf Students — 1990* (Rawlings, et al., 1991) lists 154 postsecondary institutions providing services for deaf students. Additionally, Liscio (1986) lists 287 two-year and 260 four-year colleges that provide some level of support for deaf college students. Rawlings and King (1986) note that the enrollment of deaf people in colleges increased from approximately 250 in 1950 to more than eight thousand in 1986; Walter (1992) estimates that this figure may be closer to ten thousand.

Increased access to postsecondary education has significantly improved the employment circumstances of deaf people. Research conducted before the effects of increased access could be studied suggests that deaf people did not attain occupations or earn equal compensation for equivalent jobs held by their hearing peers (Lunde and Bigman, 1959; Boatner et al., 1964; Williams and Sussman, 1971; Weinrich, 1972; Schein and Delk, 1974). Conversely, later studies demonstrate clearly the positive effect of postsecondary education on the employment and socioeconomic status of deaf people. For example, Welsh and Walter (1988) found that deaf adults with postsecondary degrees have lower unemployment rates, earn more money, and are employed much more often in white collar careers than are their counterparts without degrees. In their discussion of findings from another comparative study, Welsh and MacLeod-Gallinger (1992) state the following:

> The data presented here uniformly support the value of acquiring a postsecondary education. Deaf people who earn degrees are in the labor force more often, unemployed much less often, get higher level jobs, and earn significantly more money. Not only is some postsecondary education an improvement over a high school degree, it is clear that more college is better than less. Bachelor's degree recipients fare better than subbachelor's graduates in all ways measured in this study, and, in terms of salary, master's degree recipients fared best of all.

> (pp. 199)

However, recent studies also document persistent barriers to advanced educational training and employment. Vertical mobility remains difficult for many employees, particularly movement into positions involving management of others (Welsh and Walter, 1988). Although higher education reduces differences between the achievements of deaf and hearing people, it does not close the gaps entirely. For example, Welsh and MacLeod-Gallinger (1992) conclude that, "deaf people are still greatly under-represented in the Managerial and Professional occupations, i.e., those that require the highest education levels and pay the highest salaries" (pp. 191). The relatively lower levels of educational and employment achievements of deaf women and minorities, documented by many of the earlier studies, continue through the present (Allen et al., 1989; Barnartt and Christiansen, 1985; Crammatte, 1987; MacLeod-Gallinger, 1991); for these groups, effects of barriers and stigmas associated with deafness are often compounded by those associated with race or gender.

Furthermore, having access to the workplace does not guarantee full participation or assimilation. Studies by Crammatte (1968) and Foster (1987) suggest that even when deaf people are able to communicate with co-workers effectively in the performance of work tasks, they experience difficulty in joining informal interactions and conversations, such as those involving the office grapevine. While such involvement may seem of marginal importance in the performance of one's job, failure to be a part of the social fabric of the work environment may influence the long term achievement of career goals.

In addition to challenges associated with the condition of deafness, there are macro level changes occurring in the American work force which will have a significant impact on all workers over the next ten years, with special implications for deaf workers. First, there has been a shift from a manufacturing to a service economy. Between now and the year 2000, job opportunities in most goods-producing industries will decline, while service industries (especially education, business, and health care) will generally grow (Kutscher, 1987). Given increased demands on employees for communication and interaction in service industries, this could present special challenges to deaf people and their employers.

Second, the application of advanced technologies in the workplace has resulted in changes in the basic skills required of employees. As jobs constantly change to keep pace with technology, workers must be able to adapt quickly to changes in equipment, procedures, and the organization of their work. These requirements have given rise to a new set of basic skills, including flexibility, advanced communication skills, teamwork skills, critical thinking skills, and knowing how to learn independently (Bailey, 1990; Coates et al., 1990). Communication differences between deaf and hearing people may necessitate the use of special services in the application of advanced communication strategies and accomplishment of team projects.

Third, the arrival of the "information age" and the shift toward a global economy has brought with it the need for advanced English literacy skills. English has become the language of the marketplace, as evidenced by the facts that 80% of computer-stored knowledge is in English, and 85% of all international calls are in English (Naisbitt, 1991). Textual information will be increasingly important in the performance of work tasks, especially in the areas of telecommunication and computers. The demand for higher English literacy skills in the workplace presents a special challenge to deaf people, since as a group they have experienced difficulty in acquiring sophisticated reading and writing skills (the median reading grade equivalent for seventeen-year-old hearing-impaired students is 3.2 on the Standford Achievement Test [Allen, 1987]).

Fourth, employer-sponsored training has become an important capital and wealth producing system in America. For example, estimates of the amount spent annually for employer-based training during 1988 run as high as $185 billion (Bailey, 1990). The majority of training happens after the individual has been committed to the corporation for more than five years. The people most likely to receive some kind of employer-based training are those who are highly educated and have jobs that require a lot of skill and knowledge. Will deaf people be able to take advantage of opportunities for this training? What adjustments must employers make in order to facilitate participation of deaf employees?

In summary, deaf people have faced many challenges to full and equal employment, beginning with access to a high quality preparatory education and continuing with persistent challenges to participation in the work environment. Barriers associated with deafness are compounded by issues of minority or gender status. Advancements resulting from increased access to postsecondary education are significant, but many deaf people have not yet been able to take advantage of these opportunities, and some inequalities have proved resistent to amelioration. As the American work force continues to change, old barriers may be broken down only to be replaced by new ones. The degree to which deaf people are successful in their efforts to participate in the work force will depend on their educational opportunities, personal abilities and motivations, and the willingness and ability of employers to adapt the work environment in ways that will enable deaf people to fully demonstrate their competence and productivity.

ENDNOTES

1. Recall that two deaf employees who gave permission to interview a supervisor worked for the same person. Hence, there is a total of twenty-one deaf employees but only twenty supervisors interviewed, representing twenty organizations.

Chapter 2

HIRING, TRAINING, AND
EVALUATING WORK PERFORMANCE

They've got the power—they're hearing. You know, like from my experience, I sit down and interview with them all—and sure enough, I know that, hey, they look at me as a deaf person and they'll put my application in the file and that's the end of it. You know, they say "Well, you can't do this because you're deaf," and they don't want to get sued, so they'll just say "Hey, we'll see if there are any openings, and we'll go through the process." And they'll just put the stuff in the trash can anyhow...(Excerpt from interview with deaf employee; Foster, 1987)

F inding and holding a job, and succeeding in that job, is a challenging task. It is an even greater challenge if one is deaf, given the educational and employment barriers faced by this group. Deaf people seek employment using many of the same strategies as do hearing people, including personal contacts, professional employment agencies, and the traditional "cold call." However, they may also encounter concern and even resistance in potential employers, as a result of their deafness.

What is the perspective of employers on these issues? What do hearing supervisors think about when they meet a deaf job applicant, or when they are faced with training a new employee with whom they have difficulty communicating? How do they evaluate a deaf employee's work performance? Do they apply the same standards and expectations to both deaf and hearing workers? In this chapter, supervisors' perspectives on hiring, training, and evaluating the work performance of deaf employees are presented.

HIRING

Ten supervisors said they were involved in the hiring process. The others became supervisors of deaf persons through promotion, assignment, transfer, merging of departments, and other organizational changes.

21

Supervisors who were involved in hiring the deaf employee were asked to describe the factors they considered in making their choices and to explain their decisions. Additionally, several supervisors who were not directly involved in the decision to hire but had been told about the process by those who were involved, offered their interpretation of how the decision was made; their comments are also included in this section.

Discussions with supervisors about hiring the deaf job candidate suggest that five factors are critical to this decision: (1) characteristics of the candidate, (2) urgency and difficulty in filling the job vacancy, (3) personal recommendations and connections, (4) the perspective of the hiring supervisor towards deafness, and (5) organizational policy or mission. Most often, supervisors considered more than one factor before hiring the deaf person. While the last two factors are more clearly related to the condition of deafness, we will see that deafness influences the other factors as well.

Characteristics of the Deaf Job Candidate

Supervisors carefully considered the skills and personal qualities of candidates as part of the hiring process. Technical ability to perform the job tasks required was critical. Supervisors often commented on the effective training and good technical skills of the deaf employee in explaining the decision to hire. In some instances, having solid skills was seen as mitigating against what many supervisors perceived as the de-valuing characteristic of deafness. For example, one person said that a colleague (who hired the deaf employee) had been very impressed with the technical ability of deaf students who had worked for the company in the past as part of a cooperative educational program (co-op). He felt this experience paved the way for the deaf employee, since the colleague placed a high value on technical competence in making hiring decisions. As he put it, "if he [colleague] can get a good worker in here, black or white or deaf or what and he . . . can use him to his advantage, that is the only way he thinks—can he [worker] do the job."

Work experience, while seldom essential, was often a valued characteristic. Several supervisors noted the applicant's experience in explaining the decision to hire. One person said the deaf employee had "supervised a program in [another city] on a smaller scale but very similar in scope of services to the . . . program here," adding that this was one of the factors that "tipped the scale" in the decision to hire the applicant.

Assertiveness and confidence were also seen as important. These qualities combined to produce a deaf job candidate apparently capable of handling a variety of situations, or in the words of one supervisor, one who has "the capacity to be able to respond without any cue cards."

Willingness to learn and to work hard were viewed by supervisors as especially important, and in several cases, these qualities were the deciding factor. For example, one supervisor remembered the job interview:

> I said, let me talk to him, let me interview him. You do not have to speak to do this job. So . . . [he] came in one afternoon. I took . . . [him] through the shop. I asked him what he thought, if he could do the job. The most important thing to me is, do you want to work and are you willing to learn? There really is not anything out there that you can't be taught if you want to learn. That is the way I feel about it.[1]

When asked what made him decide to interview the deaf applicant when others were probably available, the supervisor responded, "I wasn't getting anything I wanted. There's a lot of people out there, but I think they have poor attitudes. They don't want to work, they are lazy. . . . " He said he sensed a difference in the attitude of the deaf applicant. As he put it, "I liked his personality. He said he could do the job. I believed him. He showed me some of his work that he has made himself."

Finally, sometimes the willingness to work was described as a form of compensation for the inability to hear. One supervisor expressed the opinion that deaf people must demonstrate above average motivation and enthusiasm to compete successfully with hearing people for employment:

> You see, if you're completely rational about it, completely rational, probably you can find a candidate who's gonna be equivalent who won't have this kind of impairment. That wasn't the attitude [here]. The attitude was to see whether or not [he] would be able to work. He was extremely, highly motivated. That made a big difference to me . . . if he'd been reticent at all, I probably wouldn't have hired him. All the same kinds of interview issues that come up with everyone else — come up with these [deaf] people even more importantly . . . I think, [they] have to first of all have some ability. In other words, they do have strikes against them. I don't think there's any question about it. I don't think that should be ignored, I think it's reality . . . The amount of enthusiasm and drive they show, if it's not out of range, out of proportion to reality, is very important to me.

Urgency and Difficulty Filling the Position

As noted in *Chapter 1,* during World War I, when many jobs were exceedingly difficult to fill, deaf people had many more, and much better jobs. While this period was exceptional in many ways, the notion of "supply and demand" continues to influence the ability of underemployed groups, including deaf people, to secure work. Several supervisors noted that the job held by the deaf employee had been difficult to fill. As noted earlier, one supervisor "wasn't getting what he wanted" in job applicants. Several supervisors said they did not have many candidates to consider when filling the job. For example, in discussing the difficulty in finding someone to fill a position, one person noted, "in this type of business, it is very hard finding people who will want to work where it's very hot." Another supervisor admitted that his decision to hire the deaf job applicant was in part due to the fact that "in all honesty, we were having temporary difficulty finding certain types of staff and he was the most promising of any resumes we were getting at the time." The willingness to learn the job and a limited pool of applicants is a powerful combination, as illustrated by the following story:

> He had the technician's background and he was willing to learn. With that type of drive we didn't have any difficulty. We didn't have a huge field of people to hire . . . You get maybe two or three candidates that are available at the most on a job . . . Sometimes you don't even have to talk to them, as soon as you mention "chemical area" they say they don't do those types of things. Maybe their situation was different—they didn't have to worry about supporting a family or losing their job, but [he] seemed to work out. We didn't have any difficulty with that [with him].

Personal Recommendations and Connections

The role of personal connections and recommendations in securing work has always been important. The term "networking" reflects advantages of knowing the right people, both for finding jobs and for advancing within them. Not surprisingly, deaf people used personal recommendations and connections in order to find jobs. Two supervisors recalled that there had been contact with a parent of the deaf employee. In one case, the deaf employee's father was known to the supervisor because they were in the same line of work. In the second case, the deaf person's mother "worked over in [other department] and I guess [her] mother

talked to [my supervisor, who] brought her in, interviewed her, and ...
hired her."

Other kinds of connections were also helpful in getting jobs. One deaf
person was on the board of the organization which later hired him. He
learned about the position through this involvement and decided to
pursue it. Two other deaf employees were recommended for the position
by previous supervisors. In one instance, the person was "just kind of
picked ... up through 'word of mouth' between small business owners."
In the second situation, the recommendation was even more direct:

> She had worked for one of our other shops ... that's also owned by the same
> man I work for. So when she applied for a job here I did call him and asked
> him how she worked out there, and he said she was ... super ... he let her go
> because they weren't busy at the time and she was the newest one, so he had
> to let her go. But he did give her a good recommendation.

A cooperative work program (co-op) proved an invaluable connection
for a fourth deaf employee, who was hired permanently when his co-op
ended. As his supervisor noted, the co-op was helpful to both the deaf
student and the company:

> This way they come in here and you get a good look at them and see what kind
> of worker he is and he gets a feel for what is going on in a company. It is kind of
> a two-way street.

Perspective of the Hiring Supervisor towards Deafness

An awareness of and sensitivity to the challenges faced by deaf people
played a critical role in some supervisors' decisions to hire the deaf
applicant. For example, a few supervisors had experience with deaf
people already. "I know of deaf people," one supervisor explained. "I
went to RIT, I was aware of NTID, I have a brother-in-law whose sister is
deaf and so, because I knew her for twenty years ... it wasn't like I was
completely foreign to the thing."

While experience with deafness did not necessarily decide the supervisor in favor of the deaf person, it is likely that it did influence the
decision somewhat. One supervisor, when asked whether she had worked
with deaf people before meeting the deaf employee, replied, "No, but
my mother was hard of hearing, so that's maybe why I have a little more
empathy for [her] ... I did know something [about] what it's like to be
hard-of-hearing."

In a few instances, the supervisor had some direct experience with the deaf job candidate. When these experiences were generally positive, this tipped the scale in the decision to hire, especially if other favorable circumstances, such as solid skills and a need to fill the position, existed. Initially apprehensive about hiring a deaf person, one supervisor said that interactions with the deaf employee were influential in her decision:

> When [she] first came in here and applied, I thought, "Oh, this is really different,"... [but] she had come in here as a customer a couple of times... so I knew her a little bit... Her husband had been with her too... I could see he had trouble speaking... but [she] was fine... as long as we looked at her. She could lipread and she could hear even without her hearing aid... So when she came in and asked me for a job, I really needed somebody, plus she had a lot of experience... and I had no trouble communicating with her, so I [decided to hire her].

Sometimes unexpected connections were drawn between the experiences of the supervisor and the deaf job candidate. For example, one supervisor, managing a family-owned business, recounted his father's experiences as an immigrant and the impact this may have had on the father's decision to hire the deaf employee. His father had come from Europe and had a hard time speaking English. As the supervisor observed, "I'm sure he understands that someone's intelligence really doesn't depend on their ability to communicate... Being his son, I've grown up with him and just learned to respect foreigners as well."

In another case, a supervisor whose organization provided services for deaf people described herself as having a lot of training and background "working with individuals who... are basically challenged," by which she seemed to mean people who are disadvantaged or disabled. She felt this experience prepared her to work with deaf people, adding that she was "enthused about the opportunity to work with the hearing-impaired."

Some supervisors were simply more open to the idea of hiring a person with a disability than others. The supervisor whose colleague had helped establish a co-op work program between his company and NTID and later hired the deaf employee through this program, noted that "he [colleague]... was the type of personality that would... go out of his way to initiate something like that and give somebody a chance."

Policy or Mission of the Organization

In a few cases, the philosophy of the supervisor about deafness was closely linked to organizational policy or mission. For example, one supervisor mentioned his company's policy on hiring disabled workers when describing the decision to hire the deaf applicant. As he put it, "It's our division's policy that we don't not hire people because of a handicap— we do have jobs that people can do, and so we tailored that job to help him out."

In several cases, the job involved direct services to deaf people. While this did not mean that the job had to be filled by a deaf person, it is likely that being deaf was perceived as less disabling in these positions. In fact, one supervisor in this kind of organization expressed the belief that, all other things being equal, the position should go to a deaf person:

> I felt that... if a qualified hearing-impaired person, by and large, had the same qualifications as a hearing person [had who] applied for the job, I would offer [it to] the hearing-impaired person. Basically, because of a personal philosophy that those programs that provide services to a specific population should, in fact, be headed by an individual who helps represent that specific population... if you're gonna focus on providing services for minority, they should be a minority person.

In summary, the decision to hire the deaf job applicant was the result of many factors. Technical skill was important, as were the attitude of the applicant towards learning and work and the attitude of the supervisor towards deafness. Perhaps the best way to describe the decision to hire is that it represented a "fit" between the individual and the job.

TRAINING

What strategies did supervisors use to train deaf employees? When deaf employees began work with experience and training in similar positions, the learning process was greatly facilitated. However, even experienced people need to learn the daily routines and procedures specific to their work environments, and deaf employees are no exception. Supervisors were usually responsible for this period of introduction, training, and adjustment. They were also expected to teach deaf employees new procedures and changes in policy as necessary. Supervisors' responses to questions about training are organized within this section according to whether they made special accommodations for deaf employees and the ways in which environmental conditions of the workplace influenced training requirements and procedures.

No Special Accommodations

Most of the supervisors said they did nothing different with deaf employees than with other employees. They usually used a variety of approaches to teach all their employees job routines and new procedures, including written instruction, demonstration, and assignation of a more experienced employee to work with the new person. The following quotations are examples of the various approaches taken by supervisors in teaching new tasks to deaf employees:

> EXAMPLE # 1
> Well, [I teach her new tasks] the same as anyone else ... First, I give her the notes about the new procedure, and then I go through it and I explain it point by point. Then she'll try it, and we'll go over her work and if she's made an error, we'll correct it. But it's really no different than for any of the other girls.
> EXAMPLE # 2
> All of our procedures are written for everything that happens in there ... so that it's pretty easy to follow your procedure manual and any little changes would have gone into that manual.

Use of Special Accommodations

Sometimes changes in procedures or alterations in the work environment were made to accommodate deaf employees. One supervisor found it helpful to seat the deaf employee close by, because "it was ... easier to remember to tell him things so that if I was telling something to the other fellows, I would remember to tell [him] also because he was sitting right there and I could see him—also, I could sit and show him things, like if we wanted to go over a new way of doing something." In other cases, the accommodation took the form of additional time or energy devoted to written conversation or some other one-to-one support from the supervisor. Sometimes this attention was time limited. "For the first year," said one supervisor, "I guess more than any one individual I held her hand and we walked through the process together, and then I began to move away [as] she got to know the process better." In other cases the extra support involved more permanent adaptation and accommodation:

> If I'm going to give a new procedure I am going to make sure that the procedure is written down. Now, if everybody is going to learn the procedure, I will take [her], bring her into my office and then I will explain the procedure. One on one, sign [language] and with the sheets. Then we will all go to the area and I will discuss how I'm doing it so that the hearing people see me and they understand by what they have read. I have to accommodate everybody. I have to give a little extra courtesy to [her].

Most supervisors did not know sign language. When writing was ineffective, these supervisors had to find other strategies for teaching deaf employees. In one instance, a supervisor was able to draw on the sign language skills of another worker to get him through difficult communication situations. As he observed, "If I couldn't write it out without getting lengthy . . . we do know another guy that knows sign. [That] has been a great big help because every time we have a meeting or a movie we have to have somebody explain what is going on to these people. There is no way we could write out something like that. There is no way I could communicate. [For] somebody who doesn't know sign . . . it would be impossible."

Sometimes a strategy initiated with a single, time-limited purpose in mind can have a lasting impact in a variety of areas. A supervisor described what happened when a more experienced hearing employee was assigned to work with the deaf person:

> The girl that was the supervisor in her lab then . . . assigned one of the techs to work with [her] for as long as was necessary to get her used to everybody. This girl also learned sign language very well and so that has worked out really good. So in the years that [she] has been here, this other girl that started out working with her, [they] have built up quite a rapport with each other, and as I say, learning sign language as this other girl did, it has helped a lot. The rest of us are not nearly as good as this girl is.

When asked whether the other woman learned sign language before or after her deaf colleague was hired, the supervisor replied, "She basically learned it from [the deaf employee . . . who] is an excellent teacher and is very patient and has worked with anybody who wants to learn. We basically all know the fingerspelling and that sort of thing, but she worked . . . with this [hearing employee] for probably six to eight months quite closely. [Hearing employee] basically was the one who taught her all the areas and so forth, and in that period of time, [hearing employee] learned sign very well.

Environmental Conditions

Other factors also influenced the kinds of strategies supervisors used in teaching the job to deaf employees, as well as the effectiveness of these strategies. These factors, which can be defined as environmental conditions, include feelings of companionship and team effort within the group, the physical layout of the work area, the nature of the work task, the mission of the organization, and the value placed by the organization on selected behaviors and accomplishments, such as productivity, speed, accuracy, and flexibility. For example, in one case, the size and "family atmosphere" of the organization facilitated communication of company policy:

> Well, normally I tell her what we're doing, if there's any changes in policies. Or, like, I've just come out with an employee handbook which kind of pretty much states the administrative policies of the company, which is helpful to her because sometimes she doesn't know what to do and she has to ask me. This way everyone here will know what to do . . . There's thirty people here. There's maybe fifteen that are here full time. The rest are counter girls . . . some work the morning shift, some the afternoon, and some the evening shift . . . There is thirty people, but there's actually a small group of people, and it's really not hard to communicate with a small family of people.

In another instance, the nature of the work reduced the need for extensive training. As the supervisor put it, "Once they know what to do, you only have to tell them once and they understand . . . a lot of the work is repetitive, so it really doesn't require too much correspondence." In a third case, the supervisor reduced the deaf employee's work load until he had become acclimated to the job and learned the tasks required of him:

> I caused my operation to be more inefficient by giving him twenty-five to thirty hours a week of work [for a forty-hour week], and then I took work away from that desk to help him be successful. Now we're just getting back to giving him more work. He had to become accustomed to what we do and how we do it as a learning process . . . His learning curve, compared to someone who could probably hear properly, is a little bit longer . . . Now, after two years, I think [I am giving him] jobs that he can do to give him a quality work day, give him forty hours worth of work a week.

Most often, learning the job depends on both the training skills of the supervisor and the willingness and ability of the employee to learn. In the following interview excerpt, a supervisor describes the rigorous initial training program of a deaf employee. The employee had been transferred from a department in which the work was very structured to one in which it was not:

> My operation was just the opposite. There are a whole lot of things out there to be done, but they're not identified. You have to come in and start from scratch almost. He had to learn the operation, which he did. I took him on the hands-on training program the first four months that he was working with me. He worked with all the trades people, a couple weeks with an electrician, a few weeks with pipe fitting, a few weeks with machinists, a few weeks with instrumentation people, just to get familiar with the area and know what kind of equipment he worked with. This was a big undertaking from [his] standpoint. He was always flexible to do it. He tried his darndest . . .

In summary, supervisors used a variety of strategies to assist deaf employees in learning different aspects of their job. Some of these strategies were used with all employees. Others were specifically tailored to the needs of the deaf employee. These strategies were further shaped and influenced by environmental conditions, including the nature of the work task, the pace and structure of the department, and the size of the company. Most often, learning the job involved interaction between the individual and the work environment and required adaptation and flexibility on the part of both supervisors and deaf employees. In the following section, we turn to supervisors' evaluations of the deaf employee's work performance.

EVALUATION

Supervisors were asked to evaluate the work performance of deaf employees. Analysis of their comments suggests that successful job performance requires of the worker competence in at least two areas, described here as "technical skills" and "personal qualities." Technical skills are those abilities required for the performance of specific work tasks, such as those listed in job descriptions. They are usually the focus of vocational and professional training programs and are most clearly and directly related to the job task. Knowing how to reconcile a financial statement, for example, is a technical skill. Personal qualities are no less critical to successful work performance, but they are more appropriately described in terms of attitudes towards one's work, the ability to work with others, individual work habits, and knowledge of the culture and mission of the organization. Understanding that everyone is working late due to pressure from management for increased department productivity, and being willing to participate in this team effort, is an example of a personal quality.

Different occupations place greater emphasis on different kinds of competencies. For example, jobs involving product assembly or medical lab work require high levels of productivity and accuracy. A social worker, on the other hand, is expected to exhibit high interpersonal skills and the ability to work as part of a treatment team. Most often, the skills and qualities considered essential within a particular position are closely tied to the mission of the organization and are thus most valued by the supervisor.

Sometimes changes in market conditions or organizational management result in changes in valued skills and qualities. A supervisor in an optical finishing company observed that opening of "one-hour service" labs in the malls has resulted in increased pressure on technicians to produce more eyeglasses in less time. Similarly, another supervisor remarked that changes in the job market have placed additional demands and stress on all employees within her business, as well as reduced flexibility to respond to individual problems and work styles:

> ...the job market has changed so much through the years. This used to be the kind of place where you could come and you could be in a family atmosphere. If you had problems ... you could work it out. The pressure has changed so much. I think that's the biggest thing; the demands the employers are putting on people now. No matter if you have a handicap or not. I've seen everyone just fall under the pressure, and more so for a person like [him] where he has a hearing problem. He's not picking up everything that they ... direct to him. He is experiencing more pressure that way.

A third supervisor described a new program within his company which required increased productivity from his staff and a focus on team effort.

Whatever the valued skills and qualities, deaf employees—like their hearing colleagues—have to identify them and perform their jobs in accordance with the standards and expectations of the organization and supervisor. Evaluations of work performance, therefore, reflect employees' abilities to demonstrate to their supervisors those technical skills and personal qualities viewed as essential within their companies and jobs. Supervisors' comments are presented in the following pages, using the categories of "technical skills" and "personal qualities."

Technical Skills

Most supervisors were satisfied with the deaf employee's technical skills. Some were more than satisfied, expressing the opinion that the employee was doing very well. When asked to elaborate, these supervisors referred to the individual's background and training, efficiency, productivity, precision, and progress in learning new job tasks. While different supervisors focused on different skills, the overall impression was positive. For example, one supervisor noted efficiency, stating that the deaf employee "probably does in two afternoons what someone else might take three or four [to do]." Another focused on training and experience, noting that the person "has a good solid drafting background — he knows what he is doing." A third supervisor praised the employee for her ability to follow established procedures, adding that "she does a very precise and accurate job — she's an excellent worker and she does everything right by the book and right by the letter."

Those who were more conservative in their praise tended to emphasize that the skills demonstrated by the employee were acceptable, given their background and length of time in the position. One supervisor, who had commented that the deaf employee was good in some tasks but slow at typing, added, "But you know, we can't all be fast and accurate too." Another supervisor, who said that the progress made by the deaf employee was similar to that made by hearing employees, continued by pointing out that "he has a long way to go [in terms of] just learning . . . it is just something you gain with years of experience. The only way he can get what he [has] got to get is just by puttin' in time and just learn[ing]." Some supervisors reflected on their role in facilitating the successful performance of technical work tasks. One person emphasized the importance of giving employees appropriate feedback to help them improve. Although he didn't give a glowing report of the deaf employee's performance, he felt that with proper supervision and support, the employee's work would improve over time:

> I'd say his progress [over the past year] was average . . . as much as I would expect [of] anyone . . . Again, considering the lack of background in the area that we had hired him in, you can't blame him for that to do any better. But he made very good progress. In fact, we just had a yearly rating, and he did well . . . He continually showed knowledge of the job and continually tried to [do] better . . . building on skills. He still wants to do well and he does not mind trying to do that. All he needs, like anyone else in any job needs, is

someone to tell him where to improve. You can't expect a person (it doesn't matter if they're deaf or not) to improve on something if you don't tell them what their goals are.

A few supervisors were not entirely satisfied with the technical quality of the deaf employee's work. In each case, their concern was described within the context of organizational priorities and valued skills. For example, in a setting where there was pressure for increased productivity, a supervisor said of his deaf employee, "We'd like to see [her] work a little faster." Similarly, a supervisor whose company had recently implemented a "waste containment" program was understandably eager to see an increase in the productivity of the deaf employee. His concern extended to the morale of the whole department:

> The longer people work, then the more we expect of them. We don't treat him as a handicap[ped person] after a while, and it's like, "Hey, you're one of the crowd, and we expect you to perform, work, eight hours a day." We try to give everyone ten hours worth of work to get done in eight and I need to get him up to that because everyone else is saying, "Well, who cares if he's handica- pped . . . he has to carry his own load." Ultimately, that's what we're trying to get to. So that's my goal, to get him more work . . . that he can do and still be successful . . .

Some organizations, particularly those involved in highly technical work such as architecture, engineering, and medical technology, place a very high value on accuracy—in fact, the reputation of the company rests on the precision of its work and reliability of its product. One supervisor noted that his deaf worker's inaccuracies and lack of attention to detail "creates a . . . lack of confidence" with potentially serious consequences. As he put it, "If you invest in that diagram and it's wrong, it could be very expensive . . . and time consuming."

Personal Qualities

As noted earlier, supervisors also described personal qualities as criti- cal for successful work performance. These include willingness to work hard, motivation, flexibility, the ability to work well with others, and good judgment or common sense.

The willingness to work hard was highly valued by supervisors. In some cases, they attributed the willingness to work hard to the employee's satisfaction with the work itself. As one person put it, "I think he likes it up here . . . If you have the satisfaction when you're done looking at your product and saying, 'It looks nice, I did it.' You see something that you accomplish."

Sometimes, supervisors felt deaf employees' inability to hear made them harder workers. For example, being unable to participate in the casual conversations which often take place between workers was seen as a "plus" by some supervisors. In the words of one person, "Probably . . . he is not apt to idle chatter like somebody else—he does more hours than the other people." In other cases, deafness was seen as providing a natural motivation to prove oneself to others. Below, a supervisor draws connections between the willingness to work hard and the deaf employee's understanding of his unique position within the company:

> He is the type of person, he wants to do more, he wants to be successful and he knows that we don't have too many of him around here and he's like a lead person. He's a very visible person, he's very friendly and he makes friends and he wants to be successful. So when I give him a new job, I tell him ahead of time that "Hey, I'm trying to help you by giving you this job" . . . so he can learn more. He takes it and he runs with it, and most of the time, he does a good job with it.

Frequently, additional effort was described in terms of a deaf employee's ability to identify, assess, and compensate for limitations which may be imposed on work performance due to deafness. It is important to note that these limitations were as much the result of a lack of accommodations as they were the result of deafness. Regardless of the cause, supervisors admired deaf employees who were creative in finding solutions. Below, a supervisor shares his impression of a deaf employee who found a way to compensate for his lack of access to telephone communication.

> He can't use the phone, that's very important, he runs around a lot more physically in terms of making contact with people. Now with a great deal of vigor, which he has, he still does an excellent job, but I could imagine somebody with less energy . . . not quite coping and not doing as well . . . [Later in interview] I put him in the top ten percent of [employees with regard to] amount of effort devoted to the job and time. He put in a full working day every day, and he expected to do that and that's very good, that's what you want . . . he was always there on time, he worked throughout the day, he was always trying to improve the situation, [a] very, very positive, active person.

In one case deafness, and the employee's efforts to compensate for her inability to hear her customers, was seen as resulting in superior work performance. The employee worked in a service organization with mostly hearing clients. According to the supervisor, the employee went to great lengths to discuss with clients their goals and desired outcomes before beginning a project, perhaps because she wanted to be extra careful to avoid misunderstandings. Hearing employees rarely demonstrated the same level of interest and interaction with customers. The supervisor concludes, "She really felt it was important to talk to them [clients], and so in that respect . . . she was even better than a hearing person."

Conversely, employees who failed to demonstrate high levels of motivation or commitment were perceived less favorably. Below, a supervisor describes the difficulty he had persuading the deaf employee to arrive at work on time:

> SUPERVISOR: In the first year it took . . . quite a number of discussions to get him from the point of arriving ten minutes late for work every single day to arriving on time. There is no reason in my mind why . . . you can't be here . . . why should you be different, you know? Especially when you're consistently late every day.
> INTERVIEWER: How did you resolve that?
> SUPERVISOR: We talked just in terms of, you know, this is the starting time, you're not special, there's no reason for you to act that way. Get some general discussion back and he'd be good for a couple of days, then he'd fall back on his schedule, then we'd talk about it again. It's not really something—we don't have a mechanism to penalize somebody, particularly. To me it's like a defiance, you know, there are the rules, this is the pay, we don't have a time clock per se on it . . . but . . .
> INTERVIEWER: But he comes to work on time now?
> SUPERVISOR: Generally, yeah. [But] I would say he's never been early more than two days in two years . . . it may be because he's bored with the job.

This employee's behavior created an unfavorable impression on his supervisor. The supervisor's comment that the deaf employee almost never comes to work early suggests that other employees do arrive early and that their behavior is interpreted as a gesture of commitment to the company. By failing to arrive early, the deaf employee conveys a lack of motivation and interest in his job.

Flexibility and the ability to work as part of a team were seen as important as well. Sometimes, this required that deaf employees locate and interpret their job within the framework of department activities and goals. For example, one supervisor said that hearing co-workers sometimes fall behind in their work when the phone rings constantly. The deaf employee, on the other hand, is unable to use the phone and thus is excused from this activity, which sometimes is a source of irritation to hearing workers. However, the supervisor quickly pointed out that she "always makes up for it." The interview continues:

> INTERVIEWER: ... You said that she always makes up for it. Do you think that she's aware, then, of what that causes in the group and she's purposely trying to make up for it in other ways, or do you think that she's just generally such a hard worker and she's not aware of the fact that there might be some irritation over that?
>
> SUPERVISOR: I think it's a little bit of both. I think that she is a hard worker and she would see things to be done anyhow. I also think that she is sensitive enough that she realizes that there are times when people are just to the end [of their rope] because they have been so busy and I think that she is just aware enough to know that is a problem.

Another supervisor summed up the deaf employee's qualities in this area as a "general attitude of being a part of something bigger and identifying where you fit in and doing it."

One deaf employee, who had successfully assumed a leadership role within his team, was praised by his supervisor for his ability to take control and initiate new projects without being viewed by his co-workers as pushy:

> "He went in and did a number of things that other people had not either bothered to or succeeded in doing, like getting a lot of record keeping updated and ... organized. He was looking for things to do, very aggressive but in a gentle and very positive way ... That's a very positive kind of thing if you succeed in doing it and you don't get everybody angry."

Inflexibility was viewed by supervisors as a serious weakness, interfering with both job training and work performance. The following examples are illustrative:

EXAMPLE # 1

You know, [he] was always one, well, he had his own way of doing things. Instead of listening to me, he'd just fight for his own way to do things. I mean, he was really stubborn. I'd wanna sit and show him a new way or a way that would save him time to inspect something, and he'd say, "No, I think it's better to do it this way." And I'd say, "Yeah, you can do it that way, but it takes you four times as long. How about this way?" [Later in interview] ... if he would take what's offered to him and not argue back, that would help. I mean he needs to know when to quit.

EXAMPLE # 2

[He] is a very stubborn person. It's hard at times to deal with that personal characteristic because you can't talk with him ... Our feeling is that you have to understand how drawings are put together ... in order to build on it. [He] has a feeling that he knows how to do things . . . he tends to do it [his] way . . . I think he does it under the idea that he's showing that he's thinking and creative, but it is of no benefit to us if we have to [have] things a certain way.

The deaf employees described above were perceived by their supervisors as failing to understand the protocols and valued skills in their respective work environments. In the first instance, the employee did not follow his supervisor's instructions, creating the impression that he did not respect the skill and experience of his boss. In the second case, the employee did not demonstrate an understanding of the value placed by his supervisor on the standard procedures used by the company, and as a result was perceived as a burden rather than a contributing member of the team.

Supervisors also described judgment and common sense as essential personal qualities. These qualities are critical for knowing when to ask for help and when to work something through independently. One supervisor observed of the deaf employee, " . . . if he's got a question, he just don't sit there. You get up and go somewhere and write out a question and ask. He don't come to me all the time. [But] he just doesn't sit there and let something not get done. [If] he don't know what he's doing he will ask. He is very highly motivated." Another made a similar comment regarding the deaf person in her department, noting that "she's the kind of employee that all persons would like to have. She comes to me when she needs help, but then, on the other hand, she's taken the attitude to "go for it," so to speak . . . She's every supervisor's dream."

Failure to use good judgment in determining when to ask for help and when to proceed independently created many problems. One supervisor described his frustration with—and eroding confidence in—a deaf employee who did not exhibit this quality:

Like, when I expect him to write something down, he doesn't write it down. He tries to talk with me, but I know he hasn't picked up all the things that I may have asked. I may come in . . . and give [him] a list of four things I want done. His approach at times is to—even if those things are what I feel crystal clear and I think that they are . . . with using a very minor amount of common sense, someone should be able to follow through and if I never came back to the building . . . should have them accomplished. He may [come to me] "just," as he phrases it, "to make sure what I was asking." To me, that's like, you know, I [would] write it down. [But] he has all these questions and if I tell him something and he writes nothing down and he has no questions, yet I know if I did the same thing and told him the four things, I've no idea what I'd get back, or I'd have a concern when I get [it] back, it's going very much in opposite directions to what I thought I asked for. Common sense is kind of what [he] is lacking.

The employee described above did not seem to understand the importance of taking notes. Instead, he turned to his boss with questions about what he was expected to do, which only irritated the supervisor further. Another supervisor expressed concern over his deaf employee's *failure* to ask appropriate questions and learn office routine:

SUPERVISOR: Some of the problems that we've incurred in the last two years . . . you sort of forget about the first six months because it was a learning experience for all of us. But since we became accustomed to him and we know what we need to provide to him when we give him a job or when other people complain about something not being done or whatever, we know where we've failed because the whole story hasn't been explained to him. Let me get into that for a second, because now we've worked with him for almost two years and I'm not gonna say that he uses that [deafness] as a crutch. [But] a lot of times when something does go wrong, it's like maybe he didn't know but we didn't know he wouldn't know and he didn't tell me. Okay, well, you can only use that so much because after a while, you're in our system long enough. It's very hard to be an island and not be affected by letters going over your desk and conversations, having a meeting. So that every time that's thrown at us, we sort of say, "Hey, that's no excuse." I mean, you have to have some common sense about what we do. I mean . . . you've had some . . . [college] courses, you know, and so we resist falling into that being used as a crutch, "I didn't know."
INTERVIEWER: Can you give me an example to illustrate when that happened?
SUPERVISOR: Probably it would be a reconciliation of an account, something that is reconciled every month. He'd say, "Well, I didn't know I should have reconciled it." [So I'd say] "Well, hey, you see everyone else reconciling their accounts at the end of the month, don't you think that you would reconcile that account? Why didn't you come and ask if you didn't know? [Ask] Should I be doing the same thing?"

These two stories illustrate the importance of using judgment in deciding when and how to request help. As noted in the second story, the expectation is that the performance of all employees, including those who are deaf, will improve over time. Those who fail to demonstrate growth may be perceived as lacking skill, motivation, sound judgment or, to use the words of these two supervisors, "common sense."

In summary, supervisors value both technical and personal qualities in employees. Their interest in both kinds of qualities suggests that technical ability is necessary but not sufficient for successful job performance. Personal qualities, such as good judgment and the ability to work as part of a team, are also important and require of the employee an understanding of the values, procedures, and mission of the organization.

DISCUSSION

Three points can be made about the perspectives of supervisors on hiring, training, and evaluating deaf employees. These include the themes of compensation, accommodation, and distinctions between technical skills and personal qualities.

The notion of "compensatory effort" is reflected in supervisors' remarks that for deaf people to be successful, they must demonstrate *more* of some valued skill or characteristic as compensation for being unable to hear. These may be above average technical skills, especially high motivation, willingness to work extra hard, or sensitivity to the feelings of hearing colleagues. Accepting the responsibility of being a "ground breaker," that is, the first deaf person to be hired by the company, is another example of this compensatory effect. While supervisors did not explicitly draw connections between compensatory qualities and their impressions of deaf employees, it may be that those who demonstrate these qualities are viewed more favorably in the hiring and evaluation process. Conversely, those who fail to demonstrate compensatory qualities may be viewed as lacking appropriate levels of technical skill, motivation, sensitivity, gratitude, and responsibility, *even when these levels are comparable to those demonstrated by hearing peers.* While it may be argued that to expect compensatory effort from deaf workers is discriminatory, it may be fairly common practice.

A second theme involves the use of "special accommodations" for deaf workers. Supervisors said they sometimes change the way they do business in order to hire, train, or evaluate a deaf person. Examples include redefining work loads, seating the deaf person nearby, reviewing information separately with deaf employees, and providing written explanations of work tasks. Underlying each of these accommodations is the realization on the part of supervisors that deaf people may encounter barriers within the work environment which make it difficult for them to fulfill performance expectations or otherwise function effectively in their jobs, and a willingness to alter the environment in order to enable these employees to succeed. While some supervisors made extensive accommodations, others made few or none.

The third point has to do with the importance of personal qualities in evaluating job performance. While the ability to perform technical tasks is critical, so are work habits, interpersonal skills, and the ability to understand and become a part of the company culture. Given the value placed by supervisors on these qualities, it becomes important to know whether deaf people have equal opportunities to acquire these work habits and knowledge. While it is beyond the scope of this book to describe educational programs available to deaf students or assess the degree to which they provide instruction in personal work qualities, it can be argued that the communication barriers which most deaf people face over a lifetime make it more difficult for them to acquire the wealth of social and cultural knowledge which is learned through incidental (as opposed to direct) instruction, that is, through observation and overhearing the conversations of adults and peers. The ability to read a culture through participation and observation is a skill that most people acquire naturally over many years. Children listen to their parents' conversation and those of other adults. They observe school friends, learning the values and acceptable behaviors of the group so they can more easily fit in. As adults, they use the same skills to access social and professional networks.

Deaf people are often cut off from these learning experiences, especially if they grow up in homes and attend mainstream schools where they are the only deaf person. As adults, they continue to face isolation, although they often have more choices for social alliances. For example, unless they seek out the company of other deaf adults and become part of the Deaf[2] community, they will continue to face the same isolation. Unless they work in agencies or organizations that employ large numbers of deaf people (and these are very rare), they are likely to be denied most incidental information, just as they were during their early years. As a result, the task of deciphering the culture of the work environment relative to organizational mission, administrative philosophy, and valued skills and work habits may be difficult for deaf employees, since this information rarely, if ever, appears in formal or written job descriptions. Rather, company culture is learned over time through casual conversations with co-workers, observation, and the development of close relationships with key people throughout the organization.

The communication barriers faced by most deaf people in the workplace often prevent them from accessing these social networks. As a result, it cannot be assumed that deaf people who always read the paper during coffee break or go to lunch alone do so because they prefer to be by themselves. They may also do so because they are unable to participate comfortably in the conversations of those around them. Social isolation, while often leading to loneliness, may also impede the deaf employee's ability to determine which qualities are most highly prized within the organization and may also affect evaluations of work performance. In the next three chapters, we will explore related areas in which deaf people have historically encountered barriers at work: these are communication on the job, relationships with hearing co-workers, and evaluations of potential for management.

COMMENTARY

SUSAN: I'd like to ask each of you to talk a little bit about what you remember from your job interviews.

GARY: I don't know if they knew how much hearing loss I had, but the interview went well. Sometimes I didn't understand them, asked them to repeat.

JANICE: My resume said nothing except in the bottom line, for community activities, I said I was, "Miss Deaf America second runner up," and "Miss Deaf South Carolina." That's what got their attention, and they'd say, "Oh, she's deaf." The phone number at the top with my name was the number of my hearing friends who were willing to help me to receive these phone calls. When the woman called about my application, she asked my friend, "Is she deaf?" My friend said "Yes, you can communicate with her through pencil and paper or lipreading." And that's where the woman got the idea. So she knew how to communicate with me before I got to the office. That's a trick I use.

SUSAN: So on your resume, at the top, you listed a friend's phone number rather than your own with a TDD.

JANICE: Right. The companies in my area, they wouldn't have a TDD or relay service back then, so I used my hearing friend's.

SUSAN: Did the person who interviewed you seem comfortable?

JANICE: I couldn't tell, but they told me later that they were very nervous. They didn't know how to communicate with me, but they said my personality helped them to feel relaxed. Because of my humor. And I smile, I guess. That helped them to feel better and relaxed.

SUSAN: Did you have to use paper and pencil as part of the interview?

JANICE: I depended on lipreading, unless the question was too deep or too serious. Then I'd say, "Please write it." If they said, "What do you know about computers?" or some simple question like that, then I felt comfortable. It depended upon the question. So there was a balance between writing and lipreading.

SUSAN: Did they bring a piece of paper and pencil with them or did you, or did both of you?

JANICE: That was theirs.

SUSAN: Were you nervous?

JANICE: Well, nervous about the technical questions. I didn't want to look stupid. But I wasn't nervous about the communication. I've grown up with that, around hearing friends, so that was no problem.

DAVID: I remember looking for my first full-time job after graduating from NTID. At that time, it was bad for employment. That was 1984. I interviewed with more than twenty companies. First thing when I went in, they'd hand me the electronic tests. I knew I had to bring my calculator. I found some tests were very difficult. Some were too easy. But after they gave me that test they'd say that they would contact me later. Later, I'd call and ask about the job and they'd say, "No, the position is full." So I was very frustrated. Finally, I went back to college

I was pursuing a bachelor's degree at RIT. At the same time I went around to look for local jobs. I sent the resume, then I followed up with a contact asking for a job interview. They said, "Come on in." So I told them, "I'm deaf, and I prefer to write." They said, "No problem." So I went. They were very nice. I was interviewed by a big guy who looked like Marlon Brando, you know, like a big producer. I felt very comfortable. We wrote back and forth. And then he said, "Do you think you can do the job?" I said, "I feel I'm qualified for the job." But the last question that he asked was, "I've interviewed more than ten hearing people, now you're one deaf person, why should I hire you?" I thought, "Hmm, that's a tough question." Then I thought to myself, you're lucky. I was interested in productivity. I knew that he was too. So I said, "Well, I'm deaf. I concentrate on my work. I'm skilled at that. The hearing people hear all these things, phones ringing, people talking, and they lose their concentration. I don't pay any attention to those things, I just keep focusing on my work." That convinced him.

GARY: I think that was an excellent selling point. You sold yourself well. That was good.

SUSAN: Do you think it's okay for a deaf person to indicate on their resume that they're deaf?

JANICE: Yes.

DAVID: On my resume I put down under health, "deafness."

GARY: I don't do that. I don't recommend that, because I don't want deaf people to be labeled as being different. I want them to be judged all the same, then the company itself finds out whether they're a deaf person or not.

SUSAN: What advice would you give supervisors the next time they're considering a deaf job applicant?

GARY: My advice to supervisors is to find out what kind of communication mode the person would like to use. So then the challenge is, how does the supervisor know that the person is a deaf applicant? That's a challenge. So, for example, in Janice's case they saw "Miss South Carolina." If worse comes to worse, and they don't know that it's a deaf person coming, I guess that you can sit down and try to communicate the best you can. If it doesn't work out, set up another appointment with an interpreter.

DAVID: As to having interpreters at the interview, some companies might get the wrong idea that means that during training and work, the person has to have an interpreter every single day, and that would be terribly expensive. So then they don't hire them.

GARY: Well, I agree. But the deaf person themselves has to educate the company. If it is me, then I'm responsible to explain that. When I go to the interview, I explain about the interpreting role. I tell them, "You're not interviewing both of us, you're just interviewing me. The interpreter is for me, that's all." But I understand, it's a sticky situation.

DAVID: I remember a job interview in Maryland, I brought my hearing sister, just to save on lengthy conversation time, so I brought her with me. During the job interview I told them, "I've only brought this person to save time because you don't have time for a lengthy interview, you have other interviews to do."

SUSAN: I'm wondering if you ever feel that you've been turned down for a job because you're deaf?

JANICE: Yes. I do suspect that. For example, after graduating from college, I was looking for a job in South Carolina. I had a bachelor's degree in information systems, but finding jobs was really difficult. So I demoted myself to mail clerk jobs. I took the test, and I sent it off. I heard nothing for two weeks, so I called this boss, and the boss said, "Well, I'm not really sure how you can communicate." I said, "Is that the reason? Let me come there and talk with the person." I got into the office, and we talked and then he hired me. I proved to the company that I was able to communicate. I only worked there for six months, but I wanted to educate them that deaf people could do that job.

GARY: I can't think if it's ever happened to me because I was deaf. I can't say that. Many people are inclined to say, "Well, they didn't call me because I'm deaf," and I say, "No, there are many resumes." I really can't say very much about that. I have no proof.

DAVID: I agree with Gary. People have to go by the skills, whether you can do the job.

JANICE: In South Carolina, I did have that experience. Then I moved to Virginia. There, it was a little more open minded. It was two hours from Gallaudet, so they had a lot more exposure to deafness. That helps, especially after the deaf protests. That had a big impact on all the companies.

SUSAN: Could we talk about training sessions? What happened? How did you learn new things about your job? How did your supervisor help or not help you to do that?

JANICE: No interpreter—went through training with no interpreter. They gave me papers, materials to read and to follow through, but with no interpreter. I just had to read lips myself. I felt frustrated, but that was part of my job. I was well paid, so I had to get through it. Plus, I could write a note, tell my boss, "I don't understand. You must give me time. Don't expect me to learn as fast as the other hearing employees." And they said, "Yes, okay, I understand your situation is different." So, I was perhaps a month behind the other employees.

SUSAN: Did that ever affect your evaluations from your supervisor?

JANICE: They said at the time that others would be evaluated in a certain time frame. Mine would be evaluated at a later time to make sure I had equal information or was able to learn the same as the other employees. I educated my boss. Also, I did complain that I needed an interpreter all the time. They tried their best to hire interpreters at certain times, like for a big conference or sometimes for big meetings. But for weekly training, there were no interpreters.

DAVID: I went through training in the same situation as Janice's, except that I did get more help. I worked in an engineering firm. When I started the job, I had no interpreter. There were only about fifty employees working for this company. I gave them a lot of information about deafness, communication, and the need for interpreters, but at that time I was a little nervous. You know, this was my first real job. But two technicians, co-workers, gave me a lot of written information, written by them for me.

And then I got a manual of production characteristics and specifications. They encouraged me to read a lot, as much as I could, and just ask questions. It took me a few weeks to catch up, then I was on my own.

SUSAN: You said you had two co-workers who helped you out. How did that come about?

DAVID: I was in a flexible work environment. There was no pressure. I worked at my own pace. If I had a question I could always just go to somebody. I could write it to them. At the same time I taught them some survival signs for communication. Sometimes if I had a complex technical question I'd do it on the computer, and we would communicate through the computer.

GARY: I've worked at three different companies, and each one was different. My first job was with an insurance company. I was capable of communicating on a one-to-one basis, so that wasn't a problem for me. But they did not provide any kind of services for me. Everything was the same; write notes or meet with the supervisor. Through three years, I guess my problem was that I wasn't really familiar enough with what should be done to advocate my rights for myself. My attitude now is very different. If I were to start over they'd hear from me a lot now. So that was my experience there. I was never really given any kind of opportunity— maybe not because I was deaf necessarily, but because the boss of the company was not really doing training. As I look back, I don't remember anybody in my department who was really sent out for training. My company wasn't set up that way. There was more, "Here's your job, get it done," same routine. So that was one job. Another job was a fantastic experience. It was a different field in sales. My manager was a marvelous person, very easy to lipread. We established a tone between the two of us. It was fantastic. Couldn't complain. That was the best manager I ever had, very sensitive. If I asked for an interpreter, that was fine, and they'd take care of the cost. In training, they wanted me to learn everything that I could learn about the business, so they were very supportive. Even when I was sent to Boston; I couldn't find an interpreter in Boston, so I brought one from Rochester. I went to South Carolina, had to travel all around. I always had an interpreter there full-time. So that was the interpreter situation. One thing that I did try to encourage them to do was to get captioning for the videotapes and also to solve the problems associated with listening to tapes. There was a lot of that. I remember once I went to a training meeting. Two people were giving a presentation. They had the interpreters, and then they gave out tapes. Later I said,

"You know, I can't listen to that." So they gave me a book. No one else had the book, just me, instead of the tapes. So people were very sensitive. They were very supportive.

Anyway, I guess those were two different experiences. It depends on the company, and it depends on yourself. Speaking from my experience, because I'm a supervisor now, if a person is very good at their job and proves themselves to the company, the company is more inclined to do something for them. If you prove that you can do the job, most companies will give you interpreters for training. As an Employment Advisor at NTID, part of my job is to go out and encourage companies to give equal access for their deaf employees. I know of several situations when the company did provide about five thousand dollars for two weeks of interpreting to the deaf employees.

JANICE: He's talking about companies that are based in a local northern area where people know more about the deaf. In the south they're not open-minded yet. They don't know much about deafness. Plus, I moved to Virginia, again, it's still south—it's behind in terms of deafness. That's my point. I don't agree that you must prove to the company that you're a good worker before they get the interpreter. I disagree. I think it's just that they haven't understood deaf people's needs yet. They have to be taught, but I lost my patience and quit.

SUSAN: What advice would you give to supervisors who want to provide the best possible training for a deaf employee?

JANICE: Have an interpreter ready for the training session.

GARY: I feel that the supervisor needs to build confidence in the deaf person, to let the deaf employee experience other things. From what I've seen, many supervisors are inclined to train deaf workers in one area, and then they have to stay there. So, the supervisor needs to learn and know that this person can learn new areas. I've seen that happen often. Even with my first job, I felt that happened to me. I was limited to one area. I was never given an opportunity to learn new things. So my advice would be to encourage the supervisor to let the deaf employee learn what they're supposed to be doing first, and then once they feel comfortable with that, and the supervisor feels confident about them, they should move to some new skills.

DAVID: It's hard for me to comment because I worked for a small company. But I know that in big companies, they often have large training sessions for new employees. From what I have heard, they treat deaf people a little differently. Sometimes interpreters are not provided.

They give them a book to read instead. The deaf people feel that they're not getting the full information out of the training. It's the supervisor's responsibility to have everything prepared, to have the interpreter ready, to inform everyone, so that the deaf person feels more comfortable and can get information, good information, the same as the hearing people.

JANICE: To feel part of the group, too. To feel the same, that's important.

DAVID: Yes.

SUSAN: Can you follow up on that just a little bit?

JANICE: Well, to feel part of the group, it's just like David said. You need to have an interpreter ready. The supervisor knows what information needs to be given to the employees, and should get it ready for the deaf person as well. Always make sure that the deaf person is included. Don't all of a sudden not know how to handle it, and leave them out. For example, if you're watching videotapes for training, have the captions ready, if that's possible, so the deaf and hearing people can get the same information. That would be nice.

SUSAN: I wanted to ask you if you felt the evaluations that you received from your supervisors were accurate and fair? What kinds of things did they say you did well? Did they ask you to improve in any areas? How was the evaluation handled?

GARY: I can share that. My experience was different, between the first and the second jobs. On the first job, it was more of a patronizing kind of an evaluation. It was like, I was doing a good job, and that's all. It's hard for me to say because I don't know how that person evaluates other people, but I sensed that it was more a patronizing kind of an evaluation, like, "You did good, everything's fine, keep doing what you're supposed to be doing." In another job, because I had outstanding work performance, my boss did not patronize me at all. He just wanted me to do more and more and more. I know that it wasn't because I was deaf or hearing, it was because of what I was capable of doing. So that experience was completely different. He would say, "I'm satisfied with what you're doing, now do more." Of course, the more you do, the more money the company makes. That was the bottom line for the company. So my success was there, and they kept adding more, higher expectations for me. I think the evaluation is a good time to sit down with your boss and share. It is supposed to be a positive thing. I know some people take it in a negative way. It shouldn't be that way.

JANICE: My first job experience was awful because the training wasn't really provided. As I said a while ago, the evaluation was extended by a month. They thought that by waiting longer I would learn more, but that was wrong. So, they said, "You work fine, but your learning ability is low." I said, "It's because you don't provide me with the interpreters, and I can't get the information." So that wasn't good. But then when I quit that and went to the second job, it was a lot better. I had a lot more one on one training, so my evaluation came out much higher.

DAVID: I worked five years at my old job and had six evaluations. I felt their evaluation system really wasn't very fair. During evaluation time they required me to write about my success and my strengths and weaknesses and communication during the past year. It was very hard for me to remember what I had done for the whole past year. Then after writing it, I'd hand it to my boss, and he got an evaluation from my supervisor, too. And sometimes the two didn't match. And what's more, I remember the first two or three evaluations when I sat down with my boss and the supervisor, we had no interpreter. We had to write back and forth. I remember at the second evaluation they said I had communication difficulties, that when I faced a technical problem I was afraid to ask for help. I was surprised at that. I told them that sometimes I didn't feel comfortable with the other technicians. They're very, very busy with the telephone. So sometimes if I'm stuck, I just keep quiet and go ahead and solve the problem on my own, but without informing them. They encouraged me to inform them. They said in the future there might be some technical problems that come up, and I should know how to resolve them. As time went on, I finally got a new boss, a very nice woman, who understood my feelings and my needs. When I asked for an interpreter for the evaluation, I said I'd prefer an ASL interpreter, and she understood. That was much better. By the fourth or fifth year, I got much higher performance evaluations.

SUSAN: That's very interesting. So you changed bosses part way through your job, and that made a difference?

DAVID: Yes. Big difference.

SUSAN: Was it more than just the fact that she got an interpreter for your evaluation? Did she do other things differently?

DAVID: Well, I think it was both. The interpreter was very good, a skilled ASL interpreter, so it was very easy for me to communicate, and the reversing[3] was very good. Also, she was very open-minded and sensitive to my deafness and needs. So I think there were two reasons that I felt comfortable during the evaluations.

SUSAN: You know, it's interesting, when you said that the interpreter was good at reversing your signs, I was wondering if you think that hearing people are more apt to think well of you when you have a good interpreter to voice for you because it presents you better to them.

DAVID: I agree with you. I remember one time I had a department meeting and they brought in an interpreter who signed straight English. I raised my hand to ask a question. The interpreter couldn't read me, and everybody was staring at me. I was very embarrassed, and my mind just went blank. I said, "Forget it, just forget it." For the next meeting I said, "I must have an interpreter who's skilled in ASL." They said, "What's the difference between English and ASL?" The supervisor learned about the difference between ASL and English. Next time, with an ASL interpreter, I felt like I was one of them. The communication reversal was key.

SUSAN: In this chapter, supervisors talked about technical skills and personal qualities. Which do you think is most important to successful job performance?

JANICE: Personal qualities.

DAVID: I think both are very important. The technical skills are fine. You meet that for the job qualification, but the personal skills are very important because on the job, sometimes there are changes and you may have to learn how to get along with different people. For example, if there is a restructuring in the company, you have to work with different people, or in a different part of the organization. At my old job, we used an old system for finding a part number, and there was a certain amount of paperwork. You find it in a book, and then you write it down and then get the order from the parts department. Then the computer took over that function. One man refused to learn the computer. He wanted to stay on the old method, and they fired him. He lost his job because he wouldn't be flexible in learning new skills. That applies to deafness, too. For example, one of my best friends learned printing in trade school, graduated, went out and got a job as a printer. The boss wanted him to learn their new, different kinds of skills, and the deaf person refused. He said, "No, the school taught me this, and that's what I'm staying with." Well, he was fired.

JANICE: Well, to ask the question about personal or technical skills, suppose you had to choose one, which would be most important? I think it's personal over technical.

GARY: You have to be able to get the job done or you can't keep your job.

JANICE: No, you learn it. You learn—learning how to get along is learning from people.

GARY: It's both, both are important.

JANICE: Oh, yes. Both are important, but which one is a little more important? I think the personal. I've asked all my friends, and they say the personal makes your job happier, more fun, you joke around. At the same time you're learning more, and have good teamwork.

RESOURCE LIST

Library Resources

Note: Books and articles listed in this section should be available at local public or college/university libraries or through the interlibrary loan services at these libraries. Purchase prices listed may vary and are indicated only to give the reader a general idea of cost; contact publisher directly for current cost and shipping/handling charges.

Brown, M.J. "Please speak slowly. I lipread." *ABA Banking Journal, 75,* 30, 1983.

> Brown describes the U.S. Bank of Oregon's program to hire and train deaf people as bank tellers.

Doggett, G. "Employers' Attitudes Toward Hearing-Impaired People: A Comparative Study." *Volta Review, 91*(6), 269–281, 1989.

> Results of a study conducted on thirteen employers which presents strong evidence that negative employer attitudes exist toward hearing-impaired speech, having implications for the question of reliability of employment interviews for selecting qualified applications without unfair discrimination.

Fritz, G., & Smith, N. *The Hearing Impaired Employee: An Untapped Resource.* Austin, TX: College-Hill Press, 1985. (Available from College-Hill Press, Inc., 8700 Shoal Creek Boulevard, Austin, TX, 78758; Phone 800-343-9204 [Voice]; ISBN 0-316-29367-9; Cost: $23.50)

> This manual was developed to help supervisors work more efficiently with hearing-impaired employees. It also includes a section to orient all workers to the characteristics and needs of a hearing-impaired coworker.

Halcrow, A. "This Program has Offered People a Second Chance." *Personnel Journal,* 65(5), 10, 12, 1986.

> At E. F. Hutton's headquarters in New York City, there are hearing-impaired employees who are graduates of a unique training program designed to help the company meet its human resource needs and to give employees marketable word processing skills. Halcrow's article discusses the training program.

Libous, T.W. *Employment: An Informative Resource to Assist People with Disabilities.* 2nd ed., rev. Albany, NY: Senate Select Committee on the Disabled, 1991. (Available from New York State Senate Select Committee on the Disabled, Room 815-LOB, Albany, NY 12248; Phone 518-455-2096 [Voice]; Cost: free)

> This booklet gives an overview of the federal, New York state and local laws, programs, and policies which are in place to protect the employment rights of people with disabilities. It is a "user's manual" which provides practical knowledge to the individual seeking information about the world of employment, and also serves to enlighten the employers of New York state regarding the abilities of persons who are disabled. Outside New York state, contact individual state legislatures to determine if similar materials have been published on this topic.

McCrone, W.P., & Arthur, R.L. "The Deaf Applicant: Considerations for Personnel Managers." *Personnel Administrator,* pp. 65–69, 1981 (June).

> McCrone and Arthur point out the employability of deaf workers, their stability in jobs, the uses of Vocational Rehabilitation services, and how to integrate deaf employees into the workforce.

Nester, M.A. "Employment Testing for Hearing Impaired Persons." *Public Personnel Management,* 13(4), 417–434, 1984.

> Discusses the problems that can arise from using standardized employment tests on hearing-impaired persons, who have particular difficulty with verbal tests.

O'Bryant, T. "Facts About Hiring People With Disabilities." *Worklife: A Publication on Employment and Persons With Disabilities,* 1(3), 8–10, 1988.

> O'Bryant addresses the myths and stereotypes concerning employees with disabilities.

Pati, G.C., & Adkins, J.I. *Managing and Employing the Handicapped: The Untapped Potential.* Highland Park, IL: Brace-Park, The Human Resource Press, 1981.

> This work explains to employers and others the validity in business terms of hiring handicapped workers. The text includes legal information, programs in

industry, support technology and services, training and development, job analysis and placement, and a summary of major studies on employment of people who are handicapped.

Schweitzer, N.J., & Deely, J. "Interviewing the Disabled Job Applicant." *Personnel Journal,* 205–209, 1982 (March).

Describes the usual attitudes of able-bodied people faced with interviewing disabled persons, the skills and knowledge needed, and errors to avoid. Interview techniques for hearing-impaired applicants are reviewed.

Stern, V.W., Lifton, D.E., & Malcom, S.M. (Eds.). *Resource Directory of Scientists and Engineers With Disabilities.* Washington, DC: American Association for the Advancement of Science, 1987.

This directory lists the names, addresses, backgrounds, etc. of disabled persons, including hearing-impaired persons, in scientific and engineering professions.

Pamphlets and Brochures

Crammatte, A.B. *Questions and Answers About Employment of Deaf People.* (Available from National Information Center on Deafness, Gallaudet University, 800 Florida Avenue, NE, Washington, DC 20002-3695; Phone 202-651-5051 [Voice], 202-651-5052 [TDD]; Order no. 564; Cost: $1.00)

This four-page publication discusses the types of jobs deaf people have, provides information about agencies which can help employers identify qualified deaf workers, and identifies some communication adjustments that employers and co-workers can make.

Putting Disabled People in Your Place: Focus on Deaf and Hard-of-Hearing Individuals. (Available from Mainstream, Inc., 3 Bethesda Metro Center, Suite 830, Bethesda, MD, 20814; Phone 301-654-2400 (V/TDD), Fax 301-654-2403; Cost: $2.50)

This pamphlet discusses deafness and hearing impairments, interviewing techniques for deaf or hard-of-hearing individuals, placement and accommodation, and communicating with these individuals in the workplace.

Media

Are You Listening? [video]. (Available from Gallaudet Media Distribution, Gallaudet University, 800 Florida Avenue NE, Washington, DC 20002-3695; Phone 202-651-5222 [Voice], 202-651-5227 [TDD]; loan only)

Designed to encourage employers to hire and promote deaf workers. Shows deaf employees working in factory, white collar, and professional jobs.

A Good Investment: Meeting the Needs of Your Hard-of-Hearing Employees [video]. (Available from Self Help for Hard of Hearing People, Inc., 7800 Wisconsin Avenue, Bethesda, MD 20814; Phone 301-657-2248 [voice], 301-657-2249 [TDD]; Cost: $20.00)

This eleven-minute video is designed to make managers and personnel professionals aware of hard-of-hearing employees in their organizations, special needs of these employees, and the ways in which managers can enable their special needs employees to be more productive.

Contacts

Experiential Programs Off Campus
Ely Center, Room 101
Gallaudet University
800 Florida Avenue NE
Washington, DC 20002-3695
202-651-5197 (TDD)
202-651-5240 (Voice)

The EPOC assists supervisors in working with deaf interns and co-op students from Gallaudet University. EPOC has prepared an excellent guide for supervisors, *EPOC Supervisor's Manual: A Guide for Working With a Hearing Impaired Student* (Cost: $2), which discusses how to orient co-workers, orienting hearing impaired workers, the role of the supervisor, evaluating the worker, communication, and what to do if problems arise.

IBM National Support Center for Persons With Disabilities
4111 Northside Parkway HO6R1
Atlanta, GA 30027
800-284-9482 (TDD)
800-426-2133 (Voice)

The Center is an information clearinghouse and advocacy center. The group keeps information on nearly 800 computer-related devices from hundreds of companies. It can refer callers to more than 900 other organizations that assist people with disabilities. IBM also has a touring program to raise the awareness of employers to issues related to hiring people who have disabilities.

Mainstream, Inc.
3 Bethesda Metro Center
Suite 830
Bethesda, MD 20814
301-654-2400 (TDD and Voice)

Project LINK is one program of Mainstream, Inc., which addresses the specific needs of unemployed and underemployed disabled persons, and the companies and organizations interested in recruiting disabled jobseekers. Project LINK provides services to employers, educational institutions, and community organizations (information, training, and technical assistance on diverse disability-related issues) and publishes a newsletter, *In The Mainstream,* which presents information of interest to disabled persons and people who work with them.

National Academy of Gallaudet University
800 Florida Avenue NE
Washington, DC 20002-3695
202-651-5096 (TDD and Voice)

The National Academy provides training on deafness to employers. It is also a resource for recruiting deaf employees.

National Center on Employment of the Deaf
National Technical Institute for the Deaf
Rochester Institute of Technology
P.O. Box 9887
Rochester, NY 14623-0887
716-475-6834 (TDD and Voice)

Members of the staff of NCED are available to assist employers with information and consultations regarding employment of deaf workers.

National Information Center on Deafness
Gallaudet University
800 Florida Avenue NE
Washington, DC 20002-3695
202-651-5052 (TDD)
202-651-5052 (Voice)

This resource center provides information on all aspects of deafness to a national and international clientele. The Center collects, develops, and disseminates up-to-date information on deafness, hearing loss, organizations, services, and programs related to hearing-impaired people. Call them with questions on deafness or for their list of publications.

Center for Postsecondary Career Studies in Deafness
National Technical Institute for the Deaf
Rochester Institute of Technology
P.O. Box 9887
Rochester, NY 14623-0887
716-475-6704 (TDD and Voice)

This research division of NTID maintains information on demographics and experiences of the prospective deaf postsecondary population, deaf students in college, attainments of deaf adults in the workplace and society, and educational policy and practice for deaf students. Call them for their list of research reports, or for information about deaf people.

ENDNOTES

1. All quotations are direct excerpts from interviews with supervisors. The appearance of three dots " ... " indicates that text from the full interview has been deleted within the excerpt. This practice is most often used when there is a great deal of repetition or meandering within the interview text, and care is always taken to insure that the meaning or intent of the message remains unchanged. Brackets "[ ]" are used to indicate text that has been added by the researcher. This is done in order to clarify statements.

2. The use of the uppercase "Deaf" is used to refer to a group of deaf people who share a language—American Sign Language (ASL) and a culture, while the lowercase "deaf" refers to the audiological condition of not hearing (Woodward, 1972; Padden and Humphries, 1988).

3. Reversing refers to the activity of reverse interpreting, in which the interpreter voices what the deaf person is signing.

Chapter 3

COMMUNICATION

I remember he was hollering at me one time. Something happened and he just hollered at me, and it was the first time that it really struck me that he couldn't hear like the rest of 'em. Just something about it really struck me, and I remember him saying to me . . . "You're just like the rest of them." I remember he tried to explain to me that people who are deaf are just like other people, and they want to know what's going on, too. (Excerpt from interview with hearing supervisor of deaf employee.)

Before they even met the deaf employee, supervisors were concerned about how they were going to handle communication. They adopted new strategies for teaching deaf employees work tasks, often relying on written protocols and hands-on demonstration instead of voice. Communication was also a factor in the development of relationships between deaf and hearing workers, as well as in supervisors' determinations regarding the deaf employee's potential for management.

Supervisors were asked to explain how they communicated with deaf employees using the telephone, at group meetings, and on a one-to-one basis. Additionally, they were asked to share their observations of communication between the deaf person and others in the workplace, including hearing coworkers, people from other departments, and clients. In the first section of this chapter, supervisors' descriptions of communication strategies are presented.

Analysis of supervisors' comments suggests that communication in the workplace is a function of many interrelated conditions, including environmental factors, characteristics of participants in the interaction, and the purpose of the communication. The second section of this chapter includes a discussion of each of these conditions and the ways in which they interact to produce a successful (or in some cases, unsuccessful) communication event.

DESCRIPTIONS OF COMMUNICATION STRATEGIES

Three categories of communication are included in this section: these are communication (1) using the telephone, (2) at meetings, and (3) one to one.

Communication Using the Telephone

Telephone contact is unimportant for some jobs, essential for others. The amount of phone contact required for the jobs included in this study varied according to the function of the organization, the need for collaboration and information exchange between employees, and the amount of contact with a client base. While a few jobs did not require telephone work, most did. Employers' responses to this situation varied widely.

Telephone accommodations for deaf employees ranged from no access to total access. Those who did not have special devices for using the telephone at work used a variety of strategies for notifying employers if they were unable to come to work. Most had a TDD (telecommunication device for the deaf, also called a TTY), or amplifier, at home and would either use a local telephone relay service or call directly to leave a brief verbal message with their supervisor. An example:

> She can just about call in and say, "I am not coming in today," and I will say, "Okay." I would not even attempt to get into any big long involved conversation with her over the telephone . . . that has worked out well. If I have any problem, I would just talk to her when she came in.

Accommodations for using the telephone *within* the workplace took a variety of forms. Sometimes, jobs were modified to minimize or eliminate the need for telephone contact. In other instances, responsibility for telephone work was shifted to other employees. However, being unable to answer the phone within a busy office sometimes left both hearing and deaf employees feeling frustrated and resentful. The following examples illustrate the difficulties created in these kinds of situations, as well as strategies used by deaf employees to compensate for limited access to telephone communication:

EXAMPLE # 1
INTERVIEWER: Okay, is the telephone an important part of work in the lab?
SUPERVISOR: Occasionally, [and] that becomes what I'd call a sore point. You know how it is yourself, if the telephone keeps ringing all day, it gets to you after a while . . . and of course, [she] cannot answer it at all and then the

little things that you have to do because of that phone [call, such as] look up a report or get back to somebody about something, which [she] can't do . . . You know, on those busy days, you get a little bit testy sometimes. It is kind of nice sometimes to be able to go off in your own little corner of the world and just work and not have to worry about that telephone . . . But she makes up for it in other ways . . . She sees other things to be done and forges right ahead and does it, so that it evens out . . .

EXAMPLE # 2

I don't think he ever got set up to use the phone. That would have been very, very helpful . . . every time I wanted to talk with him, he had to appear or I had to write him a note . . . he solved it by just running around. Our offices were maybe 200 yards [apart] . . . so he kept cruising up and down a number of times a day and it was frustrating for him. He would try to catch me . . . between appointments, or on the way to meetings, and this kind of thing. That's very difficult, I mean, it must be very frustrating.

Seven employees were provided with assistive devices for using the telephone at work. Putting these devices into place usually was the result of collaborative effort between the deaf employee and the supervisor. The supervisor relied on the deaf employee for advice on what was needed, and the deaf employee relied on the supervisor to follow through on the suggestions. In this vein, one supervisor made the following observation:

[She] helped us to identify what she needed. We got a [TDD] for her office. She has one in her office and one at the desk. So she doesn't need to run up front to use it. She told us about the light that goes on the phones [signal light that flashes when the phone rings to alert the deaf person to incoming calls], and we got that. So she is all set. She needed a table where she could put her TTY to sit, and so we ordered one and we got it the right height . . . She seems to be comfortable.

Getting a special device usually required that the supervisor file a request within the organization. Usually, requests were handled quickly and easily. However, there were exceptions:

. . . We've moved three times . . . and they keep forgetting to make sure that [he] has the amplifier on the phone so that he can hear it and carry on conversations for his work. I keep telling them, "You have to have the phone" and everyone always says, "Oh, yeah, yep." You know, we have ten phones, and I keep telling them, "Ten phones and then you have to have one that has the extra with the amplifier" . . . I don't think that they're educated to work with people that have a hearing problem . . . Because like the woman who is in charge of the phones, I precisely gave her a memo saying that [he] needed the amplifier phone, and she wrote back, "Fine." And when we moved and got to the new office, there was nothing. And so we had to wait for two weeks before

[he] was able to use the phone. So that's a hindrance on his performance. It's nothing that he would be blamed for, but I'm upset because they're not following through on instructions that I gave them to ensure that he would be equipped to handle his job. I guess it's just a lack of cooperation or priority. They just didn't think that it was a top priority. To me it is a top priority because it's something that one of my employees needs to have . . . it's just a little thing, but it means a lot to [him] because he has to have that to work and to feel comfortable and to handle the phone. He could answer the phone [without the amplifier], but he's missing a lot of the conversation, and he'll try to turn up his hearing aid to hear, but it's still not a really clear phone conversation for him . . . and then he really just feels totally out of it.

Providing assistive devices did not automatically insure complete access to telephone communication. For example, giving a deaf employee a TDD was only half a solution, since the people on the other end of the call were unlikely to have a TDD themselves. In these cases, deaf employees were faced with two alternatives: they could ask a hearing colleague to interpret their call, or they could use the local telephone relay service. Since the relay service was time consuming and frequently overloaded, deaf employees generally chose the first strategy.[1] Sometimes this caused problems, as in the case of the supervisor who said the deaf employee routinely used his hearing co-workers to interpret telephone calls for him, until "it got to the point where, frankly, it was a pain."

Collaboration, described earlier as important for initial implementation of assistive telephone devices, was also important for making the accommodation work over time. One supervisor said his company provided the employee with a telephone device which enabled him to converse with hearing colleagues. He continued:

That particular job which he got into with me did require a lot of conversations on the phone with various vendors, other technicians, engineers, [who] weren't necessarily in our area. I would say as much as 15 to 20 percent of his job was contact on the phone. He handled himself very well. There were times when some people [were difficult to understand] on the phone. [Even] I can't hear them half the time. But he had to say, "Look, I can't hear you, I can't understand you . . . call me back another time. [We have a] bad connection." Or he would grab me or someone else and ask us to talk to the person and tell . . . what they were saying . . . He realized his limitations and he wasn't afraid to tell other people what they were. And it didn't hurt him. Other people did not look at him as having a problem to the point of saying, "You're a burden." They accepted his limitations, and, again I have to give [him] most of that credit. He was very straightforward.

Finally, it is worth noting that some situations require initiative and creativity on the part of everyone. Several interesting alternatives for communicating with a deaf employee via the telephone were described by one supervisor:

> There may well have been ways that I could have done more to get around that [the constraints on the deaf employee regarding telephone communication], but ... I had a lot of things going on, so I didn't have a lot of time to try to think about it. But I think access [to] the telephone is available ... it's another very important area to really look over in detail. There may be ways of leaving messages ... particularly with computers now, if you have an electronic mail situation, that's excellent. A person could use it very easily. [He] could have left me messages verbally [for example, on a tape recorder], cause I could understand what he's saying. He never really tried to do that. I don't know whether it occurred to him or not. I don't know if he really had a set up for doing that, but there's no reason a hearing-impaired person that speaks can't leave [verbal] messages ... There are other ways. It just depends on how the individual wants to be. There could be light signals on the phone that would say, "Yeah, I want to speak to [person's name];" I let it ring once and then it rings again twice or something, then, he'd go to the computers and there's a message there for you.

The supervisor quoted above mentions the use of electronic mail (E-mail) through computer systems. While only one supervisor said the deaf employee had access to E-mail, this technology is worthy of attention because it is one of the most effective ways of replacing the telephone as a communication tool. Perhaps most important, E-mail places deaf and hearing people on equal footing, since it does not require the deaf person to use special equipment (such as TDDs or amplifiers). While such a computer system would rarely if ever be installed specifically to accommodate a deaf employee, supervisors who have access to such a system may find that it is worth making a terminal available to deaf workers.

Communication at Meetings

Three supervisors said the deaf employee's job does not require their attendance at meetings. Ten of the seventeen supervisors of deaf employees who do attend meetings as part of their job said interpreters were hired for meetings. However, in almost every case these were only for large meetings or meetings set up especially for deaf employees. Furthermore, interpreters at these meetings were in some cases co-workers who knew some sign language, that is, not professionally trained or certified interpreters.

Supervisors held different opinions about using interpreters at meetings. Some felt interpreters were essential; these supervisors would go to great lengths to coordinate the meeting in order to honor the deaf employee's request for an interpreter. As one person commented, "I try to accommodate [the deaf employees]. They might not *think* I try to accommodate them, but I do. I mean, who else will schedule an informal ... meeting, get the room and then get the interpreter, and *then* see if everybody can go?"

In other cases, interpreters were seen as a costly luxury, a privilege rather than an essential service or right. In this vein, one supervisor did not feel he could accommodate the deaf employee's repeated requests for an interpreter at meetings, even though he understood that it was difficult to attend and participate in meetings without this service. As he reasoned, "I don't think I should spend any more money to have a [deaf] employee work for us. I can go out and get other employees [for whom] I wouldn't have to spend that amount of money ... whatever the cost would be, [it] is too much."

Sometimes supervisors' opinions about interpreters varied according to the situation. As noted earlier, interpreters were much more frequently used for large meetings, or meetings in which the information to be disseminated was viewed as critical. The following statement is interesting, because it was made by the supervisor who described herself as going to great lengths to provide interpreters for in-house meetings. She is discussing the issue of who should pay for interpreters at professional conferences:

> Hearing-impaired people expect a lot more from hearing people ... they want to be catered to sometimes ... or [treated] special as far as interpreters [are concerned] ... When we go to ... these state meetings, it's the society [professional group sponsoring the conference] that's picking up the bill for these interpreters. It's not [our company] ... I don't think it's fair ... the [company] paid for [them] to go to the meeting. Maybe it's possible that the [company] will pay some of the interpreting fees, but don't you think maybe they should pay a little out of their pocket if they want to go bad enough?

In one instance, a supervisor who knows sign language found the use of an interpreter at meetings intrusive, adding that it absolves participants from the responsibility of directly communicating with each other and overcoming barriers associated with communication with a deaf colleague:

INTERVIEWER: When you went with [her] to [meetings to] facilitate, did you interpret?
SUPERVISOR: Oh, I did both, I mean, I was a group member as well as interpret[er]. But the point is, that sometimes, I could maybe interpret because persons felt it was more convenient to use me as a resource as opposed to focusing on [her] and conveying the information . . . [when I stepped back from doing that] . . . That just meant there was more responsibility on the group members to focus on [her] and, similarly, [she] would focus on the group.

In general, interpreters were not widely or consistently used for meetings in the workplace, especially for weekly department or team meetings. As a result, supervisors and deaf employees had to find other ways to insure that everyone had the information disseminated at meetings. Several strategies were used, including supervisor summaries of the meeting for the deaf employee, written agendas or minutes, and maximizing the potential for lipreading at meetings through seating, requests for repetition, and eye contact. The selection of one strategy over another depended on the abilities and attitudes of participants and often varied from one kind of meeting to another. Some supervisors routinely used only one or two strategies, while others used many. Below, a supervisor describes the strategies she used to insure that the deaf employee had access to information presented at meetings:

If we have a real small meeting . . . I'll get everyone together and then during the meeting I will look directly at [her] when I'm speaking, so I know that she can read my lips. Then, after the meeting, I make sure I talk to [her] separately, and I'll go over whatever it was that we talked about at the meeting. I also try always to make a point to let her know that if she feels that there is something that came up that she wasn't a part of, or some information that she missed . . . that she should let me know right away, and I'll be happy to come back or to come over and try to make sure that she has that information. If we have a really big meeting about something, then we usually set up a separate meeting for the hearing-impaired people [from throughout the organization] and a signer will come in for that meeting. If we have just a larger group meeting, for example, maybe the director of the department will come in. Well, you know, he won't know and he doesn't know about how to do things best for hearing-impaired people, so he may not know to speak more slowly, or to repeat things, or to look at them to make sure he has eye contact, so usually I will take notes . . . I always make it my responsibility and then I can go through my notes later with the hearing-impaired people.

Supervisors described problems that occurred at meetings at which there were no interpreters. For example, several supervisors recognized how hard it was for deaf employees to follow conversations when two or more people talked at the same time. As one person observed, "The problem that she has in staff meetings is that there may be ten people around a table and I may be talking and two other people may be saying something to each other, so she looks at me to [see] what I am saying and they are fooling around over there and she thinks she is missing something that they were saying—she can only get one person at a time talking." Another supervisor expressed the opinion that it may be harder for the deaf employee to ask for repetition or clarification at meetings because "in a group he's sort of singled out if he has to ask what was said, and so it's tough because he looks around and he knows the other people got it the first time and here he is having to ask for more information."

The most troublesome area for supervisors, however, had to do with changing *their own* behavior at meetings. For example, most supervisors knew they should face the deaf person when speaking, but some found this difficult. For one supervisor, the key was learning new communication habits. As he put it, "You usually speak and direct your face and orientation toward the person you want to project to. You shouldn't do that with a hearing-impaired person if that means that person [is]... blocked out. I gradually trained myself to just speak toward him, no matter what I was saying to anybody else. That's very difficult to do." Conversely, another worried that if she focused her attention towards the deaf person, the other workers would feel left out. In her words, "It's difficult, because of the eye contact. I really like to maintain the eye contact with [her], but [sometimes]... I'll find that I forget and I'll look at the other women in the group while I'm handling a meeting, and then I know I've left [her] out. And I feel badly about that, but at the same time I don't want the other girls to feel like I'm ignoring them by just looking at [her]."

Lastly, some supervisors found the effort of using special communication strategies for meetings too much work. If they were busy to begin with, the additional effort required to prepare written agendas for informal meetings or learn new communication protocols might seem unreasonable. One supervisor said the deaf employee had requested written agendas for meetings, but added that this "is much more complete than we ever have for a routine type of meeting which he might get involved in." Another supervisor, who always made sure the deaf employee sat near him at meetings and tried to remember to face the employee while speaking, added "at the same time, you've got a million things to worry about, and he's just one person."

Working through communication barriers at meetings requires the involvement and commitment of everyone. As noted in the range of comments presented so far, supervisors varied widely in their willingness and ability to accommodate the communication needs of deaf employees at meetings. Some became very involved, taking notes and hiring interpreters. Others offered only minimal support. However, the active participation of deaf employees was seen as very helpful in the implementation of solutions to communication barriers at meetings. The quotation below reflects one supervisor's positive opinion of the way the deaf employee handled communication at meetings:

> Sometimes if the meeting is around a . . . long table, the person speaking is way over there and he winds up sitting at the opposite end and misses an awful lot. Again, he would make those things known to the people . . . he would express it. He [would] say, "I can't do anything about this." And he'd say, "Oh, let's pursue this to a degree here. How do we want to get this thing solved?" [Later, same topic] He had a very realistic outlook. [He'd say,] "Why go to a meeting where I can't understand what's going on?" He'd question it, he wouldn't just go mope in a corner someplace or fake it by going to the meetings continually and not bringing anything back. He would take pains at getting it right. He would go if it was a chaired-type meeting. He would approach the chairperson . . . explain his problem that he couldn't hear and he wanted to know if they're publishing meeting notes. If so, [he would ask the chairperson,] "Would you make sure I get them? And if you have an agenda next time, would you send that out so I can look at it, and if I have things to add to it, I could add them."

Only one supervisor addressed the ability of the deaf employee to present information at meetings. This supervisor described the challenge faced by the employee in making a presentation to his colleagues:

> He has made a couple of presentations in my area, and to a group, without difficulty. He hasn't done it too much, but it took a lot of guts to try . . . He did it quite well for a first time in front of a group. It's bad enough for a person that has never made a report at all, but knows all of his 100 percent faculties, and I imagine . . . sometimes wondering when you're listening to yourself, "Am I talking loud enough for everyone to hear me? Is the person in the back bored with what I'm saying or just can't hear me? . . ." Those things happen to everybody. Some people pay attention to them and some people don't. A person in [his] case is more aware of things like that, so they're very conscious . . . about how . . . their voice is coming across, if they're talking softly or loud.

[He] would even be concerned with the pitch, the accents of the words, if they're coming out right. So it was a big experience for him.

While the primary purpose of most meetings is the dissemination and discussion of information and ideas, they are also social gatherings. So far, the discussion has centered on providing deaf employees with access to the formal dimensions of communication at meetings. However, there are also informal interactions that are very difficult to capture under the best conditions. These include the chit-chat which takes place before a meeting or during a break and the casual jokes and informal conversations reflected in the undercurrent of side comments that are a part of most meetings.

In several job settings, many hearing employees had some sign skills. It is significant that a supervisor in this kind of setting had to continually remind hearing employees to use their sign skills as soon as the deaf employee arrived at the meeting in order to include the employee in informal communications. Left to their own devices, they did not do this.

In most of the work environments, however, hearing employees knew no sign language. In these cases, including deaf employees in casual conversation at meetings required that hearing colleagues slow the pace of their conversation, take turns, and face the deaf employee when speaking (even when telling a funny story or discussing the previous night's TV show). Not surprisingly, supervisors often said deaf employees were left out of this casual banter.

Given that most supervisors found the task of insuring access to more formal communication at meetings challenging, they were even less likely to discover or use strategies to help deaf employees participate in these tangential or social conversations. They felt they could only summarize the main points of a meeting, not the casual conversations. However, feeling powerless to effect control or change did not necessarily mean that supervisors were unaware of or unsympathetic to the situation faced by deaf employees. As one supervisor noted, "I'm really aware of it [that deaf employees miss out] . . . after all, when I sit down and go over my notes with them, I only hit on the important things at the meeting—I'm not hitting on all the chit chatter, the chuckles that have gone on that they've missed out on."

One-To-One Communication

Analysis of supervisors' comments suggests that, for them, the most important communication between deaf employees and others in the workplace involved one-to-one interactions. Telephone work could be accomplished using adaptive technology or reassigned. Meetings might be handled by using agendas, minutes, or interpreters. Yet, neither communication using the telephone nor at meetings prompted the same anxiety or potential for misunderstanding as one-to-one conversation. Since supervisors had to routinely manage, evaluate, and when necessary, correct the employee's work performance, failure to communicate effectively at this level could be disastrous. For example:

> ... Supervisors ... tend to be reluctant to do that [confront the deaf employee to correct an inappropriate behavior] ... I don't know, I guess it's a feeling of awkwardness about how am I gonna explain to him that we don't do that, it's not the way we operate, or it's not allowable. Do I have to explain all that structure, or do I have to just kind of say, "No, don't do that." Will he understand me? If he says something to me, will I understand him? How am I going to do all those things that come naturally for me with a hearing person? So I'd rather not. I won't bother. And ... then that builds up to [where] he does that every single day. Have ... [I] ever stopped him from doing it? No, but he does it every single day. And then ... you have a very frustrated person who thinks the boss hates him, and the boss who says, "This has gotta stop." And the only [way] to stop it is to get rid of him.

So how did deaf and hearing workers communicate with one another? According to their supervisors, a variety of strategies were used. Lipreading and speech (voice) were mentioned most frequently, followed by reading/writing, signing and gestures. In the following pages each of these strategies is described, including the advantages and drawbacks of each as seen from the perspective of supervisors.

Lipreading and Speaking

Supervisors generally found it easiest to communicate with deaf employees when the employees used lipreading and speech. A few said they saved time using these strategies (as compared with writing messages out). Several supervisors said their employees were so skilled in speech and lipreading that they sometimes forgot they couldn't hear. As one person put it, "I don't consider her handicapped, as we communicate verbally."

However, supervisors also noted that communication with a deaf person using voice and lipreading does require adjustments. Examples include learning to face the deaf employee while conversing and to speak more slowly. One supervisor said he had to learn not to fiddle with his moustache when talking with the deaf employee, since this gesture interfered with the employee's ability to read his lips. Often, messages had to be repeated several times before they were understood.

Learning new protocols regarding appropriate ways to get the attention of the deaf person was often especially challenging. One supervisor had to correct visitors from other departments who would kick the deaf employees' desks when they wanted their attention. Another commented, "I had to learn that [she] doesn't like being grabbed by the shirt." While these approaches may seem obviously inappropriate, they were not always clearly so to hearing supervisors and co-workers.

The biggest drawback to lipreading and speech involved miscommunication. This is not surprising, since even under ideal conditions many speech sounds look identical on the lips.[2] When conditions are less than ideal (for example, conversing in a poorly lit room, in the glare of sunshine streaming through a window, or when the speaker's mouth is partially hidden by a beard or moustache), lipreading can become difficult or impossible. Some supervisors observed that deaf employees were unable to lipread hearing coworkers who spoke quickly or while turned away from them. Additionally, if the deaf person's speech was unclear, hearing people had difficulty understanding what was said. While asking the person to repeat the message might have helped in both these situations, people sometimes hesitated to do so, either because they were in a hurry or because they felt embarrassed.

Conversing in voice and lipreading was appealing to some supervisors because it most closely approximated the communication habits and norms of hearing people. Sometimes, dependency on these modes precluded the development and/or use of other communication strategies. One supervisor described his reaction to the deaf employee's efforts to teach him sign language:

> Signing is important, only because it means a whole lot to the person with the handicap. Because if you take the time to do that, it means that you're really interested in them and that's important to them. They really appreciate that. I remember that [he] brought in the handsign guidebook. He showed it to me and I brought it home. I spent some time practicing it, but I wasn't really successful. I couldn't get my hands to go right and I had a terrible time learning the signed letters. I don't know, I think maybe if I had been working

with a deaf person who really couldn't communicate at all, well then I would have been forced to learn sign. But with [him], it was different. I could understand him really well, and if I just faced him and spoke clearly and slowly, he seemed to be able to understand me. So I think in a way, I didn't bother to really pursue it because we were doing okay the way we were.

This supervisor commented at other points in the interview on the limitations of voice and lipreading for communication and described misunderstandings which occurred when the message was not given or received correctly. He attributed these communication breakdowns to the deaf person's failure to ask him to repeat his message, rather than to his failure to learn sign language.

The willingness to rely on lipreading and voice even when these strategies were ineffective was not limited to hearing supervisors. One person described with frustration a deaf employee who never took written notes during conversations, only to return later with questions designed to review or confirm points that had already been made. Of course, it is difficult to read speech and write at the same time. Unless the supervisor paused during the conversation, or the deaf person was able to either write key phrases without looking down or make quick summary notes at the conclusion of their conversation, the supervisor may have been expecting the impossible.

Reading and Writing

Eleven supervisors said they used reading and writing to communicate with the deaf employee. While this strategy was most often used in a supportive, as opposed to primary role, the amount of writing and reading varied considerably from one supervisor to another. Many used it only to confirm what had been discussed verbally. Some wrote in specific situations, such as when teaching a deaf employee new skills. A few said the deaf employee brought a pad and pencil everywhere, in an effort to facilitate conversation.

One of the advantages of written messages is that usually they are given or received correctly. In fact, several supervisors said they frequently confirmed a conversation through written notes in order to avoid confusion later about what was said. Also, if it is understood that lipreading, speech, or sign language are not options, everyone expects to write, and the awkwardness of trying to decide what will work is avoided. In both cases, writing eliminates some of the uncertainty which often accompanies communication between deaf and hearing people. One

supervisor said communication was often smoother with a deaf employee
who did not lipread or use her voice than with another deaf employee
who did:

> Sometimes I think you can communicate more with [her], who you know can't
> hear a thing you're saying, than with the other one [other deaf employee],
> whom you sometimes thought got more than she did . . . You knew [she]
> couldn't understand so if it wasn't getting through, you would sit and write it
> down. Whereas with the other girl, I think there was more [wondering] if she
> did understand you. The other girl wore a hearing aid and if everything went
> well and it was quiet in the room . . . she made out quite well. But . . . if all the
> conditions weren't good, she didn't make out so good.

On the other hand, writing out messages required greater adjustments
on the part of the supervisor and hearing co-workers. It takes longer to
write a message than to speak it. Some supervisors found it bothersome
to write out conversations, and several felt deaf employees "should learn
how to lipread better" to facilitate quick communication. Also, some
people (hearing and deaf) do not like to write or are poor writers. Even if
they write well, the tone and pace of the conversation is different in the
written mode, and it is difficult to cover a topic in the same detail. As a
result, some supervisors felt communication through reading and writing had limited usefulness and could not fully compensate for an inability to converse verbally. Even those who found writing helpful said it
had limitations.

Sign Language

While many of the deaf employees probably knew sign language and
used it outside of work, this communication strategy was useless to them
on the job unless others also were able to sign. Eight supervisors said
there was at least one person in the work setting in addition to the deaf
employee who knew some sign language. However, this cannot be
interpreted to mean that deaf employees were able to use sign fluently or
often. In some cases, hearing co-workers had learned a few basic signs,
usually from the deaf employee. In other cases, there was another deaf
employee in a different part of the building. In two instances, there was
more than one deaf person in the same department. The only work sites
in which signing was used regularly by more than two people were the
three organizations serving deaf clients.

Some deaf employees tried to teach their colleagues sign language,
with varying levels of success. Generally, a few people would become

involved and learn a few signs. In one case a hearing co-worker became a fairly fluent signer as a result of sustained contact with the deaf employee. The failure of most hearing colleagues to become expert signers is not surprising, since learning any language is time consuming and challenging, and most hearing employees do not have the time or opportunity to take intensive training in sign language at work. However, it is worth noting that several supervisors said deaf employees were gratified by even the *gesture* of trying to learn, or by the use of just a few signs by hearing co-workers. Of course, being able to have a conversation in sign language was greatly appreciated. One supervisor said several hearing people in her organization knew sign language, noting that when they stop by to visit the deaf employee, "her face lights up when these people start talking to her [in signs]."

In organizations employing more than one deaf person, supervisors were sensitive to deaf employees' needs for fluent conversation and sometimes tried to make special arrangements to place deaf workers in contact with one another by assigning them to the same lunch hour. In cases where there was more than one deaf person in the department, supervisors sometimes placed them at adjacent work stations.

Gestures

Only five supervisors mentioned gestures as a communication strategy. This may seem surprising, since pointing or using universal gestures for yes or no (for example, thumbs up or down, nodding) naturally occur in many languages, and it is hard to imagine *not* incorporating gestures when communication falters or becomes strained. One possible explanation is that most supervisors did use this approach but failed to mention it since it seemed to be such a natural thing to do. On the other hand, perhaps those who mentioned it did so because they had noticed a significant increase in their use of gestures when conversing with the deaf person. In every case, gestures were described as having a supplemental role, used to support communication in writing, lipreading, speaking, and sign. In a few cases, gesturing went beyond the use of universal signals and body language. For example, in one work setting a group of employees created a gesture to describe an employee they disliked. The deaf worker was in on this and used the gesture himself.

In summary, communication between deaf and hearing workers took a variety of forms. However, descriptions of communication strategies, services, and equipment do not explain conditions that facilitate or impede their use. Most often, several strategies were used in combination, and different situations required different methods. In order to understand why a strategy worked in one situation but not another, it is necessary to define communication as an interaction between the individual and the conditions of the work setting. In the next section, we turn to this topic.

CONDITIONS INFLUENCING COMMUNICATION

Supervisors' comments suggest that there are at least three kinds of conditions that influence communication in the workplace. These are (1) environmental conditions, (2) characteristics of participants, and (3) purpose of the communication.

Environmental Conditions

The success of communication strategies depends to some extent on the environment of the workplace, including the physical setting, type of work performed, availability of technical resources to enhance communication, and the administrative model used by the department or organization. The physical design and layout of the work setting, for example, influenced deaf employees' access to communication. Dividers that created a pattern of isolated spaces separated workers in more ways than one. Large open work areas promoted visual contact and enabled deaf employees to follow at least some of what was going on. Similarly, well-lit rooms, good acoustics, and arrangement of work stations in a circular or semi-circular fashion all facilitated participation.

Several supervisors noted that the type of work performed in their department permitted hearing employees to chat while working with their hands and looking down. Deaf employees faced isolation in performing these tasks. They could neither lipread nor use signs while working. In other settings, talking while working was impossible for everyone (i.e., because of noise in the environment), and sometimes hearing workers developed their own set of gestures and hand signals to communicate without voice. Deaf employees were on a more equal footing in these situations.

The availability of technical equipment, and/or the resources to get them, influenced communication. In one organization, workers in different departments were able to communicate through computers; deaf and hearing employees could use electronic mail for daily communication. The availability of TDDs and interpreters also influenced the range of communication strategies available to deaf and hearing workers for conversing with one another. Some organizations had large budgets for the purchase of special equipment and services, while others operated on a shoestring.

As for the influence of organizational models, some work settings were based on individual effort, in which each person worked independently. In these settings, communication was unnecessary (and perhaps even undesirable) for the performance of work tasks, and informal interactions were discouraged. As an example, a supervisor in a production shop said he never considered getting a TDD for the deaf employee, since none of the workers were expected to use the phone as part of their job. Organizational models based on a team approach, on the other hand, required people to interact and share responsibility for tasks; in these cases, everyone was motivated to find ways to communicate effectively. Thus, a supervisor in a service organization went to great lengths to get the deaf employee a phone amplifier, since his job required frequent telephone contact with branch offices.

Characteristics of Participants

The success or failure of efforts to converse depended on the characteristics of all participants. Five qualities were especially important, including (1) willingness and ability to provide and/or use information, (2) flexibility, (3) interpersonal skills, (4) commitment, and (5) familiarity.

Willingness and Ability to Provide and/or Use Information

As noted in *Chapter 1,* only a few supervisors had any experience with deaf people. As a result, their first question in response to the news that they would be working with a deaf person was generally, "How will we communicate?" Yet, by the time they were interviewed for this project, they were able to discuss communication with deaf people in depth. Many of the one to one strategies, support services, and special equipment which supervisors mentioned in their discussions of communication were unknown to them until they met the deaf employee. They learned about these options through experience, trial and error, and in some cases, through training programs and workshops. But most often, they learned about them from the deaf employee.

Not surprisingly, supervisors were generally very appreciative of deaf employees who were straightforward in discussions of potential communication barriers. They were even more grateful to employees who offered solutions, particularly when those solutions were within their power to implement. Deaf employees provided information to supervisors on a wide range of topics, including interpreters, TDDs, amplifiers, flashers for phones and doors, and sign language. They also provided tips on how to enhance their participation at meetings through seating and lighting arrangements, written agendas, and minutes. Lastly, they taught hearing supervisors and co-workers about protocols for communication one on one with a deaf person, including appropriate ways of getting someone's attention, the importance of maintaining visual access to the face and lips, and a willingness to repeat messages or write them out. Below, a supervisor describes the kinds of information provided to him by the deaf employee:

> [He] told me certain things. [He said,] "I can't hear alarms in the building." We have lots of alarms because of the chemicals . . . And he had it figured out. He said, "Look, if there is an alarm, all I can ask is if someone else hears it tap me on the shoulder and let me know."[3] He said, "I can hear some with my hearing aid but most of the time I can't and I have to rely on lipreading . . . when people talk to me I would prefer it if they were looking at me." Easy enough. Let people know that. Constraints—he had phone conversation problems, when it was nice to have a magnetic pick-up loop for the phone. We had no problem getting that for him. It took some time to get because of scheduling, but at least he made us aware of that.

Not all deaf employees were equally prepared to inform their supervisors about communication barriers or suggest ways to overcome these barriers. These employees sometimes missed important information. Perhaps equally damaging was the effect of embarrassment and annoyance felt by supervisors who made mistakes or had to deal with the results of miscommunication. An example:

> I think one of the biggest problems he had was that he kept forgetting that he had this handicap. For example . . . [he] wouldn't always ask somebody to repeat something at a meeting. He'd just be sitting there and he wouldn't be getting it, but he wouldn't come up and tell you. He'd just sit there quietly. So I always had to try to remember to get back to [him] on information. I couldn't assume he knew stuff . . . [Also], there was a presentation that we had to do, and so they set up classes for everyone in the department to learn about it and we all went to this class and there was a whole series of them. Well, everyone forgot that [he] had this problem, and he sat right through the first couple of

sessions, and after a while he came to me and he said, "This really is useless for me to be going to these sessions." And of course, I had to apologize. I just hadn't thought of it. And so I felt terrible . . . you know, [he] just didn't want to stand out I guess, and so it took him a while before he said anything. But when something like that happens, it really makes everyone feel uncomfortable.

This supervisor's response included several different kinds of reactions. His initial reaction was guilt, followed by embarrassment. He tried to see the situation from the perspective of the deaf person, suggesting that the employee probably did not make an issue of it because he didn't want to stand out. However, he also criticized the person for not requesting an interpreter earlier, or, to use his phrase, for "forgetting that he had this handicap."

The other side of the coin is that supervisors and hearing co-workers must be willing and able to use the information provided to them. As noted earlier, not all supervisors had the financial resources to hire interpreters for meetings or purchase special telephone equipment, and some felt they were unnecessary despite the deaf employee's expressed opinion to the contrary. There were also differences among supervisors regarding the lengths to which they were willing to go to change their communication styles. Some resisted even modest changes, while others brought materials home to read, attended training workshops, and made efforts to learn sign language. However, even those who were willing to adapt often found it difficult to change old habits, and several said they still had to be reminded by the deaf employee to face them while speaking or to slow down their speech, even after months or years of experience.

Generally, supervisors were more willing to make accommodations that were relatively inexpensive, did not require major alterations to the environment, and most closely approximated the communication modes and strategies used by hearing people. For example, they were more likely to provide written agendas and minutes for meetings than to hire interpreters. They also tended to prefer lipreading and voice over sign language. Since the deaf person was usually a minority of one within the hearing workplace, decisions about which strategies to use were generally made by hearing supervisors and co-workers. Deaf employees could provide information, but they could not force others to use it. While the ADA will provide deaf employees with support and legal recourse in some of these situations, the challenges inherent in any effort to change deeply ingrained and often subtle behaviors of the majority will remain.

Flexibility

Information and skill in a range of communication strategies do not guarantee successful communication. The ability to select appropriate strategies and, when necessary, switch from one strategy to another, are also critical. For example, interpreters may be provided for large meetings, but not for smaller weekly team discussions, in which written agendas and minutes are essential for communication. People who work with deaf employees daily may understand their voice very well, while those who interact infrequently have to rely on written conversation. As noted earlier, over half the supervisors said the deaf employee used more than one strategy for communication. Knowing when to supplement lipreading with written notes or fingerspelling was seen as an important skill. Supervisors especially admired deaf employees who adapted quickly to different communication situations, substituting new strategies when the first one failed. One supervisor said the deaf employee generally used sign language with co-workers and clients, but would voice a few words if they were unable to follow him, until they got back on track.

Supervisors included themselves in discussions of flexibility. They frequently used several communication strategies to insure they were understood by deaf employees. Several supervisors said they routinely review with the employee information discussed at meetings. One supervisor, who knows some sign language, said she always ends a statement by asking the deaf employee whether her signing was understood or if she should repeat her message. Another supervisor used a written "buckslip" to disseminate office news rather than the gossip grapevine, thus insuring that the deaf employee had equal access to this information. Some supervisors worked with more than one deaf employee, in which case flexibility meant learning what works for each person, and adapting accordingly. One supervisor described the difference between the two deaf people who work in her department. She observed, "[The first deaf employee] does not read lips. The other girl we have reads lips very well and if you just direct your talking to her, she can pretty much get what's going on . . . [but the first person] doesn't. You have to concentrate a little bit more. So [it changes] depending on who's in the conversation."

Interpersonal Skills

Sometimes knowing what to do and when to do it are still not enough to make communication work. People often feel awkward about approaching someone when they are unsure of how they should converse, and they become embarrassed when the conversation falters or they are misunderstood. Supervisors specifically mentioned the importance of humor, assertiveness, and being straightforward in defusing strained communication. One supervisor discussed how a deaf employee in his department used humor to reduce stress in conversations with hearing people: "His sense of humor is incredible . . . He'll tell a joke or he'll explain the sign and . . . where the sign came from. And then I've seen him give some examples of signs and then he'll show them signs that are naughty or signs that are slang signs and they'll laugh over it. It immediately puts the person at ease."

Supervisors often experienced the same feelings of uncertainty and awkwardness. However, they could not avoid the deaf person. In the following story, a supervisor explains his initial feelings of anxiety about approaching the deaf employee and his relief when the employee helped him work through his discomfort:

> How do you approach a person? You know, it's like hiring . . . any kind of handicap, a person with no arm or a person without a leg or something. I try to consider how do I approach [the deaf person] with his hearing loss up front? So I said [to him], " . . . What am I going to do concerning your hearing loss?" And [he] said, "I live with it all the time, I know all about it . . . Tell everyone about what I have" and gave me the list of things that he can't hear or he can't do . . . Right up front. I said, "Great." This took the pressure off me. He didn't make me feel uncomfortable about talking to him about it. And he said, "I've got it, I know I have to learn to live with it. I have to learn in your world . . . " Now I knew where he was coming from. That was probably one of the most important things, most gratifying things, of considering hiring someone in that capacity . . . from my standpoint, [I] did not know [what to do] except to come right out and ask him how to approach that. Other people who don't do that might have some difficulty along these lines, and it would probably be a real big help to have the hired person explain that right up front. Because that would break the ice, that would take the uneasiness off the person — I guess that would set the stage correctly.

Sometimes it was clear to the supervisor that hearing colleagues would not initiate conversations with the deaf person, if left to their own devices. In these cases, assertiveness was an important quality in a deaf employee. For example, one supervisor commented that the deaf employee always brings a pad and pencil to lunch so she can converse with hearing colleagues. Another spoke with admiration of a deaf employee's willingness to attend office parties and do his best to interact with colleagues at these events, even though the background noise made conversations almost impossible to follow.

Supervisors also felt they needed to be assertive in facilitating communication between themselves (or other hearing people in their department) and deaf employees. For example they may have to approach the employee with questions about which communication strategies work best. Several supervisors explained the deaf person's communication needs to others in the department and tried to break the ice by drawing deaf and hearing workers into conversations with one another.

Commitment

A prerequisite for the success of any communication effort is a commitment to making the effort work. Included under the general category of commitment are qualities such as motivation, sense of shared responsibility, and desire to communicate effectively.

Some supervisors said commitment must come first from the deaf person, since they really have the most motivation and expertise regarding their condition. As one person suggested, "There are just all sorts of things you can think to do [to facilitate communication] if you're motivated to do it. But I think people need to have clues because quite frankly . . . some people just don't seem to be very clever . . . and others aren't very motivated . . . If there were a number of different possibilities outlined . . . and most importantly, if a deaf person knows and is able to come up with a suggestion, that's going to be welcome . . . I think it's pivotal for them to be completely educated [in strategies and needs] because they are the most motivated people."

Other supervisors suggested that they, too, are naturally motivated to make communication work, since they are ultimately responsible for insuring that their department runs smoothly and productively. One supervisor always takes notes at meetings so she can review them later with the deaf people in her group. When asked if this was required of her, she replied, "Well no, it's not required, but you know the other team leader did it before me, and it's just something that I always keep in mind to do because otherwise I'm not sure they'll get all the information." Another supervisor recalled that her interest in communicating with the deaf employee increased when she became supervisor. As she put it,

"[Before] I was only working here part time . . . and I think I probably stayed as far away as possible in the beginning . . . we smiled and said, "Hi" and that was about it . . . then I became a supervisor and then you just knew that you had to change some things. You were going to see this person all the time, day in and day out. Also, you were responsible for reviews, seeing that she was doing the work properly."

Commitment on the part of supervisors is closely related to a willingness to use the information provided by the deaf employee. Commitment to using alternative strategies was sometimes reflected in a willingness to take time to accommodate the deaf person's special needs. Not everyone was equally open to this idea. Yet, as one supervisor noted, it is probably essential to a successful working relationship, because "if you don't [take the extra time], and [you] make it an anxiety kind of situation, then that's gonna be self-defeating. I think people . . . who are gonna work with [the deaf employee] have to be willing to take on that kind of commitment."

Several supervisors suggested that successful communication is the result of a partnership between the deaf person and supervisor (or co-workers). As one supervisor put it, "[Communication] is a two-way street." Implicit in this notion is the idea that communication breakdowns are the result of disabilities on the part of both deaf and hearing people. "We [hearing people] are handicapped also," said one supervisor, "[in] that we can't sign to him."

Finally, supervisors noted that hearing co-workers must also be committed to the success of communication efforts. Commitment on the part of co-workers was also reflected in efforts to alter communication modes and accommodate the deaf employee, even when to do so was difficult or time consuming. An example:

> I think a lot of people learn many things [by working with him]. Some people even got to the point [where] they learned some signing through working with him. When mechanics were working with [him], some of them picked up on it. Some wanted to do it, and it was easier. Sometimes signing was easier than talking. Some of them got pretty good at it. I felt good about that, developmental-wise. And acceptance also. It's very easy to turn your back and say, "I'm not gonna learn that. What do I have to do that for?" So it was good acceptance from that standpoint. There was always one or two that kind of shrugged their shoulders . . . I can't expect 100% of the people to understand the circumstances or be compassionate enough or understanding enough to get the point across. [But] most of them were very, very good.

Familiarity

Lastly, supervisors found that communication almost always improved as people become familiar with one another. As noted earlier in this chapter, people sometimes feel awkward about approaching or interacting with a deaf person. They may worry about whether they can remember to face the deaf person or to tap them on the shoulder instead of calling their name, and if they forget these things, they feel embarrassed and guilty. Sometimes it is difficult to understand a deaf person's speech. Using a TDD or interpreter may feel unnatural at first to hearing supervisors. Conversely, deaf employees may feel uncomfortable approaching supervisors with requests for special accommodations. They may be reluctant to ask people to repeat their message, because they feel this calls attention to them or makes them appear incompetent.

Yet, as people become familiar with one another, special strategies come more naturally and there are fewer stigmas attached to using them. Using the conference room with a circular seating arrangement becomes habit. Money for interpreters becomes a regular line item in the department budget. Hearing people get to know the voices of deaf colleagues and are genuinely surprised when visitors say they can't understand them. "The more . . . [the deaf employee] worked with people," observed one supervisor, "the more familiar he became with them and the easier it was for them to communicate." Other supervisors on the same topic:

EXAMPLE # 1
I can tell you when I first met her. It was my first time of dealing with a hearing-impaired person. It was about four years ago. I remember I felt really awkward. I didn't know what I was supposed to do, so I did one thing which I guess a lot of people do when they don't know any better. I spoke louder . . . eventually I learned that, of course, isn't the right thing to do. And now I hardly make any more noise than normal when I talk to [her].
EXAMPLE # 2
At first, he was afraid to talk to people in the branches, to carry on a conversation, but now he's used to it. He knows how to go about it, so he has that reassurance that he's not afraid to walk up and carry on a conversation with someone . . . most of the people that he has to work with . . . know that he has a hearing problem, and when they do come up to the department they'll work directly with him at his desk, so he's on a one-to-one contact with them.

Purpose of Communication

Generally, when supervisors discussed getting interpreters for meetings, learning to speak clearly, or purchasing a TDD, they were thinking in terms of facilitating communication relative to the performance of work tasks. Given the nature of their role within the organization, this focus on communication for work performance is understandable. Yet, a great deal of communication in the workplace is informal and social. Supervisors' comments suggest that deaf employees were far less successful in accessing informal communication than they were more formal communication related to performance of work tasks, even in settings in which special accommodations and alternative strategies were routinely used. As described earlier, deaf employees often were left out of "chit chat" and joking around at meetings. Other informal conversations that deaf people found difficult to access are those which unfold spontaneously between people when they see each other in the hall, share coffee or lunch breaks, or wait in line to use the copy machine, as well as the casual banter in which workers engage while performing routine or manual work tasks. "It's not the technical things or the big things," said one supervisor, "it's the little, day-to-day things."

While such conversations may seem unnecessary to successful work performance, they are integral to job satisfaction as well as to integration within the department or company. Perhaps most important, informal conversations often develop into communication networks that play central roles in the dissemination of unofficial yet critical information, such as changes in company or department policy, special events, and news about co-workers. Deaf employees were often completely excluded from these informal communication networks (also referred to as "grapevines"). Supervisors described the impact of this isolation as ranging from hurt feelings to more serious misunderstandings and errors related to work schedules and performance. For instance, one supervisor talked about the time the deaf person was scheduled to work alone on a weekend. At the last minute, work in all departments was cancelled due to safety problems in the building. The deaf person came in and worked for almost an hour before realizing that the building was empty. As the supervisor pointed out, a hearing worker "would have figured out the problem sooner because they would have ... gone into the computer room for something, or just to shoot the breeze, and ... noticed that no one was there ... They kind of move around a bit more, and so they would have picked up on it more quickly. But ... you know, she just more or less comes in and focuses on her work, and so she didn't [realize the building was empty]."

Sometimes supervisors deliberately used the communication grapevine to disseminate information. In these instances, deaf workers were at a distinct disadvantage. Below, a supervisor explains how he used the grapevine to modify the behavior of his employees:

> A lot of information was just filtered through the department. There are not a lot of formal meetings in this department. I think it works just as well. For example, I remember a while back, the guys were taking too many breaks and I was starting to get irritated about it, so I just turned to someone and I was way down at the end of the room, and I said, "You know, if these guys don't shape up, I'm gonna have to start assigning breaks." And I said it in just that tone of voice, not loud or angry, just real quiet. And you know, in five minutes everyone in the department was talking about how I was gonna assign breaks. So I figure that ... if people can learn that in five minutes, they can take any information and get it around the department in five minutes.

Astonishingly, this supervisor continued to use the grapevine even though he was aware that it excluded the deaf person. As he observed, "[The deaf employee] really wasn't too up on the gossip going around, and as a supervisor I used to just expect things to filter through the whole department. So if there was something going on, or a change or whatever, I just expected it to get through everyone and he wouldn't hear about it. And I know that it bothered him. I know it made him feel like he wasn't part of the team." One can only hope this supervisor did not penalize the deaf person for mistakes resulting from his lack of access to department gossip.

Deaf people were not always excluded from the grapevine. However, being included did not necessarily mean getting or giving correct information. While the potential for miscommunication is inherent in any grapevine network, communication difficulties between deaf and hearing employees can compound this situation, as illustrated by the following story:

> They get dribs and drabs of things, and then they misinterpret. Or sometimes what happens is that one of the hearing-impaired individuals will say something to a hearing person, and that hearing person misunderstood what the deaf person said. Then the hearing person comes to me with another story. Then I get all upset because of what they told me and then I go and yell at the hearing-impaired person who didn't say that in the first place. It's like [the game] "telephone."[4] When we were kids, we used to play telephone. It would

get confused at the end, [and] instead of being in Mississippi someone was in California.

Most supervisors were aware of difficulties experienced by deaf employees in accessing informal conversations and grapevine networks, and many were sympathetic. They tried to explain why deaf employees were more often excluded from informal and social communication than from communication related to work performance. One frequently mentioned reason was a general lack of attention to the communication needs of the deaf person in these kinds of conversations. In the following examples, two supervisors explain their perspectives:

EXAMPLE # 1

There're people in [the department]...who are very in tune to the fact that [she] is there and, therefore, they'll more or less direct their talking to her and tell her a few things so that she gets the gist of the conversation. [But] there are some people who are not as in tune to that...I feel very uncomfortable if someone is chatting away and not including her 'cause I think there's nothing worse than being on the outside of something and I usually get kind of nervous when I know that one of the people is just not in tune. It's not that...[it is done] intentionally. It's just one of those things that just kind of happens.

EXAMPLE # 2

When the world baseball series was on, that would be the main topic. They were all talking about the games, and [he] is very into...baseball, and then they would just carry on a conversation near him but in back of him, and they're talking and they're thinking that he's hearing them, but he's concentrating and paying attention to his work—he's not concentrating on the noise in the back. They didn't motion to him and say, "Gee, we're talking to you." They were just assuming because they were close enough to him that he was picking up the conversation, and then they'd say, "Well...what do you think about that?" And he'd go, "What?" And they go, "Aren't you listening?" And that upsets him, and that upsets me because they're not directing their conversation—their focus—to him. They just forgot, in the excitement.

The impression of both the supervisors quoted above was that hearing employees do not deliberately or maliciously exclude deaf colleagues. This impression also pervaded a second explanation, which is that it just takes too much time and effort to include them. One supervisor, who said the deaf employee uses writing for communication, observed that it "takes usually twice as long [to get the point across to her] than the chit-chat is even worth." She continues:

For example, you're sitting at the microscope doing [an analysis] and you can be chatting away with whoever you're sitting beside. Well, [in order to talk with the deaf employee] you have to stop and you have to actually be sure she gets across to what you're going to say. So consequently, the fact of just sitting there and kind of chatting away [about] what you might be going [to] do that night or what you had for supper last night, she misses all of that. Or if you're just relaxing for a couple minutes and you're talking and she wants to join in . . . sometimes it's really hard to just kind of stop and concentrate on telling her what it was you were talking about, particularly when it wasn't really anything terribly meaningful anyhow. It's just that small chit chat back and forth that we take so for granted.

Even hearing employees who knew sign language did not always include deaf colleagues in casual conversation. Sometimes they forgot to use signs when a deaf person entered the room. Some kinds of conversations were especially difficult for novice signers. For example, one supervisor observed, "It's hard to tell a [humorous] story in sign language that you just said with your voice—it's like it's not funny, the sense of humor is lost somewhere along the line."

Sometimes potentially close friendships were not realized because communication was so difficult. In discussing his relationship with a deaf employee, one supervisor observed that, "I like [him], I do like him . . . but I didn't have the . . . kind of interaction with him that I would with somebody that was attractive to me otherwise. It seemed as though all the time we had needed to really be used for communication [related to work]. There wasn't the luxury of the added two or three minutes where you could rattle off something [more casual]." In reflecting on this experience, the supervisor concluded that deaf people "ought to be aware that people may really want to interact and yet there really are barriers that have nothing to do with personality or interest or appreciation, but they're really quite subtle in terms of time involved."

At the heart of this supervisor's explanation is the belief that exclusion is not intended as a personal rejection or act of cruelty. If time is limited, the tendency is to focus on communication related to work tasks first; casual conversations become an unaffordable luxury. This is understandable, since in most work settings, mistakes resulting from failure to communicate with a deaf colleague for the accomplishment of work tasks may draw severe penalties. In comparison, there are few sanctions associated with excluding deaf co-workers from social conversations. As one person put it, "Work related, it [communication] is fine, because they have to get information from him, but when they're preoccupied with something else, like what happened the night before, they're just sort of totally wrapped up in that and they forget to direct their attention to [him] to make sure that he's part of the conversation, that he's into the group."

Supervisors varied widely in their opinions about whether they could do anything to facilitate participation by the deaf employee in social conversations and communication grapevines. Most of those who tried focused on helping the deaf person access the communication grapevine. One strategy was to use written "buckslips" to disseminate routine information which might otherwise be circulated via the grapevine. As one supervisor observed, sometimes "rumors are out and he's not aware of them, but with all the activity that happens in the division, I have a slip that I pass around with everyone's name on it so I don't have to depend on word of mouth. I give it to him on paper, any promotions, any department changes, any activity that would affect him."

Confirming or denying rumors by discussing them directly with deaf employees was a second strategy. Several supervisors said that the employee routinely comes to them to check out stories. Sometimes supervisors approached the deaf person themselves:

> Sometimes he'll be sitting with somebody and they'll start talking to him in a normal voice, and all of a sudden they'll go down to a very low whisper. They think that because he's right there he's picking up, but really he's not and then he gets [only] part of the story. So I told him that anytime he hears something, come and talk to me and I'll finish telling him one way or the other, because we had a little problem with one statement that he made. He heard it, and then he was saying it to someone else, and someone said to me, "Why is [he] going around telling people this?" It was something to do with selling a branch . . . he heard them talking about selling branches, but he got the wrong branch and then he mentioned it to somebody else, and then it came down from my very top boss, "What is [he] doing spreading rumors around?" So I had to sit down with [him] and find out what happened, and I explained to him, "Don't worry, but just make sure that anything that's told to you through the grapevine, [you check out with me]." If he's not sure that he heard everything, to come and talk to me, that we'll straighten it out so that he doesn't get into any kind of trouble, that he's well informed.

In almost every case, including deaf employees in these kinds of communication networks required extra time, effort, and attention. Supervisors were probably more likely to take the time than co-workers, because negative incidents like the one mentioned above reflected badly on them as well as on the deaf employee. Also, they probably felt more responsible for the overall well being of the deaf person and were in a better position to observe the flow of information as well as the impact of exclusion on the deaf worker. As illustrated by the following story, they were also in a position to evaluate the positive impact of simple gestures designed to include the deaf person:

> There was a problem with this outside company that we send the work out to. They had a . . . fire, or something like that. Anyway, they couldn't do our work. Well, everyone was in a dither here. They were all running around and there was a lot of excitement, and you know when something like that happens, it just goes right through the office. And it had to look kind of weird with all of us running around. Well, you know, we have three or four hearing-impaired girls in this department . . . [and] I was thinking "I bet these girls don't know about what's happened. I bet they don't understand what's going on." So I . . . wrote them a note and explained to them what had happened. Well, they were so relieved and thankful. You know, they were so grateful just to be a part of the excitement. Then they knew what's going on. . . . you know, it . . . just struck me that they didn't know and it was so easy to kind of . . . forget about them and not realize that they wouldn't know this. So, anyway, I try to put myself in their place, and to think of how they would see something.

The supervisor quoted above makes a critical point in describing herself as trying to see things from the perspective of the deaf person. Perhaps this is at the root of many of the strategies used by supervisors in their efforts to communicate with deaf employees. While it is impossible for hearing people to understand what it is like to be deaf, it may be that a willingness to *try* to understand is prerequisite for meaningful change.

DISCUSSION

This chapter is the longest in the book, and with good reason. Communication between deaf and hearing people, whether at work or in the community, is often difficult and stressful. The telephone has presented a persistent obstacle to communication across distances for deaf people; while recent technological advances have made telephones more accessible, many barriers remain. Group discussions are frequently difficult because of their overlapping and rapid-fire nature. One-to-one conversations are often fraught with misunderstandings and requests for repetition, which sometimes lead to embarrassment and a sense of personal inadequacy.

No matter what medium is used, communication between deaf and hearing people requires modification of traditional expectations and protocols. Adaptive devices are needed to access telephone conversations.

Group interactions work best when there is an interpreter present and participants gather in well-lit spaces, speak clearly, and take turns. Both deaf and hearing people must be prepared to expend the additional time and energy which are generally required to make one-to-one communication work. Communication in any medium is greatly facilitated when everyone has the patience, social skill, and self-confidence to overcome misunderstandings or feelings of social discomfort.

In short, communication between deaf and hearing people is never easy. In employment settings, communication is complicated by the constraints and pressures associated with the demands of the organization. It may be possible to avoid interaction in a shopping plaza or at a town meeting, but deaf and hearing co-workers must find a way to communicate. Failure to do so may reflect poorly on both of them, resulting in poor job evaluations, or worse yet, job loss. For deaf employees, failure to establish communication networks may also result in social as well as professional isolation, which almost certainly affects job satisfaction and career mobility.

Given these possible consequences, it is reasonable to conclude that everyone (and especially the deaf employee) is motivated to facilitate communication. Yet, supervisors' comments suggest that motivation is not sufficient to insure successful communication. Rather, communication is dependent on a wide range of individual as well as environmental factors. The selection of one strategy over another depends on the specific needs, skills, and resources of the individuals, department, and organization. For example, informing a supervisor that an interpreter would facilitate communication at meetings may be perceived as very helpful if there is money available to pay for such a service. Supervisors in small companies with limited funds may perceive the same request as unreasonable; in these situations, information about agendas and seating arrangements may be viewed as more helpful.

The most important skill supervisors and deaf employees can have is the ability to analyze the communication situations in which they find themselves and determine what will work, given the constraints and resources within that situation. Collaboration is central to such an approach. Working together, they can define the nature of the communication problem(s) and explore possible solutions, taking into account both the needs of the employee and the resources of the employer.

COMMENTARY

SUSAN: I'd like to start by asking you to talk about your experiences using the telephone at work.

DAVID: When I began the job, I asked my supervisor for a TTY, but he said, "No, that's not really a high priority, because we're trying to save money." So I didn't say anything more. But under their policy, if you're sick you have to call in before 9:00 a.m. At that time I was using a local relay service to call my office from home, and it was hard to get through, because their line was always busy. One day I tried to call in sick. I tried and tried, but the relay line was busy. Finally, I gave up. The next day my co-workers asked me, "Where have you been?" I said, "I tried to contact you through the relay service, but it was busy all the time." So they told the supervisor, and it became a first priority. They ordered a TTY for me.

GARY: At the first job I did not request a TTY, because I was the new kid on the street, and the relay service wasn't available anyway. In another job, the very first day I had to get a TDD. That was no problem for them.

JANICE: I guess my situation was very lucky. When I first got into work, they asked me immediately, "How do you communicate on the phone?" and I said, "I use a TTY." They said "Fine. Do you want me to order one?" And I said, "Yes." I said they were responsible to provide me with a TTY in my office, and they said "Fine. How many do you think we need to help you communicate?" I said "Okay, I need one in my office, you maybe need one for when I am sick and I have to call in, and perhaps in my position as a programmer, I'll need to communicate through the computer controller if I'm running a job and something breaks down, so you need one more there." Fine. They ordered three TTY's for me, one for each place. Also, my jobs ran on the computer overnight. If my job blew up, they had to call me at home. They used a beeper. I felt the vibration. So then I could call the computer controller and talk to her on the TTY. It was beautiful. I was really lucky.

SUSAN: Did you teach your co-workers how to use the TTY?

JANICE: Yes. Also, I wrote it down for the computer controllers because there were different people for each shift. I taught the boss, too.

SUSAN: Were they comfortable, do you think?

JANICE: Oh, yes, they were very good. And also, when I quit that company and went to another job, the same thing happened. As soon as I got in, they asked what to do. I said, "I need a phone flasher and a TTY." Fine.

SUSAN: Some supervisors said they reassigned the deaf person's telephone work to hearing people, which created problems if the hearing people resented the extra phone work. I'm wondering if you've ever had this experience?

JANICE: No, I haven't experienced that. My second job required communication with people in other buildings. They all knew I couldn't communicate with them, and it was impossible for everybody to have a TTY, so I asked a person to take notes for me, and they were very happy to do it. I'd write out a program for someone in another building. If they didn't understand the communication through my friend, they'd actually come over to my building for a serious, indepth discussion with me. Everyone was happy to support me.

SUSAN: Did you ever feel like the hearing person resented having to make those notes? Did you do other things for her in return?

JANICE: They never said, "Remember you owe me," or, "I helped you in the past," or anything like that. They were always just real happy to help. It was very nice of them. To be honest, they were very generous.

GARY: As an Employment Advisor, I've had calls from supervisors asking how they should deal with hearing people who resent having to accept all of the deaf person's phone work. My suggestion is to let the hearing person give some of their work to the deaf person, to even out the work. Second, I suggest they be careful with the job description. For example, if there're three workers, one deaf and two hearing, one of the hearing workers has to stay to answer the phones during lunch. The deaf person can go out every time. So, it's always an issue. Also, it goes back to the hearing person's attitude. Janice happened to be fortunate in that the people were very friendly and helpful. In some places, people are not. I also know of a deaf supervisor who solved the phone problem by encouraging people to communicate through electronic mail.

SUSAN: Do you have any advice for supervisors regarding telephones and deaf employees?

JANICE: Well, supervisors should be aware of how to use a TTY and understand how important the TTY is to deaf people.

GARY: Supervisors should decide what kind of phone communication is required on the job, and see if there's a way around it by using a relay service or electronic mail. There are many different ways to get around the phone—explore them. At the same time, supervisors should be sensitive and ask the person what kind of telephone needs they have. TTY's don't answer all needs. Some can use the phone, some can't.

JANICE: Where I was working, there was no good relay service. So your alternatives depend on where you're from. In the future the national relay service will be available twenty-four hours a day. It'll be beautiful.

SUSAN: Did you attend meetings as part of your job?

JANICE: I've had awful experiences with meetings. My two different jobs required weekly meetings. They always told me they couldn't afford to hire an interpreter. So, I just put up with that problem. I'd try to overcome the communication barrier by asking them to write out what they were expecting to talk about before they arrived at the meeting. If I had to present on my projects, I would write down and make copies of everything I was planning to talk about so I could hand it out. But they wanted me to use my voice. It felt a little uncomfortable because I know that I don't speak as well as hearing people, but I accepted it. I got through it, but imagine for other deaf people who perhaps really can't talk at all or for those who can't lipread well. You need to solve that problem at meetings for someone who is completely deaf. An interpreter is the best solution really.

SUSAN: Did you read lips? Is that how you understood what they were saying?

JANICE: Remember that I had the paper with their presentations written out. So when they spoke fast I'd just read what they had written. I got maybe 50 percent of what they said.

GARY: At the first job we only had meetings every six months. I'd ask for an interpreter, but they never provided one. I don't know why they didn't. I guess it was because I was the new kid on the street.

JANICE: Well, you weren't really deaf enough maybe.

GARY: I understand what you are saying, Janice, but I don't think that was it. In the other job, I usually had an interpreter. When I was going to a meeting, they knew they had to provide an interpreter. Sometimes at the last minute they'd have a meeting, and ask me to come, and I'd say, "No thanks." If it was a small group discussion, I'd try to sit in. If it got out of control, I'd walk out, because I knew that it would be a waste of my time.

SUSAN: Can you remember when you walked out of a meeting? What was the reaction of your boss?

GARY: There were no hard feelings. He knew that it was not worth my time to just sit there, understanding nothing. Of course, when meetings involved large numbers of people, of course, it had to be set up far ahead, and there were interpreters. But small group meetings might be set up at the last minute, and they couldn't get an interpreter for those. When the manager wanted me to share some information, we'd discuss one-on-one what I was going to say, and then I'd run the meeting, which let me control the flow of communication. That worked, because they had to be sensitive to my communication needs and talk slowly as I was the lead speaker. If the manager wanted to add something, he would try to speak directly to me, to make sure I understood exactly what was happening. I'd stop him if I didn't understand, and ask him to repeat. In a small group, people would be sensitive, but only when I was in control of the meeting. Also, I have given presentations to thirty or forty people with no interpreter. In those situations, my friends would sit down front. I'd try to lipread, but if there was a question I didn't understand, I'd ask my friends to repeat for me.

SUSAN: Gary, how did you get the information which was discussed at the smaller meetings?

GARY: My boss would sit down with me and talk to me directly. One on one, I'm fine, because the person is usually familiar with my communication system; they know how to talk with me. It's funny, some people in the office who I didn't know that well would tend to talk louder. They thought that would help. One guy kept doing that, and I'd say, "What?" and he kept getting louder and louder. My secretary and manager knew me—knew that I'm deaf. So they knew that I couldn't hear and that it is worthless to raise their voice with me, so they were sensitive to it.

JANICE: It's funny. I had a different experience. It was with a girl who'd been on the job about two weeks or so and there was some gossip. She said to me, "Come here," and whispered it into my ear. I said, "Wait a minute, I have to lipread you." She said "Oh, I forgot." When she stepped back and started to speak, I had to remind her, "Don't forget to turn off your voice!" It's such a habit for them to whisper in your ear.

DAVID: My job didn't require many meetings. But there was a quarterly meeting, when the president of the company would give a presentation about job performance, business sales, and so forth. After the presentation, the president would always come around to me with an interpreter and ask if I understood the presentation.

SUSAN: Was there an interpreter for the quarterly meeting?

DAVID: Yes, but I had a hard time participating during the meeting because it went so fast. I'd take in the information through the interpreter, and then I'd think about it, you know, figuring out what they meant. By the time I'd want to say something, they'd gone on to another topic. I told them after the meeting, "I'd like to talk with you. I have some questions." That way I could ask questions and understand better.

GARY: Some presenters are sensitive. They try to make sure the interpreter is at the same pace with their speech and, at the same time, they remember the deaf person is deaf. I've gone to conferences with ten thousand people, and with the interpreter there, some of the presenters will realize I'm deaf right away. Sometimes they'll come up to me, and that's nice. But others are afraid to come up to me because they don't know how to communicate with me. They think they have to depend on the interpreter. Sometimes they talk to the interpreter instead of to me. I say, "No, communication one-on-one is fine." And they say, "Oh, you can talk?"

JANICE: People from outside companies who give presentations sometimes are insensitive. I went to a conference where the participants were insensitive to me. They'd talk very fast and/or mumble. I'd say, "Stop, stop, please talk slowly, say it again." And the interpreter would have to keep interrupting for that.

SUSAN: Supervisors said deaf people are sometimes left out of the joking and side comments that take place at meetings. I'm wondering if you've had that experience.

DAVID: Well, I had a few co-workers who are good signers, and they would always think of me. They'd hear something and interpret what was being said. I set up a sign language class when I started the job. I started with sixteen people (sixteen out of fifty employees) who were real interested in learning signs. I divided them into two groups and taught them during lunch hour, a half hour to each group. As time went on, the group got smaller. Some people found it hard to learn signs, some lost interest, and some were too busy. So it got down to five. They were from different departments. There was one co-worker from my department, and the rest were from other areas, like research and development, sales, marketing, and accounting. Whenever something was going on in their area, they'd let me know. So I had a lot of information during the meetings. I didn't miss much gossip or news.

SUSAN: Was it your idea to set up the class?

DAVID: Well, it began with the people themselves. There were many people who were interested and motivated, and they came to me and expressed their interest. So I talked with the president of the company. I told him I was thinking of setting up a sign language class, but I would need books. He said, "Fine." He paid for the sign language communication books, and gave everybody a copy. Then we set up the time and so forth.

SUSAN: How good did those five people get at sign language?

DAVID: Four of them were between beginners and intermediate level. The person who worked in my department was between intermediate and advanced. Not ASL, but good signs. He and I sat next to each other every day, so he knew more.

JANICE: My situation's very much like David's, except everyone was from my department. There were three programmers, a developer, and a researcher. I set up classes because they came to me and were interested. Like David, I set it up during the lunch hour.

GARY: During breaks or before the meeting started, I'd communicate with the interpreter. Also, I had my friends; there was always at least one who would sit next to me, so I'd converse with them one-on-one.

SUSAN: A few supervisors said they didn't hire interpreters because they felt it shouldn't cost them more to employ a deaf person. Others said it was just too expensive. What is your opinion?

DAVID: That's a very touchy topic. A small company lives on a tight budget, and, depending on their sales, they may not be able to afford an interpreter. It's very important that deaf people inform employers about the expense, so they can prepare for it. The big companies have the money, but I still believe it's the deaf person's responsibility to educate them about the expense.

SUSAN: When you say "educate," what do you mean?

DAVID: Well, they should explain that interpreters are expensive, but that they will need them for meetings, and maybe for one-on-one communication, so that the deaf person can participate equally with hearing people at the job.

GARY: I'm still struggling with that myself. I tell my students, "You can't go to the job and demand to have an interpreter." I tell them to try to get the supervisor to be sensitive to it. Twenty years ago it was a different ball game. Today a lot of places have been exposed to interpreters. If the supervisors at a small company want to see a deaf person hired, succeed, and be equal to hearing people, then they will try to provide interpreters. If interpreters absolutely cannot be provided, then they should have a buddy system, some friend who is an expert in sign language who can convey the information. A third option would be to use the computer. You have to learn to be creative. Also, I've seen more and more companies hiring full-time, in-house interpreters. Someone was telling me just this morning about a company that has an interpreter full-time, but they only interpret for twenty of their forty work hours each week. I wonder what they do the other twenty hours. Paperwork? Are they an interpreter/secretary?

JANICE: Really, it's important that they only interpret twenty hours a week to prevent Repetitive Motion Injury (RMI).

DAVID: Most companies feel that to hire an interpreter by contract is cheaper, because you've got to pay a full-time interpreter benefits.

JANICE: I think they break even. Freelance interpreters charge sixty dollars an hour, so maybe the full-time interpreter's salary would be a little less in the long run.

SUSAN: How do you handle one-to-one communication?

DAVID: I was thinking about the supervisor who said if communication between the deaf employee and his supervisor breaks down and problems go unresolved, the situation can blow up. That happened to me. When I was young I worked for a small photographic firm. After a few months the old supervisor was fired, and a new supervisor came in. The two of us kind of cold-shouldered each other. There was no communication. They gave me a piece of paper and told me what to do, and I did it. I had two positions, one as a stock clerk, and another that involved heavy carrying jobs. That second position took a lot of my time, so by the time I was finished with that part of my work, I didn't have time for the clerking. It was very frustrating, because I kept getting farther behind. My supervisor began to write notes to me, saying, "You're not doing your job." I said, "I'm covering this other position first and then going to my clerking job." He said it didn't matter, didn't even give me a chance to talk, just turned around and left. I was so frustrated. It went on for a couple of months. One day I got a letter. I'll never forget it. I opened it up, and it said I was fired because I was a lousy worker, and I had a bad attitude. I was shocked. I decided not to struggle with it, I just left. If I were to go back to that job now and it happened, I'd get a lawyer and take him to court. But my concern is that I'm not the only person—I believe that happens to other deaf people, too.

JANICE: I grew up with lipreading. When hearing people don't understand me, or when I don't understand them, I ask them to write it down. Otherwise, no problem. I understand people. Writing is our back up.

SUSAN: Supervisors said sometimes people don't want to write because it takes a long time, and they get frustrated. Did you ever sense that people were frustrated with you, or didn't want to write?

JANICE: No.

DAVID: Yep. I depend on writing for one-to-one communication. I have a pad of paper or an index card in my pocket, and when I need something, I go to somebody. If they look like they don't want to do it, I just leave them. I wait until the right time, when they look friendly and are glad to write. I have to catch them in the right mood.

SUSAN: You said you went to them for information. Do you ever find that people will take the time to write down a joke or a funny story or a piece of gossip?

DAVID: No. I didn't bother them for that, either. I wrote for information, that's all. I know many hearing people don't like to write. Some are awkward with writing, so I didn't take their time doing that.

GARY: My tendency is to ask them to write a word down, if I didn't get it. Then I tell them how to say it again so I can lipread it.

JANICE: I teach them to fingerspell. Then, if we don't understand a word, we can spell it out. If two words look the same on the lips, like "were" and "where," they can spell it.

DAVID: In the past, many deaf people didn't have computers and TDDs. They depended on writing.

JANICE: Yep. My father always had a pad of paper.

DAVID: Now today, if you do that, you look like a nerd. Sometimes I'm embarrassed, you know, but I have to think of myself. My father, who is deaf, always says, "Without the paper you'll be frustrated. No communication. You'll feel isolated. Put that paper in there, it's for communication."

SUSAN: Do you feel you miss important information related to your work because you are left out of informal conversations?

DAVID: Yes. I told some of my co-workers, "When news comes up, new rules, anything related to the job, I'm always the last person that gets the information." And they said, "Oh, really?" Next time, they let me know immediately. Next time I got the news first.

GARY: I had what they call a buddy system, meaning that you have some good friend who's willing to sit with you during coffee breaks and share information about what's happening. Best to take somebody who has worked for the company a long time, has a good personality, and works well. Even now, I advise deaf people, "Get a buddy. Get somebody to help you know what's going on in the company." There are a lot of strategies that work well, but the deaf person has to be assertive. Not aggressive, because aggressive is negative. Sometimes the supervisor picks a person who they feel could work well with deaf people. That can help a lot.

JANICE: We had bulletin boards in certain rooms. So the boss, who didn't have time to call people together, would just put things up on the bulletin board. We'd walk around and see that. If somebody didn't see it, we'd just share that. We'd ask, "Do you know about this?" And they'd go and look. So most of the time we just used the bulletin board for rules. But as for gossip, David, you're right, I was always the last person to find out about the soap opera that was going on around my office.

SUSAN: Did your work performance ever suffer because you didn't have the same information as everyone else?

GARY: Well, it's the same thing that Dave said, "I'm always the last to know." But related to work itself, I've never had that experience, no.

JANICE: Oh, I've had some bad experiences. We had cubicle offices. I'm sitting there typing, learning out of books and from the people who teach me. But the hearing people yell out, "Hey, why isn't this working?" and somebody else over in another cubicle hears and starts to work on it. That's really not fair. It was very frustrating.

DAVID: When a new production method was introduced, even though I had more seniority than the others, the hearing people preferred to communicate with other hearing people. Then later they told me about it, but I didn't get the full information the way they had. The boss would sometimes come and say "What are you doing?" I'd say, "Well, I'm doing what you told me." And he'd say, "No. You're not." And I felt really lousy. I complained. I said to the boss, "Next time the engineer comes, you come to me. Write it down on a piece of paper." He said, "But sometimes the engineers don't feel comfortable with that, they prefer to talk." And I said, "Yeah, I'm really stuck. Next time I would like to join in and be able to look." He understood and let me join in. So when I had a question, then I had the opportunity to ask.

JANICE: Same problem in my experience. Every time I couldn't solve a problem with my program, I'd call some senior programmer, who would come over—perhaps they didn't understand either, maybe they'd call other people, and they'd start talking among themselves and leave me out. They're debating back and forth, and I've missed the whole discussion and valuable information. I couldn't keep up. Sometimes I'd have the nerve to say, "Hey, stop. You were supposed to talk to me. This is my program." They'd say, "Oh, I'm sorry." Then they'd repeat, "She said, he said." But still it's summarized, you know.

GARY: I had no real bad experiences, but there were communication problems at that first job, and that's why I left. I didn't really have the opportunity for hands-on experience working in other projects, because they felt communication was a problem for me. I didn't fight the system, because I didn't know what could be done. If I was going through it again now, my attitude would be different. I'd be a lot more outspoken, knowing what could be done.

SUSAN: I'd like to conclude by asking if you have advice for supervisors regarding communication.

JANICE: A buddy system is the best system. Also, they should hire an interpreter when they plan to have lengthy conversations and meetings.

GARY: Yeah, that's very common advice. Second, they should be sensitive in talking with others who haven't worked with deaf people, so they are not hit between the eyeballs by the experience. Prepare them. Third, they should get an interpreter at least for the first day, so the deaf person can understand the process, the company, and everything related to the job. Last, they should ask the deaf person what kind of communication support they need and what methods they feel most comfortable with. At the same time, the deaf person needs to be open and not hide their deafness. They should be straightforward about it. It's a two-way exchange.

DAVID: Yes, I agree with you. If the supervisor has never met a deaf person before, it's the deaf employee's responsibility to give them information which will help them become more comfortable and learn about different communication methods.

RESOURCE LIST

Library Resources

Books and articles listed in this section should be available at local public or college/university libraries or through the interlibrary loan services at these libraries. Purchase prices listed may vary and are indicated only to give the reader a general idea of cost; contact the publisher directly for current cost and shipping/handling charges.

Cagle, S., and Cagle, K. *GA and SK Etiquette: Guidelines for Telecommunica-*

tion in the Deaf Community. Rochester, NY: The Authors, 1991. (Available from the Authors; Phone 716-385-7949 [TDD]; Cost: $8.95)

> The authors, both deaf, explain how to use a TDD and avoid cultural misunderstandings.

Castle, D.L. *Telephone Strategies: A Technical and Practical Guide for Hard-of-Hearing People.* Bethesda, MD: Self Help for Hard of Hearing People, 1988. (Available from Self Help for Hard of Hearing People, Inc., 7800 Wisconsin Avenue, Bethesda, MD 20814; Phone 301-657-2248 [voice], 301-657-2249 [TDD]; Cost: $6.00)

> This booklet deals with the practical as well as technical aspects of communicating on the telephone for hard-of-hearing people. Castle covers equipment, managing telephone communication breakdowns, communicating with different people, and other methods of making telephone calls.

DiDio, L. "Deaf Students Talk Over 10NET LANs." *Network World,* 5(14): 15–16, 1988.

> DiDio's article discusses Gallaudet University's use of electronic networks for interaction between deaf students and teachers. Local networks permit interactive conversation in everyday English.

Garretson, M.D. (Ed.). *Eyes, Hands, Voices: Communication Issues Among Deaf People.* Silver Spring, MD: National Association of the Deaf, 1990. (Available from National Association of the Deaf, 814 Thayer Avenue, Silver Spring, MD 20910; Phone 800-942-ASDC [V/TDD]; Cost: $20.00)

> Published as a special issue of *Deaf American* (vol. 40, nos. 1–4, 1990), this work discusses the role of American Sign Language in the education of deaf students and among the deaf population. The thirty contributions (articles, letters, and poems) in this work reflect the wide and sharply differing range of perceptions on communication among deaf persons.

Harrington, M.J. "Type-Talking is a Gallaudet Favorite" *Computerworld,* 24(43): 43, 1990.

> This article discusses the use of computer networks to facilitate communication, training, educational programs and to apply real-life work situations to the educational environment.

Jamison, S.L. *Signs for Computing Terminology.* Silver Spring, MD: National Association of the Deaf, 1983. (Available from National Association of the Deaf, 814 Thayer Avenue, Silver Spring, MD 20910; Phone 301-587-6282 [V/TDD]; Cost: $10.95)

This is a comprehensive dictionary of computer related vocabulary, developed by an employee of the IBM Corporation in cooperation with many nationally recognized experts on sign language. Also available are three videotapes which cover prefixes, suffixes and vocabulary, A–Z. Each video is $39.95.

"Making Connections: Fax Project Provides a Vital Link for Deaf Business Owners." *Gallaudet Today, 21*(3), 7, 1991. (This whole issue of *Gallaudet Today,* devoted to the topic of deaf professionals, is available from *Gallaudet Today,* Gallaudet University, 800 Florida Avenue, NE, Washington, DC 20002-3695; Phone 202-651-5671 [V/TDD]; Cost: $3.00)

This article discusses the importance of the fax machine as a communication tool between hearing and deaf people.

Newell, W. *Basic Sign Communication: Student Materials.* Silver Spring, MD: National Association of the Deaf, 1983. (Available from National Association of the Deaf, 814 Thayer Avenue, Silver Spring, MD 20910; Phone 301-587-6282 [V/TDD]; Order No. SL034; Cost: $17.00)

This student manual was designed as part of a comprehensive curriculum of basic sign language instruction. It contains practice materials on use of sign language vocabulary.

Newell, W. *Basic Sign Communication: Vocabulary.* Silver Spring, MD: National Association of the Deaf, 1983. (Available from National Association of the Deaf, 814 Thayer Avenue, Silver Spring, MD 20910; Phone 301-587-6282 [V/TDD]; Order No. SL032; Cost: $10.95)

This vocabulary dictionary depicts over nine hundred basic signs introduced in the three levels of instruction presented by the curriculum package. The dictionary is very well illustrated and is useful as a general reference text.

Registry of Certified Interpreters. Silver Spring, MD: RID Publications, 1991. (Available from RID Publications, 8719 Colesville Road., Suite 310, Silver Spring, MD 20910-3913; Phone 301-608-0050 [V/TDD]; Cost: $14.95)

This booklet lists interpreters who have been certified by the Registry of Interpreters for the Deaf, by state.

Riekehof, L.L. *Joy of Signing: The Illustrated Guide for Mastering Sign Language and the Manual Alphabet.* Springfield, MO: Gospel Publishing House, 1987. (Available in cloth cover from Gospel Publishing House, 1445 Boonville Avenue, Springfield, MO; LC 86-80173; Phone 800-641-4310 [Voice]; Cost: $16.95. Available in paper cover from Harvard University Press, 79 Garden Street, Cambridge, MA 02138; ISBN 0-674-19424-1; Phone 617-495-2600 [Voice]; Cost: $8.95)

This well-known dictionary contains an explanation of sign language structure, signs arranged by category and illustrated with line drawings, and origins of each sign and how it is used.

Sheie, T.P. "Adapting Training for the Hearing Impaired." *Training & Development Journal,* pp. 100–102, 1985 (January).

Outlines communication strategies and methods for training hearing-impaired employees and including them in professional development activities.

Sternberg, M.L.A. *American Sign Language: A Comprehensive Dictionary.* New York: Harper Collins Publishers, 1981. (Available from Harper Collins Publishers, 10 E. 53rd Street, New York, NY 10022; Phone 800-242-7737 [Voice]; ISBN 0-06-014097-6; Cost: $50.00)

The largest American Sign Language dictionary to date, this work contains more than fifty-four hundred entries and cross-references, illustrated and described, an introduction to sign language, seven indexes in foreign languages, and an extensive bibliography.

Pamphlets and Brochures

ABC Fingerspelling Cards. (Available from National Information Center on Deafness, Gallaudet University, 800 Florida Avenue NE, Washington, DC 20002-3695; Phone 202-651-5051 [Voice], 202-651-5052 [TDD]; Cost: up to 25 copies free, then 100/$1.00)

This is a set of cards that shows the twenty-six handshapes for the letters of the manual alphabet and the numbers one through ten.

Castle, D.L. *Maximizing Telephone Accessibility for Deaf and Hard-of-Hearing People.* (Available from National Center on Employment of the Deaf, National Technical Institute for the Deaf, Rochester Institute of Technology, P.O. Box 9887, Rochester, NY 14623-0887; Phone 716-475-6219 [V/TDD]; Cost: up to ten copies free, then $.35 each)

Castle describes strategies for communication, covers information about the TDD, discusses how to make a TDD call, explains TDD etiquette, describes dual-party relay systems, and gives some resources for additional information.

Castle, D.L. *Signaling and Assistive Listening Devices for Hearing-Impaired People.* (Available from Alexander Graham Bell Association for the Deaf, Inc., Publication Sales, 3417 Volta Place N.W., Washington, DC 20007; Phone 202-337-5220 [V/TDD]; Cost: single copy free, 10/$2.50, 25/$4.00, 50/$6.00)

This pamphlet describes wake-up alarms, multi-purpose signalers, telephone-doorbell devices, etc., plus sources for receiving additional information about these devices.

Communicating with Deaf People: An Introduction. (Available from National Information Center on Deafness, Gallaudet University, 800 Florida Avenue NE, Washington, DC 20002-3695; Phone 202-651-5051 [Voice], 202-651-5052 [TDD]; Order no. 550; Cost $2.00)

This twenty-page illustrated publication introduces the various ways deaf people can communicate, including gesture and facial expression, speechreading, Cued Speech, fingerspelling, American Sign Language, and other manual communication systems. It discusses new technologies and their potential contributions to communication, sign language in other countries, regional signs, and the development of sign language in the United States.

Have You Ever Wondered About . . . How Deaf People Communicate. Series 2. (Available from National Information Center on Deafness, Gallaudet University, 800 Florida Avenue NE, Washington, DC 20002-3695; Phone 202-651-5051 [Voice], 202-651-5052 [TDD]; Order no. 492; Cost $1.00)

This illustrated publication introduces the different ways deaf people can communicate, including gesture and facial expression, speechreading, Cued Speech, fingerspelling, American Sign Language, and other manual communication systems.

Let's Communicate: Tips. (Available from Division of Public Affairs, National Technical Institute for the Deaf, Rochester Institute of Technology, P.O. Box 9887, Rochester, NY 14623-0887; Phone 716-475-6853 [V/TDD]; Cost: up to 100 copies free, then $.25 each)

"Tips" includes the manual alphabet and a few commonly used signs for use in communicating with people who are deaf.

Locating Sign Language Classes. (Available from National Information Center on Deafness, Gallaudet University, 800 Florida Avenue NE, Washington, DC 20002-3695; Phone 202-651-5051 [Voice], 202-651-5052 [TDD]; Order no. 230; Cost: $.50)

This one-page publication suggests some starting points for locating sign language classes in any locality.

Tips You Can Use When Communicating with Deaf Employees. (Available from National Center on Employment of the Deaf, National Technical Institute for the Deaf, Rochester Institute of Technology, P.O. Box 9887, Rochester, NY 14623-0887; Phone 716-475-6219 [V/TDD]; Cost: up to 25 copies free, then $.35 each)

This brochure will help integrate deaf employees into the work environment. Suggestions for using visual cues to enhance communication during meetings and for installing telephone amplifiers on deaf employees' telephones are included.

What You Should Know About TDDs. (Available from Division of Public Affairs, National Technical Institute for the Deaf, Rochester Institute of Technology, P.O. Box 9887, Rochester, NY 14623-0887; Phone 716-475-6853 [V/TDD]; Cost: up to 10 copies free)

This brochure explains what TDDs can do, how to choose the best equipment based on needs and environment, advantages and disadvantages of TDDs, and problems that can occur when using TDDs. Agencies and manufacturers that can help with selection are listed.

Media

Contact the following distributors for information about loan or purchase of media:

Gallaudet Media Distribution
800 Florida Avenue NE
Washington, DC 20002-3695
202-651-5227 (TDD)
202-651-5222 (Voice)

Some films and videos are available for purchase; purchase price is indicated below. Others are available only on a loan basis. Contact Gallaudet Media Distribution for purchase/borrowing information.

Captioned Films/Videos for the Deaf
Modern Talking Picture Service
5000 Park Street North
St. Petersburg, FL 33709-9989
800-237-6213 (TDD and Voice)

Some films and videos are available for purchase; purchase price is indicated below. All media listed may be borrowed from Captioned Films for the Deaf; an account must be established with CF/VD before borrowing. Contact CF/VD for purchase/borrowing information.

Basic Sign Communication [video]. (Available from Captioned Films/Videos for the Deaf; Cost: $400 for the complete set)

Originally developed as a supplement to NTID's Basic Sign Communication Curriculum and tested by the National Technical Institute for the Deaf, this sequential videotape learning system contains six videotapes with thirty-two complete lessons of natural sign English/Pidgin Sign English. These are vocabulary tapes.

Dactylology: Words on Your Hands [video]. (Available on loan from either Gallaudet Media Distribution or Captioned Films/Videos for the Deaf).

This series of fingerspelling lessons depicts various individuals signing. Lessons include an introduction, manual alphabet practice, three- and four-letter words, prefixes and suffixes, syllables, etc.

Deafness and Communication [16mm motion picture]. (Available from Gallaudet Media Distribution; loan only)

This eleven-minute color film is intended to educate the public on the nature and severity of hearing loss and some of the channels of communication open to deaf people.

Joy of Signing [video]. (Available from Gallaudet Media Distribution; loan only)

This series of videotapes follows the text *The Joy of Signing* by Lottie Riekehof. Each shows how to sign different words and how the words are used in sentences. Only two videos may be borrowed at one time.

Specially For You: A Guide to the Use of the Telephone for the Disabled [video]. (Available from San Francisco Public Library, A/V Support, Civic Center, San Francisco, CA 94102; Phone 415-557-4292 [Voice], 415-557-4433 [TDD]; Cost: $75.00)

This eleven-minute video shows how the telephone can be modified for use by disabled people, including hearing-impaired individuals. Amplifiers, flashing lights, and TDDs are demonstrated.

Technical Signs Videotapes and Manuals. (Available for loan or purchase from Captioned Films/Videos for the Deaf. Contact them for cost of individual tapes and availability of accompanying manuals.)

These videos are part of a national project, based at the National Technical Institute for the Deaf, designed to collect, evaluate, select, and record signs used in academic and career environments. Each tape consists of six to twelve lists of words in the same technical area. Areas covered include anthropology, biology, business, career education, communication, economics, employment, engineering, English, fine and applied arts, human sexuality, legal terms, mathematics, photography, physics, printing, psychology, general science, religion, secretarial, social work, TV/media, and theater. Manuals for some of the videos are available separately.

Using Your TTY/TDD [video]. (Available from Sign Media, Inc., Burtonsville Commerce Center, 4020 Blackburn Lane, Burtonsville, MD 20866; Phone 301-421-0268 [V/TDD]; Cost: $29.95 for VHS/Beta, $44.95 for ¾")

This narrated and captioned videotape introduces the TTY/TDD in a clear and practical manner. It explains making and receiving TTY/TDD calls, as well as proper TTY/TDD etiquette.

Contacts

Communication Disorders

National Institute on Deafness and Other Communication Disorders
  Clearinghouse
National Institutes of Health
Building 31, Room 3C-35
9000 Rockville Pike
Bethesda, MD 20892
301-402-0252 (TDD)
301-496-7243 (Voice)

> NIDCD facilities and enhances the dissemination of information on normal and disordered processes of human communication. Established in March 1991, the Clearinghouse is a national resource center for information about hearing, balance, smell, taste, voice, speech, and language for health professionals, patients, industry, and the public.

Interpreters

Registry of Interpreters for the Deaf
8719 Colesville Road, Suite 310
Silver Spring, MD 20910
301-608-0050 (TDD and Voice)

> The national RID office will be able to direct employers and people who are deaf to local area interpreter referral services.

Relay Services

Effective July 1993, every state must have an in-state, out-of-state, and international relay service available; hearing-impaired people thus will have the same access to phone services that are available to hearing people. In a relay service, communication access is provided by people who communicate simultaneously with hearing people by voice and hearing-impaired people via a TDD. For information about relay services, the following sources are available:

• Inside front cover of local phone book will provide relay telephone numbers.

- Each phone company serving the local area will have brochures. Contact their special needs centers.
- AT&T National Special Needs Center (800-833-3232 [TDD], 800-233-1222 [voice]) can provide information. AT&T also has videos available which show how to use the relay service.

Telecommunication Devices for the Deaf (TDDs)

Telecommunications for the Deaf, Inc.
8719 Colesville Road, Suite 300
Silver Spring, MD 20910
301-589-3006 (TDD)
301-589-3786 (Voice)

Many telecommunications stores, such as Radio Shack, carry telecommunications and assistive devices for people who are deaf. TDI encourages the development of devices and services which enhance the ability of deaf and hearing-impaired people to communicate by telephone. They coordinate all groups interested in telecommunications for hearing-impaired users, publish an annual TDI International Telephone Directory, and are a good resource to find local firms which sell and repair telecommunication devices.

Telephone Services

AT&T National Special Needs Center
2001 Route 46
Suite 310
Parsippany, NJ 07054-9990
800-833-3232 (TDD)
800-233-1222 (Voice)

This Center sells and leases telephone and communication equipment for use by persons with disabilities.

Tele-Consumer Hotline
1910 K Street NW
Suite 610
Washington, DC 20006
800-332-1124 (TDD and Voice)
(202-223-4371 in the Washington metro area)

This hotline is a free consumer information service for all consumers in need of assistance in dealing with telephone shopping requirements. They answer questions on equipment which will help those with an impairment communicate more effectively and publish a number of free publications, including a *Special Needs Factsheet*, a *TDD Relay Center Comparison Chart* on present relay services, and a *TDD Directory Listing* which describes available TDD directory books containing emergency numbers, government and special agencies, travel agencies, banks, schools, libraries, and lawyers who have TDD numbers.

ENDNOTES

1. The situation will be greatly improved by July, 1993, when Title IV of ADA requires common carrier phone companies both in state and state-to-state to provide relay services.

2. For example, the words "pat," "bat," and "mat" all look alike.

3. There are many solutions to this kind of problem, including alarms which flash in addition to making noise and special devices which can be worn or carried by deaf employees and vibrate in order to alert them, should the auditory alarms sound.

4. This is a game requiring several players (the more the better). Players generally sit in a circle or stand in a line. The game is begun when the first player makes up a phrase and whispers it to the player next to him/her, who passes it to the next person in the same fashion. The last player must voice the phrase he or she receives out loud. The goal is to pass the phrase from one player to another without changing it. However, the phrase spoken by the last player is usually very different from the phrase made up by the first player, having been distorted as it was passed from person to person.

Chapter 4

RELATIONSHIPS WITH HEARING PEOPLE AT WORK

SUPERVISOR: . . . I think probably what I should have done is had a meeting with the girls and explain about [her], rather than just let her come in here cold . . . I should have talked to the other girls alone first, so they'd know what to expect, know a little bit about her, maybe.
INTERVIEWER: What would you have told them?
SUPERVISOR: Well, I think I would have told them that she was . . . very talented . . . and that I think they should have all been helpful to her . . . I would have wanted them all to be a little bit kinder to her—not kind [in the sense of] condescending, but just a little more patient with her . . . I didn't tell any of the girls about her because I didn't want them all to be watching her. I didn't know how to handle it myself. (Excerpt from interview with hearing supervisor of deaf employee.)

While people do not seek employment in order to make friends, they often find friends or, at least, acquaintances, in co-workers. Certainly it is easier to go to work every day if one can look forward to friendly faces and good conversation over breaks and lunch. Furthermore, as noted in *Chapter 2*, success at work is not evaluated on the basis of technical performance alone; the ability to get along with co-workers and be a part of the team is also valued by supervisors. Employees who demonstrate solid relationships with colleagues and the ability to work in groups may be more positively viewed by their supervisors than those who are seen as isolated from or rejected by peers.

Supervisors were asked to describe their perceptions of how the deaf employee related to co-workers. While several said the deaf employee got along well with others, most qualified their response by noting that there were constraints on interaction between the deaf person and his or her colleagues. Descriptions of interactions between deaf and hearing employees covered a wide range of relationships, including incidents of open hostility as well as close friendships.

Communication plays a central role in the development of relationships, and many of the factors that emerged as influential in the development of relationships between deaf and hearing workers are closely related to the conditions affecting communication presented in *Chapter 3*. Accordingly, there are areas in which the current discussion of relationships overlaps the earlier discussion of communication. The difference between the two chapters is one of focus. In *Chapter 3*, the focus was on the development of formal and informal communication strategies and networks. Here, the focus is on how environmental conditions and individual characteristics promote or inhibit the development of relationships.

Analysis of supervisors' comments suggests that several factors contribute to the range and quality of the relationships which develop between deaf and hearing employees. These include (1) environmental conditions, (2) characteristics of the deaf employee, (3) characteristics of hearing co-workers, (4) supervisor support and intervention, and (5) the length of time within the environment.

ENVIRONMENTAL CONDITIONS

Environmental conditions affect the potential for relationships to develop between deaf and hearing workers. Examples include the size and physical layout of the organization, the type of work performed, the break patterns established by the supervisor, and the "spirit" of the organization, department, or work group.

Some environmental conditions facilitate interaction and the development of relationships. One supervisor described her department as operating on a "family" model, in which people look out for one another. This supervisor said staff take pride in their team spirit, adding that she felt this spirit helped the deaf employee become part of the group. Another said interaction within her department was facilitated by the small number of staff and the physical layout of the office (everyone shared one large work area, thus insuring visual access to office activities by all employees). A third noted that the deaf employee "opened up" more and began to initiate conversations with co-workers after she left a filing job for a position that involved more interaction with staff in other departments.

Sometimes, however, even after concerted efforts to modify the environment to suit a deaf employee have been made, questions about how to behave remain. In these cases, even a simple interaction can become strained. For example, one supervisor worried about how to approach the deaf employee when the employee was not wearing his hearing aid, even though he had taken many steps to insure that the employee would be forewarned:

> You know . . . sometimes it's a question of how do you get someone's attention. We purposely put him in a location where at least you . . . don't have to come up behind him. You can come up from a spot where he can see you coming. Either he can see you . . . or you tap on his table . . . [But] I know at times . . . [he] will turn off his hearing aid. When he does that, he has no hearing whatsoever. I don't know where that leaves him in the environment, if you forget the world. If you tap on his shoulder, he might go right through the ceiling. I have no idea.

Other environmental conditions constrained the development of relationships between deaf employees and their colleagues. For example, tasks within some work settings made possible casual conversations between hearing employees while they worked; several supervisors noted that this encouraged the development of cliques within the group and isolated the deaf employee. As one person observed, "The problem is that a lot of things they were doing were like looking at a stack of paper and putting [sheets] into number order. So while they could do that and talk at the same time, [she] couldn't, because she couldn't watch them and read their lips and watch what she was doing at the same time. So there was a lot of chatter going around that she was not . . . part of. She felt bad at times that she was left out of that."

When more than one deaf person worked at the company, supervisors noted that deaf employees preferred to work or go to lunch with each other, and one said that she purposely assigned the deaf employee to breaks that coincided with those of another deaf person. When asked to explain this decision, she said, "They're buddies. I mean, if I was a deaf person I'd certainly want to communicate with a deaf person at lunch. As a matter of fact they come down [to the cafeteria] and all the deaf folks are down from all different departments . . . [and] they sit at the table together." The assignment of deaf people to breaks at the same time was intended to be helpful, and, quite likely, was viewed as helpful by the deaf employees. It also reflects an assumption on the part of the supervisor about the preferences of deaf people and promotes the development of separate social groups within the organization, making it even less likely that informal relationships will develop between deaf and hearing employees. This is not necessarily negative. However, one must consider whether deaf employees in these circumstances are forming alliances on the basis of shared interests and personal attraction (as do most people), or because there is nobody else in the environment with whom they can communicate.

CHARACTERISTICS OF THE DEAF EMPLOYEE

Another set of factors which supervisors suggested contribute to the development of relationships between deaf and hearing employees have to do with the personality, attitudes, and interpersonal skills of the deaf person. Several supervisors attributed the success of the deaf person in making friends at work to his or her assertiveness and generally outgoing personality. As one person put it, "He is a social person . . . he'll go to lunch or do whatever, he is not an island at lunch." Some further examples:

EXAMPLE # 1
INTERVIEWER: Lunch times, break times, do you feel as if [she] is included as much as the other women? I mean, to what degree does her deafness interfere with that kind of stuff?
SUPERVISOR: She doesn't let it interfere . . . When she knows who she's going to lunch with, she'll grab a piece of paper if she knows she's going with so-and-so . . . She kind of handles it all by herself. She does not go and just sit and eat her lunch without joining in. And see, there again, I think it's her personality. I think some people might find it . . . easier to just go and sit and eat your sandwich and be quiet. But [she] doesn't let that happen.
EXAMPLE # 2
He fits in. I think he allows himself to fit in to a degree . . . I don't think he lets his handicap get in the way . . . [I think he] accepts what he has without using it as a crutch or a reason for not doing as good as [someone else] . . . He accepts what he has, but at the same time he's not gonna let it slow him down in getting involved. So he could very easily say, "I'm not gonna go to that party if I'm not gonna hear anybody," or, "I'm gonna hear a lot of noise. Why should I go?" . . . He doesn't have that problem. He will go because he's with some people that he works with and he enjoys a good time. I know that, 'cause at the last couple of Christmas parties he'd go to, he'd definitely want to go, and he says he wants to be with the group. But it would be so easy for the reasons I stated . . . [to say,] "I'd like to go, but gee, I don't hear the stuff or anything." I never, ever heard that from him.

Conversely, those who did not initiate contact with hearing colleagues were perceived as "loners." In some instances, this phrase was used in a descriptive, as opposed to explanatory, mode in that supervisors simply noted that the deaf employee spent time alone without speculating as to why. One supervisor said of the deaf employee in her department, "She's a loner . . . at break time, she'll go in the lunch room and turn on the TV, which is no problem; it's what it's there for. But as far as sitting down with a group of people at a table, she may, but she'll be like down on the end sitting there. Like the last couple of days, she's been eating lunch outside."

In other cases the term "loner" was used within a context which seemed to infer a choice, or preference, on the part of the deaf person. As one person commented, "[He is] much more alone . . . I don't know, maybe it's survival or whatever at noontime, but he'll tend much more to be alone at noon, maybe sitting in the area of people [rather] than in any way talking with them." A second supervisor offered a more detailed description of the deaf employee's behavior:

SUPERVISOR: For the most part, he'd just sit and read [at lunch]. He'd go up to the cafeteria and he'd bring his lunch down here and he'd just sit and read a book or a newspaper.
INTERVIEWER: Do you think he ever felt lonely?
SUPERVISOR: No, not really. He's a really strong-willed person. I think that he was that way because that's just the way he wanted to be. He was the kind of guy, I don't know, [it was] just his personality.
INTERVIEWER: Well, when the guys went out for drinks or something like that after work, do you know if he ever went with them?
SUPERVISOR: I don't know. I don't think so. I would doubt it . . . You know he was more of a loner.

The second supervisor cited above stated that the deaf employee was a loner because he had that "kind of personality." However, later in the interview, this supervisor offered a different explanation, one focusing more on the communication barrier between this employee and his co-workers. He observed that the employee would "read during lunch, then during the day he didn't gab. He'd sit right there and work. You know, I almost felt like he kind of settled for that. Like, if he didn't have the problem with the hearing and stuff, maybe it would have been different for him. Also, it was difficult for him with people telling jokes and stuff. I mean, he didn't catch on right away."

These two explanations reflect different perspectives on the part of the supervisor. Perhaps most important, each explanation has different implications for intervention. If one believes that a deaf employee is a loner by choice, then it is unlikely that attempts would (or even should) be made to draw him or her out. However, if one believes that the person stays to him or herself because it is difficult to participate in casual conversations, then efforts to include the person in social interactions by talking more slowly or using gestures, writing, and other alternative communication modes are in order.

Several supervisors said the deaf employee held a basic attitude of distrust towards hearing co-workers, often reflected in an expressed opinion that co-workers were talking about them behind their back or deliberately leaving them out of conversations. These assumptions on the part of deaf workers about hearing colleagues—whether deserved or not—understandably interfered with the development of positive relationships. The following account is illustrative:

> She got to know me pretty well. The other girls she didn't talk [to] very much, she just kind of stayed to herself. Because she had to communicate with me because of the orders and the situation in the office. But basically she always thought people were talking about her behind her back. [She thought] she wasn't very well liked, and I think it was just her imagination because she was very well liked ... It's just because of her hearing problem. I think that she [felt] a lot of people talk[ed] about her, and they didn't, because I never heard anything. [I] even tried to ask the girls and they said, "No, I never talk about her." But the office has a clique and maybe she wasn't included in the clique, so that's kind of basically why she stayed to herself, I think, and that's why she thought she was being talked about.

Conversely, a feeling of trust and basic rapport was seen as very helpful in working around potentially difficult or frustrating situations. For example, one supervisor described his relationship with a deaf employee as one in which "[he] accepts and trusts that we're not trying to make barriers for him." He continues:

> And therefore, if I say to him, "Oh, yes, I knew that two days ago—haven't had a chance to tell you, and here's the information," [he] is under no assumption that I've done that because I didn't want him to know or because I thought it was not important, or that he was not important [enough] to know that information, or that I was in some way avoiding dealing with him on that issue. But rather that it was an honest oversight or that I was too busy. He accepts that because I guess he trusts our relationship as being an open one.

Some deaf employees were perceived by their supervisors as having good interpersonal skills. They were able to employ strategies which facilitated interactions with hearing co-workers and overcame barriers related to communication and feelings of nervousness or awkwardness. The strategy mentioned most by supervisors was the ability to use or respond to humor. Some examples:

EXAMPLE # 1
SUPERVISOR: She gets along very well. Absolutely no problems at all. As I say, she has a really great sense of humor and she really is awfully funny. I really am so upset sometimes that we can't communicate more. I'm sure that she has a lot of funny things she could tell us. But she does get along very well. I can't think of anyone in there that she does not get along exceptionally well with.
INTERVIEWER: Can you give me an example of her sense of humor?
SUPERVISOR: What was she saying one day about someone being a coward, and she kept talking about a yellow streak and it took me a while to figure out that she was talking about a coward with a yellow streak down his back. But she comes up with these things that you really don't expect. By the time you do figure [it] out . . . the whole situation is long gone and you're sitting there laughing about it.
EXAMPLE # 2
SUPERVISOR: He likes to joke, I like to joke. Easy personality. He is a character . . .
INTERVIEWER: Do you remember a joke he did?
SUPERVISOR: . . . Yesterday there was a piece of plastic, two foot in diameter circle. There was a circle cut out so what you had was a ring. He put this under his butt and walked around the shop like that . . . He likes to show off a little bit like that. It's just a little attention-getter, good for a laugh.

Similarly, several supervisors perceived the ability to "joke around" as indicative of a related ability to build positive relationships with fellow employees. In describing the deaf person in his department, one supervisor said, "He takes a joke, he fools around with everyone, he partakes in all our departmental activities, so he fits in." In short, the ability to manage strained interactions, whether through humor or other strategies, was seen as an interpersonal skill which facilitates the development of positive relationships between the deaf employee and others. Deaf employees who handled these situations with grace and humor were valued by their supervisors.

CHARACTERISTICS OF HEARING CO-WORKERS

The personality of hearing colleagues also played a role in the development of relationships at work. Sometimes deaf employees had difficulty getting along with hearing people for reasons which their supervisors felt were unrelated to their deafness. For example, one supervisor noted that "some people [hearing or deaf] are just mean," adding that both deaf and hearing co-workers have trouble getting along with these difficult people. Another described a troubled relationship between the deaf employee and her hearing co-worker as more a function of a "personality conflict" than a function of deafness:

> SUPERVISOR: Well, [she] has had problems dealing with some of the people here. You know, some of the people here are not willing to bend, and at the same time, sometimes [she] is not willing to bend either.
> INTERVIEWER: Can you give me an example?
> SUPERVISOR: Well, one that stands out the most is ... I remember this happened not long ago ... she told me that she was having a problem with one of the girls in her group, and it had to do with the newspaper. Well, she told me that she was all done with this girl. She wasn't going to be friendly with her anymore. She wasn't going to talk to her anymore. And apparently, what had happened was that she'd been reading this girl's newspaper over her lunch hour. And the girl came into the lunchroom and just grabbed it right out of her hand, and said, "Don't you read my newspaper. You get your own newspaper." Well, [she] was very upset, but she came in the next morning and there were no newspapers left when she came in the morning. They were gone, so she couldn't buy one. So I advised her. I said, "Look, you're going to get one sent to your house then ... have one delivered. There's no point in arguing with this person. If that's the way she wants to be, then that's it. And the only solution is to just make sure you have your own." I know that between those two girls there's really a personality conflict anyway ... they just don't like each other.

In other cases, difficulties with hearing co-workers were attributed primarily to deafness. One supervisor suggested that routine obstacles which must be overcome by everyone are compounded by communication barriers. In her words, "If in fact one has very limited access to the network ... by way of maybe just their personality or maybe their novelty on the job or whatever the reasons are, that's further compounded by ... the communication issue. The person who is new on the job tends to be an outsider and then ... is unable to communicate in day-to-day language, then it probably underscores the probability that a hearing-impaired person will not be part of a network."

A few supervisors reported instances of friction related to hearing co-workers' lack of awareness of and sensitivity to the needs of the deaf person. The following story raises the issue of individual rights and the conflict of perspectives which can occur between deaf and hearing co-workers:

> SUPERVISOR: I remember that she didn't want to go over to the other building when she had to move. She was very, very bitter when she went over there. And you know, the girls in that team, the four of them, they work in two separate rooms. Well, [she] said that she didn't want to be in with the other

girls. So now there're two rooms over there and she works in one room all by herself, and the other three operators work together in the other room. Oh sure, there's a door in between, but still she's completely separated. She said that the radio hurt her ears, and so eventually she had to take out her hearing aids because the other three operators would play the radio all the time, and you know, it was funny 'cause we really hadn't thought [about] it that way. I mean, they just kind of figured, well, she can't hear, so why would the radio bother her . . . she can't hear our voices, so what's the difference. When I was talking with another girl the other day, and I thought . . . maybe it's a question of the tone or the pitch of the radio. Maybe someone comes on and they're singing a song and the tone of the voice is what makes it hurt her ears. But in any case, she said that it bothered her. And you know, I'm still not sure if it was okay to tell her that if it bothers her, to take the hearing aid out, which is what they ended up telling her. But the other girls, they say that they have their rights too, and so they feel they have a right to play their radio if they want to, and they shouldn't have to turn it off for her.

INTERVIEWER: Well, did she say that it was the noise that made her want a separate room, or was it something more?

SUPERVISOR: Well, she said that it was the noise, that it had to do with the radio bothering her, but you know . . . I think it's more than that. I think that she knows that the other people are talking and chatting, and she wants so much to be included. And I think really that kind of was part of it all . . . you know, it's always kind of nice to be able to talk with the people you work with. Even though I know that she's not real good friends with them socially, I'm sure that she'd feel it would be kind of nice to talk with them. You know . . . I know that I can never really understand or know how she really feels. I can imagine and I can sympathize, but I'll never really know what it's like to be deaf like that, and to be in that world.

While it is impossible to ascertain all the details of the incident described above, it is probably a case of a relatively small misunderstanding, compounded by insensitivity on the part of the hearing workers, ballooning into a major dispute. The supervisor was most likely correct when she speculated that the pitch or tone of the radio was what bothered the deaf employee. However, the really hurtful part was probably the request by the hearing employees that the deaf person simply remove her hearing aids. Since the aids enabled the deaf person to pick up more of what was going on around her, the hearing workers' suggestion implied that they would prefer to listen to the radio than communicate with the deaf person. Put another way, they found it more acceptable that the deaf person cut herself off from the sounds around her than for them to give up the radio. The deaf person was forced into a "no-win" situation; she could choose to further shut herself off to auditory stimuli by removing her hearing aids and staying in the room with her hearing co-workers, or she could keep the aids on and physically isolate herself by working in a separate room. The fact that she chose the latter suggests that she was so offended or demoralized by the behavior of her hearing co-workers that she preferred not to be around them any more.

Another supervisor described an incident in which a deaf employee was harassed by hearing co-workers, and the reaction of the deaf employee to this experience:

> . . . you know, he really didn't like a lot of people here, from my observation. For the most part, he just kept on working. I think he felt that his co-workers were less understanding of his problem than supervision. I can remember I would send him to do something in another part of the building . . . I didn't know it, but they would do things over there, like they would drop something real loud behind him to see if he would hear it, sort of playing games with him, and it really bothered him . . . This went on for a long time before he told me about it. What happened was, one time I told this guy in this department to go and tell [him] to go over there and do something, and he went and he told [him] and [he] said, "I ain't going over there anymore." And so this guy came back to me and said, "He won't go." I got mad. I said, "If I tell you to do something, you're gonna do it." So I hauled him into my office, and then he told me what had been happening. He told me all about it, and I said, "Oh my God! Why didn't you tell me about this before? I would have stopped it." I told him [that] of course I wouldn't send him over there and subject him to that kind of thing [again].

It seems that the deaf person was unwilling to tell his supervisor about the harassment until the situation came to a boil. One has to wonder why. Was the deaf person fearful that he would not be believed, or did he feel that to discuss the situation with his supervisor might be perceived as "tattling" and would put his relationships with other hearing co-workers at risk? Perhaps even more interesting is the supervisor's reaction. Instead of confronting those who were harassing the deaf employee, the supervisor chose to avoid the situation by not sending the deaf person into that area. While this might have been the easiest solution, it implied a tacit acceptance of the behavior, since the harassment was not publicly or formally recognized and punished by management.

More often, however, supervisors' descriptions of interactions between deaf and hearing employees suggest that difficulties in establishing relationships were less a function of malice or insensitivity on the part of hearing colleagues than of ignorance, social discomfort, and a general unwillingness to invest the time and effort required to communicate and develop a relationship with a deaf person. As one person put it, "Sometimes, other people tend to shy away because they really don't know how to act or behave around a hearing-impaired person." And another example:

> ... she would come to me quite often and just [say] she wasn't making new friends. She was taking it really personally and I would just try to explain it to her that I don't think that it was anybody being deliberately nasty or ... deliberately leaving her out of things, but everyone was so busy and it does take ... a lot of time and effort and really paying attention to be able to listen and be able to understand what she is saying ... I understand her very well and I think she pretty much understands me, but that's from really sitting down and looking in her face and having her watch me and it was very time consuming. So I don't think it was that people were deliberately leaving her out. I don't think anybody really went out of their way, to be honest, to make an effort to really get to know her that well. I just tried to tell her that it wasn't anything against her. It was just that people simply did not have the time to invest.

Similarly, several supervisors noted that hearing staff simply forgot to include the deaf person in social interactions. One supervisor commented that "it's very difficult to remember to include [the deaf person] in the conversation. You know she can lipread very well, and so ... you can tend to forget at times that she's really hearing impaired, and you know, you have to remember to talk slowly or to face her or maybe to move your lips better. And yet, it's easy to forget that she has these needs." Even when hearing workers are aware of and able to meet the communication needs of the deaf person, they sometimes forget to use what they know. For example, a supervisor who works in an environment where many of the hearing employees know at least basic sign language said that people in her department "forget that she [deaf colleague] can't automatically participate in the conversation unless you use your sign. Well, turning on that little light mentally as soon as she gets there [staff room] doesn't always happen. And consequently, I don't think [she] spends a lot of time in the staff room. She doesn't take her breaks there."

SUPERVISOR SUPPORT AND INTERVENTION

Many supervisors said they offer direct or indirect intervention with the goal of facilitating the development of relationships between deaf and hearing employees. For example, some supervisors provided what they felt was a positive role model for hearing employees through their own effort to communicate with the deaf employee. Several supervisors found themselves in the position of mediator between deaf and hearing staff. The following quotation is illustrative:

> People forget that [he] has a hearing problem, and they don't look at him on a one-to-one basis sometimes when they're talking. And he just feels that no one likes him, that he's out of it because no one talks to him, and that's why I say the problem is really training other people in our area to make sure that when they're talking to him, to direct themselves to him because he cannot pick up sounds when they're in back of him or on the side of him unless he's aware of what's going on. Then he's turning around to make sure he sees what's happening, to pick up on the lipreading. So that's really the hard part, training them and talking to them, and then talking to him [deaf employee] and telling him that people are not being rude to him, that they just forget. It's so easy to just yell what you want, to just talk to each other. It's not that they're trying to block him out of the conversation. It's just force of habit, just to carry on a conversation. And you think that everybody can hear you and hear what you said. And forgetting that [he] does have a problem and we have to direct ourselves a little bit towards him. Sometimes that's a real barrier between both sides. For [him], he feels like they're neglecting to inform him. It's relationships, too, you know. In a working relationship, minor little things where they probably don't really want to block him off. They just forget. And he feels badly, and then I go up and talk to them and then they feel badly. And you know, no one's really at fault . . .

In some instances, an intervention which proved helpful initially became a barrier to interaction over time. A supervisor who knew sign language and often acted in the role of interpreter for the deaf employee came to the conclusion that this practice made it more difficult for the employee to establish her own relationships with hearing co-workers. The supervisor eventually stopped attending meetings with the employee in an effort to force hearing staff to interact directly with the deaf person. This story has implications for the use of interpreters to facilitate communication at meetings and other group events. While the interpreter can be helpful in these situations, there is also the risk that deaf and hearing co-workers will become dependent on the interpreter and will therefore be less resourceful in developing direct relationships with one another and alternative communication strategies.

In other cases, supervisor intervention took the form of protection from strained interactions and compensation for the deaf employee's social isolation. One supervisor said he and another supervisor handled most of the communication with the deaf employee, thus providing a buffer between the deaf person and his hearing co-workers. Several others said they had developed strong mentor relationships with the deaf employee, which sometimes continued even after the employee or supervisor left the department. A few went out of their way to become friends with the deaf employee. In the following excerpt, a supervisor relates with humor a story about the communication difficulties she encountered when she went to lunch with the deaf employee and the "price" she paid for this interaction:

> A long time ago when she and I worked closer together, I used to invite her to lunch, and she seemed to really enjoy that. But you know, it was kind of funny because I remember that whenever I would go to lunch with [her] . . . I would notice that, well, for example, say I got something that was kind of difficult to eat, like a salad or something . . . I really found that I'd never get to eat very much because it was hard for me, and we only have a forty-minute lunch break. So I really always thought that was funny because I'd never get to have a full meal if I went to lunch with her. I didn't want to miss something that she might say that was really important and so I had to really concentrate on the conversation.

While the supervisor does not complain or suggest that this harmed the relationship, her experience illustrates the time and effort often required to sustain a friendship with a deaf colleague, even when the activity is as basic as a conversation over lunch.

As described earlier in this chapter, one supervisor responded to the discovery that the deaf employee was being harassed by hearing co-workers in another department by not sending the deaf employee to that part of the building. In other cases, however, supervisors took a more proactive role in responding to what they perceived as inconsiderate or improper behavior. Below, a supervisor describes what she did when she observed hearing workers ridiculing the deaf employee:

> A few times . . . people were pretty rude to her . . . that really bothered me . . . like, they might talk to her if she was walking away from them, and . . . say she was in here [lunch room] and walked out . . . and the girls called to her and said something . . . [and] she just continued to walk. They might laugh and mock her a little bit . . . Well . . . I had to straighten the girls out on that . . . for one thing, [deaf employee] was brighter than most of the girls that worked here, because . . . it's unusual that [someone in that job] has a college education, and so I explained to them that [that] girl was far brighter than they were 'cause most of them had only gone through high school, and so if [she] didn't answer them, it was because she didn't hear them—not because she couldn't . . . I think knowing that kind of helped the other girls respect her a little more.

Why did this supervisor take such an aggressive stand in responding to the harassment, while the other supervisor chose a more passive approach? One possible reason is that she was dealing with people she managed directly (recall that in the first story, the incident had taken place in another department). Or perhaps it was because she knew the deaf employee better or because she had observed the behavior first hand. Maybe it was simply because she felt she could predict the response of her employees, that is, she knew a direct approach would work.

A third supervisor, when confronted by a deaf employee's loneliness and sense of social isolation in the department, chose a more moderate response, based on her understanding of how the employees in her group would respond. She felt that subtlety was the key in changing the behaviors of her staff:

> SUPERVISOR: There were times when she was very unhappy. She would come in here just about in tears and myself, I wasn't really sure if I say anything [if] I would make a bad situation worse . . . I wasn't sure what I should expect them [hearing workers] to do, and what I should expect her to do . . .
> INTERVIEWER: What advice would you give to another supervisor who was facing the same kind of a problem with a hearing-impaired person? The issue of people feeling left out or not included?
> SUPERVISOR: I think I would just advise patience and a little bit of understanding. I would not interfere between them and the other employees. I would try to [help] in a non-intrusive [way], maybe try and get them together a little bit. I think it really makes it worse if you were to . . . meet with the rest of the staff and say, "Now, [she] is hearing impaired, let's all be nice to her." I don't think that is the correct approach at all. I would go out at certain times and be talking to [her] and maybe somebody else would walk by and [I would] say, "What do you think about this?" and try to get them involved in a conversation that way, but nothing too direct. I'd try a subtle approach first.

Clearly, the decision of whether and how to intervene is complex. The selection and success of strategies depend on the politics of the situation and the personalities and interpersonal skills of all parties, including those of the supervisor.

LENGTH OF TIME WITHIN THE ENVIRONMENT

Finally, supervisors said time and experience in the environment had a generally positive effect on the development of positive relationships between the deaf employees and their hearing colleagues. As with communication, relationships between deaf and hearing employees were more likely to flourish the longer they worked together. Feelings of distrust and anxiety were overcome as people became more comfortable with each other. As one supervisor put it, "After [deaf employee came], I think everyone realized that she was just like all the rest of us. It didn't take long for that fear of the unknown to be gone." Similarly, hearing co-workers became more aware of and responsive to the communication needs of deaf employees over time, which in turn led to improved relationships.

Time was especially helpful in combination with other factors. For example, one supervisor described the deaf employee as initially mistrustful of hearing co-workers, despite the supervisor's efforts to convince her they were not talking about her behind her back. The supervisor noted that the deaf employee became more relaxed after she was given a bridal shower by hearing colleagues. The combination of a friendly gesture, increased familiarity with co-workers, and the continued efforts of the supervisor helped ease strained interactions and build more positive relationships over time. The supervisor concluded, "After the [bridal] shower she got to know more of the girls, and she would go up and ask them questions before she got married about what they went through before they got married and things like that. So she . . . opened up a little bit after a while . . . I think she basically has to get to know someone and see what they're about before she can really open up to them."

The supervisor who reprimanded hearing workers for making jokes about the deaf employee behind her back in the lunch room told an interesting story about another situation in which she felt the deaf person misinterpreted the behaviors of her hearing co-workers, and the effect of time in helping to overcome hard feelings. She recalled that the deaf employee complained that hearing co-workers were using her work materials. Since there had already been bad experiences with teasing in the lunch room, the employee was naturally sensitive and on the alert for further harassment:

> SUPERVISOR: She was very meticulous about how she left her things, and if she came back in the next day and thought someone was using her station, she'd get very angry. And I think in the beginning she may have thought . . . because she was different . . . hearing-impaired, that people were going to pick on her.
> INTERVIEWER: How did you handle that?
> SUPERVISOR: Well, I would just personally go over and help her find whatever it was she was looking for . . . I have never seen anybody at her station or do anything to her . . . that's one thing the girls in here do [is] share each other's things sometimes, but they always put them back. And maybe she did think that—she didn't know them after all—maybe she did think they were going to take things from her. I don't know.

The supervisor concluded by saying that the situation was eventually resolved because "after she became used to working here, then she became more trustful of the other girls." This improvement was due to several factors acting in combination over time. First, the supervisor continued to support the deaf employee and constructively mediate disputes arising between her and the hearing employees. Second, the deaf employee learned the routines and accepted rules about sharing work materials and, with the help of the supervisor, had her suspicions consistently disproved. Third, she also got to know co-workers who treated her fairly and were more mature than the younger girls who had teased her in the past. However, it is important to note that these changes did not occur quickly, nor did they happen by themselves. Change was achieved in large measure as a result of the supervisor's consistent attention to the problem and intervention.

DISCUSSION

Supervisors offered a variety of explanations for the range and quality of relationships which they observed between deaf employees and their colleagues at work, including environmental considerations, characteristics and interpersonal skills of the deaf employee, sensitivity and awareness of hearing co-workers, supervisor support and intervention, and time and experience within the work setting. While it is probably true that these factors affect relationships between all employees (deaf or hearing), the condition of deafness further complicates existing constraints. For example, a deaf person who has experienced a lifetime of difficult or strained interactions with hearing people may bring to a new job a greater distrust of colleagues than would a hearing person who has not had these painful experiences. Similarly, most employment environments and work tasks are designed and organized with the communication styles and needs of hearing people in mind and may therefore not be suited to the needs of deaf employees for visual access to office activity and conversation.

Moreover, the constraints imposed by communication differences, and the impact of these constraints on the ability of deaf employees to access and participate in informal social networks in the workplace, cannot be underestimated. Since most relationships are dependent on frequent and casual conversation, a deaf person who has difficulty communicating with hearing colleagues is at a great disadvantage. Overcoming these obstacles requires of both deaf and hearing employees creative and resourceful management (and often restructuring) of the environment, as well as a willingness and ability to initiate or respond to overtures of friendship, even when to do so is time consuming, initially awkward, and/or inconvenient. Since time is generally a precious commodity in the workplace, interventions designed to enhance opportunities for deaf people to meet and get to know hearing people at work may be difficult to implement. However, this should not preclude making the effort.

Finally, it should be noted that relationships in the workplace are frequently the foundation for career mobility. The phrase, "It's not what you know, but who you know," holds more than a grain of truth, and employees who perform their jobs with skill but remain isolated from colleagues are often viewed as poor candidates for promotion or management. As a result, the challenges faced by deaf employees in developing relationships with co-workers cannot be viewed as solely an issue of job satisfaction. While the social isolation of deaf employees and ensuing feelings of loneliness are issues worthy of attention, there are additional reasons for addressing the topic of relationships at work. Indeed, facilitating the ability of deaf employees to access the social network in the workplace may also be essential to their career development over a lifetime of employment.

COMMENTARY

GARY: When I read this chapter, I noticed that people seemed to be positive in their perspectives. At the same time, there were some difficulties for deaf employees. For example, if there were other deaf people working there, they tended to get together for a break or lunch. Working alone, sometimes they were alone.

JANICE: I've always been the only deaf person in my job, so I've never had experience with having other deaf employees in my department. Most of the time I ate lunch with my hearing friends in the department. And in the second job, I often went to lunch with the supervisor, as well as with my co-workers. I felt very comfortable in those situations.

SUSAN: If there are two deaf people in the department, should they be assigned to the same lunch break?

JANICE: I think it depends on the people. Often, hearing people assume that deaf people must want to be together, but sometimes they may not even like each other. They might have totally different personalities. Just because they're both deaf, that doesn't mean they should always be together.

DAVID: My father was deaf and worked for a government printing office. There were many deaf people working there. During break time or meal times, the deaf people would tend to get together and talk politics and so forth. My father would go off and interact with the hearing people. He was deaf, but he grew up in the hearing world. He liked to interact with hearing people. He had a pad of paper and would talk about all kinds of things through writing. Meanwhile, the deaf employees had their own clique, where they would back stab and talk about each other. One time, none of his hearing friends were around, so my father went and sat down with the deaf people during break. And they said, "Hey, why are you joining us now?" Dad said, "Well, you know, I've been interacting with the hearing all along, but today my mind is on a lower level, so I decided to join you." They didn't say another word.

GARY: The supervisor should not decide that two deaf people would want to be together. The deaf people should decide for themselves. The deaf person can go to the supervisor and say, "I'd like to have lunch at the same time as the other deaf person," but the supervisor shouldn't make that assumption. Of course, not everyone will want to associate with other people. Some deaf people prefer to eat alone.

DAVID: Yes, I second that.

SUSAN: Did you become close friends with any hearing people at work? And if so, how did you get to know them?

JANICE: They were interested in learning sign language. They wanted to communicate with me, as equals with each other. So, we went out to lunch together. We would visit, and also it would help improve their communication skills. At the second job, the supervisor learned sign language, so quite often she and I would go to lunch together. I think really the best way to develop communication between employees is by going out frequently, getting together during free times, like breaks or lunches.

SUSAN: Did you invite them initially, or did they invite you?

JANICE: They invited me. I was brand new, so I was the stranger. But they invited me, and they broke the ice. It felt warm.

SUSAN: Can you remember the first time you went out with them? How did the relationship and communication get going?

JANICE: Well, I think it was because of my background. I grew up in a mainstream school. I knew how to interact with hearing friends. It sort of was no big deal, really. All I had to do was learn who they were, that's all.

DAVID: I got to know people through hobbies, shared interests. For example, I used to own a '65 Mustang, a classic car. When I brought the car to work, someone said, "Whoa, look at this. Look what David's got." Another worker had a '62 Corvette. He and I became really good friends, through the hobby. Another person and I became friends because we were both interested in model trains. So, it started really with the hobbies, when we were introduced. If we found that we had the same hobby, we became good friends.

SUSAN: So when you wanted to talk about your hobbies, how did you communicate?

DAVID: We started with writing, because I was new on the job and nobody knew any sign language yet. When I started teaching the sign language classes during the lunch hour, they started to learn signs. This one guy, who had the same hobby as me, joined the sign language class, and he was very motivated. We became good friends. He signed well. We communicated with signs then.

GARY: I remember I became good friends with this one person, and I went to lunch with him. Sometimes there would be three of us, four of us, two of us, six of us. It varied. At the beginning I tolerated a large group up to six or seven. When it became difficult to follow their conversation, I'd ask, "What are you talking about?" I missed a lot. After a year I decided to break off. Go off on my own and use my free time for myself. I'd read, go for a walk, do my own thing. Sometimes I'd go to lunch with one or two friends, but with three or four I didn't really feel comfortable. It was frustrating.

JANICE: That's an important point. When it's less than three people, that's best.

GARY: Yes. If it was just the two of us, communication was easy. Most of the time I'd ask just one person to lunch. They knew I didn't really want other people because it presented communication problems for me.

JANICE: With three of us, I was always sort of in the middle, and I was kind of controlling it. Better than four or five. I had more control by having just one of me and two of them.

SUSAN: How did you control the conversation?

JANICE: Well, for example, with two people, I can look from one person to another to see who's talking. When I'm talking, both the people can look at me, and they can hear each other. If you have lost something, the other person can catch it. See? It's a trade around. Rather than if there're three or four people, then I get lost. I don't know who's saying what to whom. But with two, both people are looking straight at me.

SUSAN: Do you encourage them not to talk at the same time? Do people respect that if you say, "Please don't both talk at the same time"?

JANICE: Yes. Sure. Also, they remember to talk clearly, make sure I understand what they're saying. They are more conscious of what they're doing.

SUSAN: Do you think that if a deaf person doesn't go on breaks or to lunch with hearing people because they find it frustrating to try to follow group conversations, their behavior may be misunderstood? For example, do you think they may be perceived as wanting to be by themselves, or stuck up?

JANICE: No. Once I have lunch with the supervisor and explain the situation, I think she will explain to other people about my experience with groups, that I get lost and can't follow the conversation. Because at my company they would have summer banquets, Christmas parties, etc., and in a group I would always say, "Forget it," and I'd go off. Then they'd come up to me, one or two at a time, to give me their attention because they knew that I couldn't follow the conversation when there are too many in a group. Once in a while we'd celebrate an employee's birthday with a party, and I'd just go to my office. Pretty soon a couple of people would come, and they'd try to be nice to me, tell me what's been said, show me some pictures, and so on.

DAVID: Well, in my opinion, many deaf people choose to be alone. Maybe because ninety percent of deaf children are raised by hearing parents and communication is difficult at home. Then they go to main-stream schools, where communication is difficult again. They don't have opportunities to really talk with people, so they just kind of get used to not talking. They don't complain about it, don't mind.

GARY: I think people are smart enough to know what kind of person you are. I think the supervisor can judge if a person, deaf or hearing, is a loner. And you don't have to go on breaks or lunch together to learn about someone's personality. You can find out through work. Also, regarding group conversations where it is difficult to follow what is happening, I guess you just learn to live with it. I don't want the supervisor to assume that you solve the problem by hiring another deaf person. That doesn't always solve the problem. It depends on the people themselves. I'm sure Janice and David have heard stories where deaf people say, "I don't want to be with other deaf people at all."

DAVID: Yes.

JANICE: Well, some deaf people would rather be alone. If another deaf person comes over, they talk and talk and talk. It's hard to cut them off.

GARY: There were two other deaf people at my first job. I met one of them for lunch. Went to his building. But I never bothered to go and meet him for lunch again. Once in a while I'd bump into him and talk, but to find time to sit down, go over there, no, I just didn't bother. I just didn't have any particular desire to go over and meet the other deaf people. Now, if I went back to work there at that environment, I'd probably go running during my lunch hour.

SUSAN: Do you think supervisors evaluate people on their ability to get along with other people and show that they're a team player? Is it harder for deaf people to show that they're team players?

JANICE: It's hard for a deaf person. If we had a project involving a group, it was difficult for me because there were five people involved, and every time we met I always lost track of what they were debating and discussing and how they were solving problems with the program. So, in my job evaluation, my rating for teamwork was low compared to the other people, due to my communication problems, the fact that I could not follow the conversations. I told my supervisor that this was not fair, and the supervisor understood.

GARY: I guess I'd say that supervisors know that communication is the main issue. It's not intelligence, it's communication. When something's going on, we want to pick up on things and know what's happening, but we don't get the chance. So, we have a little bit less of an opportunity in that area. I hope I never have to have those problems again in the future. You know, problems with being really equal to other people in the job, being able to run programs, being involved in team meetings, being equal in communication. I remember the frustration I felt trying to solve those problems. You could do it, but it's not easy.

SUSAN: David, did you have to do teamwork?

DAVID: No, I did more individual work.

SUSAN: I was wondering if there was anything about your work settings that affected your ability to meet people?

GARY: The size of the company, the number of employees, makes a big difference. In my past job, there was an open environment, fifty, sixty people all sitting around in a big open space. Tables all around. You could easily see who was and wasn't there, which was good. But at the same time, so many things would be happening, and I'd just be focusing on my work and miss it. For example, the president of the company would walk by, and I'd hear nothing. Somebody would tap me and I'd be surprised to learn what was going on. So that was a disadvantage.

JANICE: Yes. The hearing people would hear it, but I wouldn't. It is not an advantage for deaf workers to have an open space when there are so many people. When I moved to a small company, it made a big difference. Size is very important.

GARY: I advise my students to look for jobs at small companies. They're more homey. People are more sensitive. In my old job there were almost three thousand employees in my building alone. I didn't even know their names. Many of them didn't know I was deaf.

DAVID: Yes, I prefer working for a small company, because there's a real family environment. I worked in an open floor, but it was a small company. I studied the people's behaviors, the way they dress. Kind of got to know them, their personality. I enjoyed that. There were only fifty employees in the whole company. I knew almost everyone, and they knew me. I would see the president of the company every day, and sometimes we'd talk. It was a really wonderful experience for me.

SUSAN: Did people form cliques?

JANICE: No, we'd all go out together, as a department. Sometimes the director of the department would join us.

DAVID: If I saw people in a group, I'd take a look. If I saw my friend there, I'd join them, and my friend would just start interpreting. If I didn't know anybody, I didn't bother to join them. I'd just go off on my own.

SUSAN: Supervisors said humor was really important for making friends. They told several stories about how deaf people made a lot of friends because they were able to crack jokes to break the ice. What is your experience with this?

DAVID: Oh, yes. I'm very good at identifying people's ways and habits, like the way they walk or talk, and I can mimic them. I make my co-workers laugh when I do an exact copy of somebody.

GARY: I have to agree. Humor really can bring warmth to a friendship. People respond to that, so I always try to throw some humor in. Also, it's my personality to be the first to speak, to start the conversation.

DAVID: When I was teaching the sign language class at work, I would always use a funny story to teach the concept of deaf humor and culture. For example I told the story about the sign for the word "but" (which starts with index fingers touching and then moving up and apart). The story goes as follows: There is a deaf person driving who comes to a train crossing where the gates are down. He waits and waits, but nothing happens. The gates remain down. Then a policeman comes by and the deaf person decides to ask him to open the gates. The deaf person goes up to the policeman and writes down on paper the words, "Please but." Of course, he is thinking in signs, and the sign for "but" looks like the two gates opening up. So I often use a funny story like that to teach sign. They love it. They laugh. That's very important in relations with hearing people, because then they become really fascinated, and that helps to form a good relationship.

JANICE: My jokes are always based on daily situations. I never use traditional jokes. Instead, I just build on whatever comes up that day, just teasing over everyday things.

SUSAN: Imagine a young deaf person comes to you for advice. They say, "I'm starting my first job, and I'm the only deaf person there, and I'm worried. How can I make friends? Where do I start?" What advice would you give them?

JANICE: I would say, "What's important is that you already know one person there—the person who hired you. So you broke the ice already at the interview. Go up to that person, because they can introduce you to the others. And that's where the communication with others will start."

GARY: My suggestion would be to use the buddy system. I'd tell them, "Find a person that you feel comfortable communicating with, and get to know them."

JANICE: Yeah, but how can you start a buddy system the very first day?

GARY: Well, there are several ways you could do it. One, a person could volunteer to work with the deaf person. Or, two, the supervisor could help the deaf person to get close to someone as a mentor.

SUSAN: I want to talk a little bit about some of the stories that supervisors told in this chapter, to get your opinions. Do you remember the story about the deaf woman whose hearing co-workers told her to turn off her hearing aids if their radio was bothering her? The deaf person ended up working by herself in the next room. What did you think about that situation?

DAVID: My situation was different. The boss would catch me reading the newspaper during work, and he'd tell my supervisor, "Tell him not to read the newspaper." I told the supervisor, "That's my radio." He asked me what I meant. I said, "You work, and you turn on the radio, and you listen and work and listen and work. What do I do? I concentrate on my work. Where's my radio? I use the newspaper. I don't read it while I'm working. When I work, I can do important, top priority things, because I'm not distracted by the radio. When my work's finished, I read the newspaper." And he said, "Oh." I said, "You can do both, but you don't concentrate on work very well while you're listening to the radio. When I put the newspaper aside, I concentrate on the work."

JANICE: My friend in the post office saw that people had radios. He said, "Where's my enjoyment? Hearing people listen to the radio while they sort the mail or do other jobs that don't require full concentration. I should have the same opportunity. I should be able to bring a pocket TV, so I can watch it while I work, just as they listen to the radio." That hasn't been resolved yet.

GARY: I guess there're many questions about deaf people being alone, like in that story about the hearing people who wanted to listen to the radio. I think that's okay, if the deaf person chose to go off on their own.

SUSAN: I was wondering if you thought that the hearing people had a right to ask the deaf person to turn off her hearing aids?

GARY: No. Nope.

JANICE: No. They don't have that right. If they do, then the deaf person should have an equal right to tell the hearing people to turn off the radio. So they need to find a solution between them. Regarding the deaf person going in another room, well, that's fine as long as the deaf person is happy with that and can concentrate more and it's quieter. That's fine. But if the deaf person needs those two hearing people in order to do her work, then you have to tell the supervisor, and the problem has to be solved.

GARY: I remember reading somewhere that if the deaf person becomes friends with co-workers, sets up good relationships with them, and co-workers are sensitive, then the deaf person would stay and work there longer because they have established a common ground. They don't want to start all over again at some other company. That's sad in a way, because the deaf person may not really be growing in their job. They stay at the same company and do the same work every day. They're comfortable with their environment. They don't want to get out of the environment, even though they may have better opportunities elsewhere. They just don't want to explain about communication and Deaf culture all over again. So that's a negative thing for us. It's easier for hearing people to move around. Deaf people are more limited because they're afraid to start over again.

DAVID: That's true. I agree with you. I felt that way, myself. I was comfortable at my old job. I didn't want to go through it all over again to find a new job. But I know that's negative in terms of my career, promotions, and so forth. It is negative to stay in one place all the time. I have to struggle with that feeling.

SUSAN: Remember the story about the deaf person who was teased whenever he went into another department? People would make loud noises behind his back and so forth. When the supervisor found out, he felt terrible and did not send the person there any more. What do you think of that story, the way it was handled?

JANICE: That kind of behavior is new to me. That's a low level job. I've had high level jobs. I've never been responsible for carrying things around. Also, in high level jobs, you treat each other professionally. Maybe in low, blue collar jobs, where they have high school educations, they tease each other. I've noticed that.

GARY: I think the person who was screaming at the deaf employee— they're really just nutballs.

DAVID: If I was in those shoes, I would just have it go in one side and out the other. I'd let them waste their breath yelling and having fun. I'd just go on and do my own job, and ignore them.

SUSAN: If you were the deaf person in that situation, would you be satisfied with the supervisor's response?

DAVID: No, because it would limit my job, and I would be more bored at my job. I'd like to do something different than the same monotonous grind every day.

SUSAN: So what do you think the supervisor should have done?

DAVID: Well, I'd complain to the people who are making fun of me. But it's the supervisor's job to criticize them.

SUSAN: Some supervisors said that hearing people don't intend to be mean or cruel, but sometimes they don't become friends with deaf people because it just takes too much time. For example, if you try to tell a joke in writing, you lose the whole point.

JANICE: Yes, that's normal. It works both ways, you know. As a deaf person, when I meet a hearing person, I think, oh, it just takes too much time to write it all out and express my feelings compared to the ease of sharing ideas in sign language with another deaf person. It's the same for hearing people. It's fifty-fifty. That's the nature of communication itself.

DAVID: In the hearing world I'm always chasing hearing people, trying to become friends with them, trying to figure out what they're saying. Now, in the deaf world I feel like you hearing people should chase us for a while. It's mean maybe, but I grew up suffering, and now it's your turn to suffer.

JANICE: It's kind of a reverse situation, seeing how hearing people feel now, working at a place with many deaf people, like NTID. They come in and try to look for friends. I wonder how it feels to come into the deaf world. It must be a nice experience for hearing people to see how we feel in their world. We're always chasing them around.

DAVID: Remember, the hearing world is big, and the deaf world is small.

JANICE: Yes, but suppose God made everybody deaf, then the hearing people would be handicapped.

SUSAN: Imagine a supervisor comes to you and says, "I've got a deaf person coming in next week, and I want to make sure they're able to build relationships and friendships here, just like hearing employees. What can I do to make that easier for them?" What do you think they should do?

GARY: My advice would be to let the deaf person decide how to become friends, how to get along with other people, how to meet people and join groups for lunch. Let them decide for themselves. The supervisor can try to make sure the deaf person feels comfortable, but to say, "You have to go to lunch with somebody," or to put pressure on the hearing people, is not fair. For example, they can explain to the hearing employees that a deaf person is coming to work and suggest that if anybody wants to work with that deaf person, they can volunteer. But don't put somebody on the spot.

JANICE: I guess I've been lucky with my supervisors in the past. They were very sensitive. I think their concern was rooted in their personalities. Some people are cold. Some are withdrawn. If so, that makes communication harder for the deaf person. So the supervisor has to decide who can be the most help. If the supervisor feels they don't have the right skills for it themselves, maybe they can think of another person who has a wonderful personality and is warm with people. Fine. Use that person to make the deaf person feel welcome to the department.

DAVID: Really, I don't have any advice for the hearing supervisor. But, I do have some advice for the deaf employee. The deaf employee should be open-minded, not close-minded or staying just to the deaf world and rejecting everything else. If they're going to get a job, they're going to be in a hearing world. It will be very frustrating. I'd rather that they be open-minded, learn, see what the hearing world's like, get involved with hearing friends, know their communication—English, writing, whatever communication methods they prefer. That way they can easily interact with the hearing people.

RESOURCE LIST

Library Resources

Books and articles listed in this section should be available at local public or college/university libraries or through the interlibrary loan services at these libraries. Many of the books and articles listed below were written by or about deaf people and present the perspectives of these individuals on their lives in a hearing world. Purchase prices listed may vary and are indicated only to give the reader a general idea of cost; contact the publisher directly for current cost and shipping/handling charges.

American Annals of the Deaf. (Available by subscription from *American Annals of the Deaf,* KDES PAS-6, 800 Florida Avenue NE, Washington, DC 20002-3695; Cost: contact publisher for current cost)

> The *Annals* is one of the most important journals dealing with aspects of deafness. It is the official organ of the Conference of Educational Administrators Serving the Deaf and the Convention of American Instructors of the Deaf and is focused toward the professional in the field. The April reference issue, which can be purchased separately, contains directories of educational programs and services for deaf people, supportive and rehabilitative programs, and research programs and services for the deaf.

Benderly, B.L. *Dancing Without Music: Deafness in America.* Washington, DC: Gallaudet University Press, 1980. (Available from Gallaudet University Press, Gallaudet University, 800 Florida Avenue NE, Washington, DC 20002-3695; Phone 800-451-1073 [V/TDD]; Cost: $12.95 paper copy)

Benderly's book is a well-researched and balanced account of deafness written in a lively, anecdotal style that makes it a good choice for those encountering this disability for the first time. The focus is on the debate between manual and oral communication proponents and how this has overshadowed the needs of deaf people in a sound-based society.

Conference: Sociology of Deafness. *Social Aspects of Deafness.* Washington, DC: Department of Sociology and Social Work, Gallaudet College, 1982.

Papers from the Gallaudet College Conference on the Sociology of Deafness are collected here in six areas: deaf children and the socialization process, social aspects of educating deaf persons, the deaf community and the deaf population, socioeconomic status of the deaf population, interpersonal communication and deaf people, and deaf people and social change.

Deaf Life. (Available by subscription from MSM Productions, Ltd., 85 Farragut Street, Rochester, NY 14611; Cost: contact publisher for current cost)

Deaf Life is a popular journal about deaf people and matters of interest to the deaf community. It is published primarily for people who are deaf and is printed in large type with a simplified vocabulary.

Gannon, J.R. *Deaf Heritage: A Narrative History of Deaf America.* Silver Spring, MD: National Association of the Deaf, 1981. (Available from National Association of the Deaf, 814 Thayer Avenue, Silver Spring, MD 20910; Phone 301-587-1788 [Voice], 301-587-1789 [TDD]; ISBN 0-913072-38-9; Cost: $20.95 paper copy)

Gannon's very comprehensive book details the history and culture of deaf people in the United States from the early 1800s to the present. It can be used as a reference tool, a textbook on deaf culture, a course in orientation to deafness seminars, or as interesting literature for the general public.

Written by a retired judge whose hearing was impaired by a war injury, this book compiles a rich and enjoyable anthology of both factual and fictitious accounts about people who are deaf, written both by deaf and hearing people.

Greenberg, J. *In This Sign.* New York: Holt, Rinehart, & Winston, 1970.

Although a novel, this story successfully points out the real life problems and frustrations faced by a family with deaf parents and a hearing child.

Groce, N.E. *Everyone Here Spoke Sign Language: Hereditary Deafness on Martha's Vineyard.* Cambridge, MA: Harvard University Press, 1985. (Available from Harvard University Press, 79 Garden Street, Cambridge, MA 02138; Phone 617-495-2600 [Voice]; ISBN 0-674-27040-1 cloth copy, 0-674-27041-X paper copy; Cost: $19.50 cloth copy, $8.95 paper copy)

This book accounts for the high incidence of hereditary deafness on Martha's Vineyard for over two hundred years. Almost everyone, hearing and deaf alike, used an efficient sign language, invented or borrowed.

Higgins, P.C. *Outsiders in a Hearing World: A Sociology of Deafness.* Beverly Hills, CA: Sage Publications, 1980. (Available from Sage Publications, 2111 W. Hillcrest Drive, Newbury Park, CA 91320; ISBN 0-8039-1421-0 cloth copy, 0-8039-1422-9 paper copy; Cost: $28.00 cloth copy, $14.95 paper copy)

As the son of deaf parents, Higgins is one of the few sociologists possessing sign language as well as personal social skills necessary to enter the deaf community and complete this study. Higgins examines the lives of deaf people, their community and identity within it, deaf peddlers, stigmas attached to being deaf, and interactions between deaf and hearing people.

Holcomb, M., and Wood, S. *Deaf Women: A Parade Through the Decades.* Berkeley, CA: Dawn Sign Press, 1989. (Available from T.J. Publishers, 817 Silver Spring Avenue 206, Silver Spring, MD 20910; Phone 800-999-1168 [V/TDD]; ISBN 0-915035-28-6; Cost: $19.95 paper copy)

This book is an enriched compilation of information, history, and anecdotes involving deaf women in America, past and present.

Holcomb, R.K. *Silence is Golden Sometimes.* Berkeley, CA: Dawn Sign Press, 1985. (Available from T.J. Publishers, 817 Silver Spring Avenue 206, Silver Spring, MD 20910; Phone 800-999-1168 [V/TDD]; ISBN 0-915035-06-05; Cost: $7.95 paper copy)

This humorous book helps to enable hearing people to understand the "deaf experience": the problems and frustrations of those who must cope with and live in a predominantly hearing society.

Jacobs, L.M. *A Deaf Adult Speaks Out.* 3rd ed., rev. and expanded. Washington, DC: Gallaudet University Press, 1989. (Available from Gallaudet University Press, 800 Florida Avenue NE, Washington, DC 20002-3695; Phone 800-451-1073 [Voice]; ISBN 0-930323-61-0; Cost: $12.95 paper copy)

Jacobs brings the perspective of an insider in the American deaf community to very comprehensive chapters on the etiology of hearing loss, modes of communication, deaf people as a minority group, the characteristics and social lives of deaf adults, the portrayal of the deaf community, and a directory of programs and services for deaf people.

Lang, H.G. *Silence of the Spheres: Deaf People and Deafness in the History of Science.* Champaign, IL: University of Illinois Press (in press).

This book is an examination (through biographical research) of barriers faced by deaf men and women in pursuing careers in science, engineering, and mathematics. It is a historical analysis of the contributions deaf persons have made in various fields of science and a description of coping strategies used to overcome attitudinal, communicative, and other barriers.

NAD Broadcaster. (Available by subscription from the National Association of the Deaf, 814 Thayer Avenue, Silver Spring, MD 20910-4500; Phone 301-587-1788 [voice], 301-587-1789 [TDD]; Cost: contact publisher for current cost)

Published eleven times a year, this newspaper presents in depth news of the deaf community in America. Information about telecommunication devices for the deaf and other assistive devices can be found here.

Padden, C., and Humphries, T. *Deaf in America: Voices From a Culture.* Cambridge, MA: Harvard University Press, 1988. (Available from Harvard University Press, 79 Garden Street, Cambridge, MA 02138; Phone 617-495-2600 [Voice]; ISBN 0-674-19423-3; Cost: $17.95)

Padden and Humphries, both deaf, describe examples of American Sign Language and of the cultural life of deaf people. Also, they elaborate on the culture of deaf people in their world views: how deaf people describe themselves and think about their lives in the hearing world.

SHHH. (Available by subscription from Self Help for Hard of Hearing People, Inc., 7800 Wisconsin Avenue, Bethesda, MD 20814; Phone 301-657-2248 [Voice], 301-657-2249 [TDD]; Cost: contact publisher for current cost)

This bi-monthly magazine is geared toward people who cannot hear well but who are committed to participating in the hearing world. Issues of national concern to hard-of-hearing people and articles aimed at better communication with hearing individuals are included.

Schein, J.D. *At Home Among Strangers.* Washington, DC: Gallaudet University Press, 1989. (Available from Gallaudet University Press, 800 Florida Avenue NE, Washington, DC 20002-3695; Phone 800-451-1073 [V/TDD]; ISBN 0-930323-51-3; Cost: $19.95)

This comprehensive portrait of the deaf community as a complex social network of deaf people across the United States includes chapters on deaf culture; family life; education and rehabilitation; economic life; medical, legal, and interpreting services; and a theory of deaf community development.

Silent News. (Available by subscription from Silent News, Inc., PO Box 23330, Rochester, NY 14692-3330; Phone 716-334-7736 [TDD]; Cost: contact publisher for current cost)

This monthly independent national newspaper reports on news relevant to deaf people and deafness, especially on the latest legislative, technological, medical, and sports developments. It serves both the general deaf public and those involved professionally in the field of deafness.

Walker, L.A. *A Loss for Words: The Story of Deafness in a Family.* New York: Harper Collins Publishers, Inc., 1986. (Available from Harper Collins Publishers, Inc.; 10 East 53rd Street, New York, NY 10002; Phone 800-242-7737 [Voice]; ISBN 0-06-091425-4; Cost: $7.95 paper copy)

Walker's autobiography portrays her experiences with her deaf parents, her exposure to deafness, the general deaf community and culture, folklore, and her interpreting service job.

Watson, D. (Ed.). *Readings on Deafness.* New York: Deafness Research and Training Center, New York University School of Education, 1973.

Many of the chapters in this book were written by deaf individuals. The readings were designed to help the general public better understand the deaf culture, deaf educational methods, and support services available for people who are deaf.

Wilcox, S. (Ed.). *American Deaf Culture: An Anthology.* Silver Spring, MD: Linstock Press, 1989. (Available from T.J. Publishers, 817 Silver Spring Avenue 206, Silver Spring, MD 20910; Phone 800-999-1168 [V/TDD]; ISBN 0-932130-09-7; Cost: $15.95 paper copy)

This collection of classic articles is selected to provide a variety of perspectives on the language and culture of deaf people in America.

Pamphlets and Brochures

Awareness Bookmarks. (Available from National Information Center on Deafness, Gallaudet University, 800 Florida Avenue NE, Washington, DC 20002-3695. Phone 202-651-5051 [Voice], 202-651-5052 [TDD]; Cost: up to 25 copies free, then 100/$1.00)

This is a set of five colorful bookmarks which introduce information on hearing loss, the manual alphabet, and sign language.

Deafness: A Fact Sheet. (Available from National Information Center on Deafness, Gallaudet University, 800 Florida Avenue NE, Washington,

DC 20002-3695; Phone 202-651-5051 [Voice], 202-651-5052 [TDD]; Order no. 085 (English), 554 (Spanish) or 543 (French); Cost: $1.00 each)

> This six-page fact sheet introduces readers to the deaf community, types of hearing loss, educational implications of deafness, communication methods, and special services.

Directory of National Organizations of and for Deaf and Hard of Hearing People. (Available from National Information Center on Deafness, Gallaudet University, 800 Florida Avenue NE, Washington, DC 20002-3695; Phone 202-651-5051 [Voice], 202-651-5052 [TDD]; Cost: free)

> This directory lists organizations which provide information on deaf or hard of hearing people and/or specific professional or consumer areas of interest. The information provided by this listing was gathered from the individual organizations.

Foster, S. *Dealing with Barriers in the Workplace: Strategies Used by Deaf People in Response to Difficult Situations at Work.* (Available from Center for Postsecondary Career Studies in Deafness, National Technical Institute for the Deaf, Rochester Institute of Technology, P.O. Box 9887, Rochester, NY 14623-0887; Phone 716-475-6704 [V/TDD]; Cost: free)

> This research paper describes and discusses the responses of deaf people to difficult and frustrating situations and conditions in the workplace. The paper suggests how responses of deaf people might be used in counseling and intervention with other deaf adults who are experiencing difficulties at work.

Media

Contact the following distributor for information about loan or purchase of media:
Gallaudet Media Distribution
800 Florida Avenue NE
Washington, DC 20002-3695
202-651-5222 (Voice)
202-651-5227 (TDD)

> Some films and videos are available for purchase; purchase price is indicated below. Others are available only on a loan basis. Contact Gallaudet Media Distribution for purchase/borrowing information.

Across the Silence Barrier [video]. (Available from Gallaudet Media Distribution; loan only)

This 55-minute video studies some of the educational and cultural problems faced by deaf people and some of the many ways they communicate.

American Culture: The Deaf Perspective [video]. (Available from San Francisco Public Library, A/V Support, Civic Center, San Francisco, CA 94102; Phone 415-557-4292 [Voice], 415-557-4433 [TDD]; Cost: $400/set, $125 each; rental $25 each; twelve-minute sampler reel, free preview)

> This series of four videotapes includes "Folklore," which examines the jokes, humor and stories that form the folklore of the deaf community; "Heritage," which examines deaf people as a cultural group with a common history and shared language; "Literature," which examines literature created by people who are deaf; and "Minorities," which explores the cross-cultural perspectives of the deaf community in America.

Creative Interpretation of Literature in Sign Language [video]. (Available from Gallaudet Media Distribution; loan only)

> Deaf actor Bernard Bragg and author/actor Robert Panara perform poetry and literary excerpts in sign language.

Have You Heard About the Deaf? [video]. (Available from National Association of the Deaf, 814 Thayer Avenue, Silver Spring, MD 20910; Phone 301-587-1788 [Voice], 301-587-1789 [TDD]; Cost $39.95 VHS/Beta)

> Narrated by Jack Gannon, author of *Deaf Heritage*, this videotape uses slides, old film clips, and interviews to present the cultural accomplishments of thirty-seven hearing-impaired individuals throughout history. The package includes a Teacher's Guide.

An Introduction to American Deaf Culture [video]. (Available from Sign Media, Inc., Burtonsville Commerce Center, 4020 Blackburn Lane, Burtonsville, MD 20866; Phone 301-421-0268 [V/TDD]; Cost: $59.95 each, $269.95 for the set of five videotapes)

> This series is an excellent resource for deaf studies, interpreter training, and sign language programs. Each tape is produced in sign language and reverse interpreted (voiced over). The series includes: "Rules of Social Interaction," "Values," "Language and Traditions," "Group Norms," and "Identity."

The Invisible Barrier [video]. (Can be borrowed or purchased from Gallaudet Media Distribution; Cost: $40)

> This thirty-minute color, sound, signed, and captioned video presents some of the problems, frustrations, and pleasures in the day of a deaf professional couple coping with the hearing world. The point is made that both deaf and hearing people must work to overcome the communication barrier.

Invisible Handicap [video]. (Available from Gallaudet Media Distribution; loan only)

> This twenty-minute video provides the hearing world with basic information about deaf people: who they are, where they work, and how they communicate.

Listen [16mm motion picture]. (Available from Gallaudet Media Distribution; loan only)

> This is a twenty-eight-minute documentary on hearing loss, its causes, psychological meanings, and ways to cope with the problem.

My Third Eye [video]. (Can be borrowed or purchased from Gallaudet Media Distribution; Cost: $44 VHS/Beta)

> This widely acclaimed program from the National Theatre of the Deaf provides entertaining insights into the world of the deaf through skits, a circus side show, and a sign language sing along.

Contacts

National Information Center on Deafness
Gallaudet University
800 Florida Avenue, NE
Washington, DC 20002-3695
202-651-5052 (TDD)
202-651-5051 (Voice)

> NICD provides accurate, up-to-date information about deafness and hearing loss to persons with hearing loss, parents, professionals, and the general public. Each year the Center responds to thousands of requests for information and referral. Fact sheets, resource lists, reading lists, and other materials are available for nominal fees by writing for the publications list.

President's Committee on Employment of People with Disabilities
1331 F Street NW, 3rd Floor
Washington, DC 20004
202-376-6205 (TDD)
202-376-6200 (Voice)

> PCEPD serves an advocacy and public awareness role in fostering job opportunities for handicapped people. It works with autonomous committees on employment of disabled people at state and local levels and produces its own publications.

Chapter 5

EVALUATIONS OF THE DEAF EMPLOYEE'S POTENTIAL FOR MANAGEMENT

DEAF EMPLOYEE: My project manager is trying to boost me up.
INTERVIEWER: Really, promotion?
DEAF EMPLOYEE: Yes. I'm trying to hold it down.
INTERVIEWER: Why?
DEAF EMPLOYEE: The load of responsibilities . . . more work, more depth, more engineering level. I am qualified, yes, but you can develop a high stress to it. It's a lot of pressure, and I don't like pressure.
INTERVIEWER: Pressure from what?
DEAF EMPLOYEE: Communication between one person to another person. Become a middle man . . . Suppose I misunderstood them . . . it would be totally my fault because I'm vulnerable when it comes to [being] hearing impaired. (Excerpt from interview with deaf employee; Foster, 1987.)

Deaf people, like hearing people, vary in their interest in and potential for movement into management positions. Some people don't want the pressure or responsibility, while others seek it. However, the important question is whether deafness reduces the likelihood that a deaf person would be considered for management. Some deaf people feel they do not have equal opportunities, either because they face discrimination from employers, or because they doubt their ability to handle the communication associated with the job. What do supervisors think?

Supervisors were asked to evaluate the deaf employee's chances for promotion with a focus on movement into supervisory or management positions. Frequently, they noted that there were no current openings for promotion, in which case they were asked to describe in very general terms whether they felt the deaf employee was capable of moving up, should an opening occur.

Half the supervisors *did not* think the deaf employee had potential for management, although one qualified his response by noting that the employee had not been with the company long enough for him to make a

141

final determination. Of those who felt the deaf employee *did* have the potential to enter a management position, six qualified their responses with a discussion of barriers to mobility that would have to be overcome before the person could be promoted. Further analysis of supervisors' comments suggests that there are at least four conditions that affect deaf employees' chances to move into management positions. These are (1) technical skills of the employee, (2) personal qualities of the employee, (3) communication skills, constraints, and/or accommodations in the work environment, and (4) attitudes of others. In this chapter, each of these four conditions is discussed.

TECHNICAL SKILLS

As noted in *Chapter 2,* technical job skills are most closely related to the daily performance of specific job tasks and often are described in terms of accuracy, speed, and productivity. Management jobs, however, were seen as requiring additional technical skills. For example, advanced technical training or certification or familiarity with a series of machines, rather than the ability to operate a single model, were sometimes a prerequisite for promotion. Additionally, work experience became a more central consideration:

> [He] would be a very comfortable supervisor/manager to work for. [But] I think that his knowledge base for administration and management is probably pretty limited. He has a lot of potential for growth; he doesn't have a whole lot of time to get a whole lot of training in doing that. He's a good case coordinator, considerate of other people who have to be involved with the system, so he's a good systems manager, but as far as actual knowledge of management styles, actual techniques, [he] hasn't had the appropriate exposure or training in those. To be a successful manager, those kinds of things have to be available in his repertoire.

Most supervisors evaluated the employee's technical work performance as satisfactory or better. While some supervisors noted that advanced skills or improvements were necessary for promotion, they were generally optimistic about the person's technical competence and ability to acquire additional skills over time.

PERSONAL QUALITIES

Personal qualities are more resistant to clear-cut definition than technical skills. They rarely are itemized in formal job descriptions and vary in relative importance according to the culture and mission of the organization. Examples of personal qualities from the earlier discussion in *Chapter 2* include the ability to work well with others, flexibility, good judgment, and the willingness to work hard. In discussions about the management potential of deaf employees, supervisors expanded their descriptions of personal qualities to include (1) assertiveness, (2) the ability to work under pressure, (3) ambition, (4) interpersonal skills, and (5) an understanding of management culture within their organization. While some supervisors felt extremely positive about their deaf employee's personal qualities, most expressed concerns in one or more areas. Furthermore, these perceived areas of weakness were interpreted as constraints on the deaf employee's potential for movement into positions of supervision and management.

Assertiveness and Self-Confidence

The ability to be at once self-confident and assertive was viewed as an important personal quality in managers. Assertiveness was seen as potentially helpful in managing some of the communication challenges which a deaf supervisor may face:

INTERVIEWER: Do you think that [she] could handle that job if she had the technical certification? Could she be a manager or supervisor?
SUPERVISOR: I think [she] probably could. I think she has the type of personality that she probably could. It would be difficult just by the very nature of going to meetings, interacting with other managers and supervisors. It would be difficult. I don't think it would be impossible . . .
INTERVIEWER: You said that she has the kind of personality that would enable her to do it. What are the qualities that you think are necessary, which she has that would enable her to be a manager?
SUPERVISOR: Well, the fact that she's very outgoing and the fact that she does not let anyone stand in her way if she wants to understand something. She will indeed find out. That's why I think that if she did have to go to these meetings, I'm sure that she would be sure that someone like [hearing employee who knows some sign language] was with her. [Or] I'm sure that she would just [do] . . . like she does when she goes to lunch with the other people—she takes her piece of paper and whatever is necessary [to communicate].

Conversely, a lack of assertiveness was seen as a constraint to advancement. One supervisor described the impact on a deaf employee's chances for promotion of his unwillingness to accept risks and confront co-workers when necessary:

> INTERVIEWER: If [he] was to stay here, what do you think the chances are that he could be promoted within the company?
> SUPERVISOR: Right now, from our area, low. There's nothing that is open. But within the [company], if he became . . . how can I say it? Not tough, but a little bit more aggressive. He is a little shy. He holds back. He's timid in taking that vital step forward to help him make his work a little easier, or if he has a confrontation with somebody (it could be words against one another), he'll immediately just back off or won't try to express his opinion. He's afraid that if he says something wrong and they don't agree with him, that they will put him down. And so, right now, that's the only thing I can see where he'd have a hard time advancing himself. Detail work, technical skills—fine. But it's just that interrelationship where some people are a little bit more aggressive than others.

Being assertive was sometimes described as a corollary of self-confidence. For example, one supervisor said the deaf employee was easily manipulated by colleagues, noting also that the employee was very dependent on the supervisor for support and encouragement. As she described it, "In order for [her] to move into a management [position] . . . she would need support in terms of encouraging her. The social skills are there. Now when I say I held her hand for the first two years in this job, I literally held her hand. And even with what she does I think she's comfortable with a lot of that because of the kind of support she gets from me."

Ability to Deal with Pressure

Closely related to assertiveness and self-confidence is the ability to deal with the pressures of management, including meeting deadlines, making unpopular budget decisions, and evaluating, reprimanding, or firing staff. Several supervisors said these tasks would present problems for the deaf employee. As one supervisor said of a deaf employee, "I don't know if she could be assertive enough to do that. I don't think it would be so much a communication problem as, I don't know if I should call it a shyness problem or what . . . [For example, if] you can't suspend people, [or] you can't fire people. I have had occasion to do both."

Another supervisor said she felt the deaf employee could not handle the pressure associated with management:

> INTERVIEWER: If . . . your job were to become open, do you think that [he] would be able to handle that kind of work?
> SUPERVISOR: . . . Well, . . . no. Health-wise, he cannot handle a lot of pressure, and in [our department] there is a lot of pressure, 'cause there's a constant time frame that you have to have meeting deadlines. They can come up and say, "I need this in two hours." And it's a three- or a four-hour job, and you just have to say, "Okay." And [he] would find it difficult to work with. He would get too nervous and upset with it . . . I don't think he'd be able to cope with it.

Ambition

Being able to manage is one thing; wanting to manage is another. Several supervisors described the deaf employees who worked for them as lacking the ambition for promotion. One supervisor described the employee as satisfied with his current job and unwilling to accept the problems that come with management positions. As she puts it, "Some people just don't want that kind of heat." This supervisor, who has worked with more than one deaf person, offered the opinion that this lack of desire for management or administration positions may be part of what she describes as, "The 'Deafness syndrome' . . . they feel that they've achieved where they are now and that's enough for them." One has to question this kind of stereotyping and its influence on decisions made by this supervisor regarding the deaf people with whom she works. Her comments also raise more general questions about society's response to deafness and whether decisions made by deaf workers with regard to promotions are reached under conditions of equal opportunity.

Supervisors also said that ambition includes being willing to "promote oneself," put in extra hours when necessary, and take the initiative in tackling new or difficult jobs. As a result, those deaf employees who did not demonstrate these qualities were generally perceived as unlikely to be promoted. One supervisor said the deaf employee in his department, " . . . doesn't push, or ask you if he can do [more] . . . he [only] does whatever you ask him to do." Employees lacking initiative were also seen as requiring more of the supervisor's time:

> Well, to evaluate him right now probably on a scale of one to ten, he's probably . . . cause I would have to compare him to other people, he's probably a four or a five. He does his job, he's competent, and part of my job is to make him more aggressive and more competent so he can go out and do more . . . You

know, aggressive in asking for new jobs, tackling more difficult assignments. If I have to go to him to ask, "Do you have more free time?" that's contrary to being efficient and effective . . . You have to come to me and you let me know if you have this free time and I'll give you another job to do. Sometimes he doesn't, sometimes he does. So that's a goal that we have . . .

Sometimes doing extra work and taking on new jobs is not a sufficient indication of an interest in promotion. For example, one supervisor said that in his company, employees are expected to declare their ambition for promotion by talking to their supervisor, at which point the person will be considered for management training and advancement. In his words, "If that's the route he'd wanna go . . . then he would have to come to a manager and say, 'Look, I wanna someday be given the opportunity to be a supervisor,' and so they would start him getting trained and be given jobs, visibility, training classes, ultimately to be a supervisor."

Ambition involves being willing to take risks. In the following quotation, a supervisor whose uncle is deaf explains why she believes deaf people may be unwilling to risk their job security in order to take on a new position, even when that position involves higher pay or more responsibility:

> The fear of risk, I can identify [with that] . . . because the prevailing issue in my aunt's family through growing up was my uncle leaving one job to go to another. As typical of deaf persons in the work force who are really serious about working and taking care of their family, he was one of the best people in his trade, and often . . . other employers would ask him to change jobs. He said no. They would offer him more money, they offered him less work . . . [But] he would not take the risk . . . One person said, "Look, we'll even go fifty-fifty. It's a business and you will be co-owner; I could be your ears, and you, by and large, do the trade." My uncle would not take the risk . . . So the message here is that when it comes to security, when it comes to providing for one's family, that took priority over job opportunity, upward mobility in the job workplace . . . He really was determined to provide shelter for his wife, and he had little children at the time. So security in the home and well being is much more a priority. That's part of the value system.

A similar explanation for the persistence of deaf people within a single job was offered by another supervisor. She explained that deaf people must be better than hearing people and work doubly hard if they want to get ahead at work. She concluded by noting, "That's why, when you look at the stats, you'll find that the deaf person represents one of the lowest turnover rates in an organization. They tend not to quit a job, they tend to represent the least amount of confrontation and conflict. It's because deaf persons don't have the luxury of going from one job to the other and quitting right away and taking the risk, because . . . [there are] so many hurdles to encounter."

Interpersonal Skills

Supervisors said that the ability to get along with people, coordinate their efforts, and motivate them to do a good job is critical to success in management positions. As one supervisor put it, "Supervision is 70 percent relationships." Another described supervision as the creation of a "win-win" situation for both manager and staff. He continues:

> If you wanna maximize [your employees'] effort, they need to know that they're wanted and needed and respected. Good money is not the problem; they get paid enough. So what's gonna keep them happy, keep them motivated during a job? They need to win and I need to win. I need to get the job done, they need to be happy and to know that I appreciate them doing the job. That takes different forms, but that's why I say "win-win," we both win. If I win all the time and they lose, they're not gonna be happy, and then I'm not gonna get my work done, and my boss is not gonna be happy. Long term, [in order to become a manager] you have to gain more experience and confidence in how to deal with people . . .

Sometimes, being a manager involves a discovery of the delicate balance between leading and being a part of the team. One supervisor described this difficult interpersonal skill as involving two elements, "learning how to be a part of the network . . . [and] learning how to be a star without being a star." As she explained it, if "a star shines too much, then—depending on the security and well being of the other colleagues—they may [become] resentful . . . You have to learn how to be a star and . . . cooperate and share what you've learned." It is important to add that this supervisor felt the deaf employee in her department had the qualities necessary for management.

Of course, being able to relate well to people and develop good relationships with co-workers requires regular contact and relaxed, positive interactions. The barriers to communication and relationships between deaf and hearing employees described in earlier chapters therefore have potentially severe and negative implications for the vertical mobility of deaf workers. Deaf employees who were seen as unapproachable or socially isolated from the rest of the group were viewed as poor candidates for management. One supervisor, who described the deaf employee as a "loner," relates this characteristic to the person's potential for management. As he put it, "Managers have to be really people-oriented, and you have to be interested in learning about people and know how to get along with them. If you're a loner personality, then you can't draw on those experiences; and him, I don't know. That would have been maybe a problem." Another supervisor, who viewed the deaf employee as part of the Deaf community, as opposed to being part of the larger hearing community, questioned whether the person had sufficient experiences to prepare her for management responsibilities:

> There are so many different types of people that you have to deal with in these jobs—irritated people, nice people, bad people—really a variety. So there are many people, and I don't know if she [deaf employee] has ever dealt with those kinds of problems before. It's not that she couldn't learn, it's just that I don't know if she's ever had that experience. You know, [she] is really involved with the deaf people . . . She and her husband really do a lot with deaf people, and she's a very outgoing person. But you know, I've noticed that a lot of hearing-impaired people . . . maintain their own group, and sometimes, you know, to mix the two, I don't know if it would work out . . . It's kind of like people coming in from another country, it's the same type of thing. And those people who are working here and they're from another country, and they go home at night—it's a completely different world for them. And I have trouble communicating with some of those people here, too.

There is a double irony in these comments. As revealed by supervisors' comments in earlier chapters, deaf people frequently experience difficulties accessing the informal conversations and social interactions which routinely occur among their hearing peers. Yet, if they respond to this situation by withdrawing from social encounters with hearing people or gravitating towards other deaf people, they may be labeled "loners" and perceived as poor candidates for management.

Moreover, the perspective that a deaf person who interacts mostly with other deaf people lacks sufficient experience for management reflects a belief that the social context of the deaf subgroup is inadequate for full participation in the larger society. This belief is a good example of the resistance in many organizations, and indeed in society in general, to the acceptance and promotion of individuals with different social and cultural backgrounds. The same reason has been given for failure to promote women and members of ethnic and racial minorities into management positions, the rationale being that one must be able to think like a man (and/or a Caucasian, hearing person) in order to supervise men (and/or Caucasian, hearing persons).

Understanding Management Culture

Finally, supervisors referred to a set of skills which can be described as "understanding management culture" in their discussions of career advancement; these include discovering and supporting the values and goals of the organization, learning how the organization operates and what is required to get things done, and understanding what is expected of managers within one's division or company. Many skills associated with management culture have been touched on already in discussions of other related job skills. For example, knowing that one must directly express to one's supervisor a desire for promotion in order to be considered for management positions reflects an understanding of how the organization operates. Making difficult decisions regarding budget allocations requires a broad vision of the goals of the organization and the ability to analyze individual requests for support within the framework of those goals. The ability to critically evaluate and assist in improving an employee who is not performing his or her job properly indicates an understanding of company standards and a commitment to meeting those standards.

In short, management culture is a perspective, reflected through a demonstration of broad understandings about the organization as well as an application of specific job related skills such as those discussed earlier in this section. One supervisor suggested that "a manager . . . sometimes has to push and has to be a little more cold sometimes to get a job done; it takes a certain personality, a certain drive." Another expanded on this notion with the observation that "managers can't please everybody; managers sometimes have to take a hard-nosed stand; managers sometimes have to place the job above the family; managers sometimes can't take an easy way out immediately in dealing with stress." A third supervisor summarized her discussion of the related qualities required for promotion into management by stating that "it's how you play the game," noting that the rules may change depending on the number of employees in the work group and the size of the organization. The value attached to specific related job skills varies from one department or organization to another. The deaf employee who seeks advancement must be able to assess each setting and determine an appropriate course of action.

COMMUNICATION SKILLS, CONSTRAINTS, AND ACCOMMODATIONS

The communication barrier between deaf and hearing people in the workplace was frequently cited by supervisors as a constraint to promotion, particularly into positions of management. For example, several supervisors noted that much of their work involves the telephone. Most assumed that a deaf employee could not handle this part of the job. Even supervisors who were aware of telephone relay services or provided the deaf employee with a TDD tended to view these accommodations as having limited usefulness (such as for calling in sick or phoning deaf friends or family members). TDDs and relay services were seen as inefficient for the amount and quality of telephone contact required of a supervisor. For example:

> SUPERVISOR: If it was just on paper, clear cut, it would be no problem. There are a lot of sales people, there are a lot of phone conversations that are coming in from all aspects of the hospital. If you were in clinical microbiology and you needed to find out from . . . [a deaf histology supervisor] a certain procedure and you didn't have a TTY but you knew the deaf person had to use a TTY, do you think you would go to the [deaf] supervisor or would you go and call one of the hearing individuals in the lab and ask them the procedure?
> INTERVIEWER: You think that's what would happen?
> SUPERVISOR: Maybe, but I don't know. [She] is capable of being [a] supervisor, [she] knows her stuff very well. I'm not in her position. I don't know how she would handle ordering. I do all the ordering. I've got to pick up the phone . . . and I've got to say, "I need twenty 20-liter containers." She would have to call [local relay service] and [the operator] would have to say [for deaf employee, in relaying the message,] "I would like . . . " She probably could do it, but there are a lot of middle people involved too.

Writing skills sometimes take on greater importance in management positions. The ability to write reports, memos, and employee evaluations clearly and fluently was critical to the performance of many management tasks. Employees who do not write well are at a disadvantage when decisions are made about promotions. In describing the deaf person who worked for her, one supervisor observed that her "writing skills are not great. There is a lot of evaluation writing [in supervisory job]. A lot of memo writing. A lot of writing people up for various things."

Direct communication between individuals was seen as another barrier to promotion. Supervisors noted that their responsibilities include training, monitoring, and evaluating employees, all of which involve one-to-one communication. They expressed concern that the deaf employee might have trouble fulfilling these responsibilities. For example, one supervisor wondered whether the deaf employee "would be able to train people . . . [or] to explain things in enough detail for them to understand." And another person, when asked whether he felt the deaf employee could ever take on a management role in his department, responded by saying, "I think that would be . . . difficult because [if you are deaf] you are going to be writing [instead of speaking]. I've got people pulling me in every direction, sometimes asking me this and . . . I am giving them directions and . . . I am walking over here and I am giving this guy directions on what to do. It would be a little slower process [if the manager were deaf and had to rely on written communication]." Sometimes demands that come with management responsibilities were seen as more subtle:

> INTERVIEWER: If [he] was able to master the technical things, are there other things that you look for in someone who you should consider for a supervisor?
> SUPERVISOR: The only thing that comes to my mind would be communication skills. Be able to go talk to an employee . . . who may be doing a bad job. You know, [give them] a friendly word of encouragement. Or for somebody to come up to me and say, "Hey, I need this. I need help." That's a touchy thing, the communication.

It is important to note that communication is not in and of itself a barrier to promotion. Rather, it is an interaction between deaf employees and their colleagues. It becomes a barrier only when the communication characteristics and skills of the deaf person are incompatible with those used by others within the work environment. Accommodations such as having hearing colleagues learn sign language, computers, TDDs and interpreters often eliminate the communication barrier. One supervisor suggested that computers could be used within his company in place of the telephone for direct communication between the deaf employee and other departments. Another emphasized that if the deaf employee met the necessary management and administrative qualifications, then "the agency would be happy to provide him an interpreter for all the work he needed to do—that would go without saying."

In short, the degree to which communication differences were viewed as barriers to promotion varied from one work setting to another. The supervisor who said his company would provide an interpreter to a deaf administrator worked in an agency offering direct services to deaf people, and it was not unusual to find a willingness to accommodate a deaf employee within these kinds of settings. Other supervisors, however, were less willing to accommodate the communication needs of deaf employees, which suggests that organizational priorities and goals are important factors in determining the accommodations made available to deaf employees.

ATTITUDES OF OTHERS

The last condition for promotion of deaf employees concerned the attitudes of others, including supervisors and co-workers. Several supervisors stressed the importance of their role in preparing the deaf person for success at work and for promotion. An example:

> Promotion is . . . a lot of it is learning skills which do not require hearing. As a technician, you do a lot of report writing, and [he does okay] in that, so I would say it should not bother him at all as far as advancing. By getting more education in this line of work, which has been laid out already—trying to get him to a better position by giving him a technical knowledge that he needs as a technician—we do those things, and that's my responsibility to any person. I can't expect them to function well without having the education necessary to do it along the lines. He has a technician's diploma, but it's in a broad range. If I want a person to do things in a narrower band, I should be more responsible in making sure that person is trained in those particular skills.

As noted in *Chapter 3*, it is not always easy for hearing and deaf people to communicate with one another. Successful communication often requires the commitment of time and resources, the use of alternative communication modes, and a willingness to work through awkward or embarrassing situations. Perhaps most important, for communication to be effective, all participants must be patient. This is true for all communication, but takes on even greater importance in situations where the deaf person is in a management position. One supervisor said of the deaf employee, "[She] could probably do that [manage other people] as long as everyone is patient . . . If they said something once, and the hearing individual couldn't get it right . . . you have to re-say it. Patience runs thin sometimes, you have to be patient. [She] probably could do it. Nothing is impossible."

The degree to which hearing people would be willing to accept a deaf person in a management role was seen as affecting chances for promotion in some cases. In the following quotation, a supervisor expressed his concerns about how the hearing workers would respond to the idea of a deaf manager. He had no doubts about the individual's technical skills:

SUPERVISOR: He has the technical potential. I don't know about ... not being able to communicate. Talking would be a problem. I don't know ... I would probably say that most people would probably be negative about it. That is my personal feeling.

INTERVIEWER: Because of the communication?

SUPERVISOR: Yeah, people don't want to change. People are against even having our CAD machines in here. So you get the old generation against the younger guys going into the CAD system, and it is like [the older guys say,] "That thing isn't going to work. We did it manual for years." [They have a] "Why should we change?" attitude ... it's probably not just [company's] attitude, it's an attitude in any place. "We have done it all these years this way, why should we change?" [As regards a deaf supervisor], they probably would say, "That will never work. How is he going to talk to somebody or how is he going to explain to somebody? How is he going to give somebody a review?" There probably is going to be quite a bit of problems.

Again, the overall philosophy or attitude of the company and supervisor will probably determine the degree to which conditions such as the attitude of co-workers become barriers to promotion. It would be naive to presume that attitudes can be changed by issuing orders. However, the standards set by the supervisor and the degree to which prejudice is tolerated by management will, eventually, influence the attitudes of all employees, deaf and hearing.

Two supervisors drew comparisons between the negative attitudes which might mitigate against the movement of a deaf employee into management and those faced by women, African Americans, and members of ethnic minorities. In the following example, a supervisor speculates about the receptiveness of what he refers to as the "social structure" in his office to these kinds of situations:

There may be people on staff who interact very well with this kind of person as a co-equal but who might have all sorts of problems in terms of having him be a supervisor. I just don't know, but I know enough about people to know that they are really strange, and so you don't know what's gonna happen till you do it. Same thing about having a woman supervisor with a crew of males or something. It seems very straightforward, but it may not be ... There's no question in my mind that [he] has the potential. Whether the social structure will allow him to is another matter ...

The reference of the supervisor cited above to social structure is really about discrimination and disruptions of the status quo. Implicit in his remarks is the notion that placing a woman, member of ethnic or racial minority, or person with a disability in a position of supervision may offend the people who are to be supervised, and that their response may seriously thwart the effectiveness of the new supervisor. In the following quotation, another supervisor offers her perspective on what the deaf person can and must do in order to become an accepted and effective manager:

> The fact of the matter is that persons who are disabled, as well as those who are ethnic minorities, have stereotypes they have to [overcome] . . . So . . . that would be an additional hurdle that [she] would have to conquer here . . . Let's say, for example, she were to apply for the [position of] director of this agency. She has to be interviewed by the Board of Managers, comprised of a search committee . . . Invariably, the question will come up, "Can a hearing-impaired person do this job?" And even if she can demonstrate that with all the assistive devices necessary to do the job she could do well, invariably, someone will think (I'm willing to wager you subconsciously), "But she's deaf" . . . It's almost like the Jackie Robinson syndrome in my opinion. As women and Blacks and persons who are disabled or any minority have to compete in the workplace, they have to do doubly well. So [she] really does doubly well in my opinion, in part because it's her personality. Also in part because she's cognizant that she has to prove herself. . . . So, unless she demonstrates that she's able to do the job doubly, I mean that she's just so outstanding and so superb and if she can walk on water and exist on no oxygen at all, I mean she's just super, *super,* probably would a person then say, "She's executive caliber."

This supervisor's observation reflects the notion of compensatory effort and competence which was raised in the earlier discussion of hiring and evaluating deaf employees in *Chapter 2.* The same points have been made about women and members of ethnic or racial minority groups in the workplace. It could be argued that to expect superior skills from deaf employees as a kind of compensation for being unable to hear is, in itself, discriminatory.

DISCUSSION

Four points can be made about the conditions that supervisors suggest are important if deaf employees are to move into management. First, while the conditions described by supervisors apply to anyone seeking management positions, deaf people may have special needs or difficulties in developing an awareness of these conditions and/or in meeting the requirements or overcoming those elements which are more likely to present specific difficulties to deaf employees, such as those related to communication. For example, learning that overtime or a willingness to take on new tasks is considered essential for promotion within a company is casual information, in that it is not part of a job description and is not likely to come up in conversations directed towards routine performance of one's job. Rather, such information is more likely to be shared through informal conversations with peers, as part of the communication "grapevine." Yet, supervisors acknowledged that it is often difficult for deaf employees to access this kind of information network. As a result, deaf employees must find other strategies for getting the casual information which they need, perhaps by purposefully building and drawing on the relationship with the supervisor as a mentor who will then become a source of information, as well as of guidance and support.

Second, the comments of supervisors suggest that technical competence is necessary but not sufficient for the career advancement of deaf persons. Both technical skills and personal qualities were identified by supervisors as ingredients for successful work performance. However, the weight attached to each varied according to whether the discussion was focused on managerial or sub-managerial jobs. Specifically, supervisors placed greater importance on personal qualities in evaluating the employee's potential for management.

Third, the potential for promotion reflects a combination or interaction of the conditions described in this section. For example, it is necessary to have both an understanding of the process of promotion within the organization *and* the ambition to pursue this process in order to successfully move up the ladder. The following story is illustrative:

> I'm sure [she] is a very, very frustrated girl. But it's not because nobody has tried. She's gone over to Industrial Relations different times, asking for transfers, but you know it's really difficult to move hearing-impaired people around . . . She was told that she could work in the Computer Room, but that would require shift work, and she doesn't want to do that . . . Her cousin has a really good job in another company, and I think that she is so proud of him and she'd really like to be proud of herself the same way . . . but I've told her that, "You have to go through the ranks to do that, and you have to start in the Computer Room, and that means you have to do shift work." And she said, "Oh, no." She feels she doesn't want to do that. She says, "I'd like to learn the computer, but I don't want the shift work, so I don't bother to go over there." But she's got to understand that that's the only way to get ahead.

Similarly, the following examples illustrate powerfully the interaction between several kinds of conditions and their effect on supervisors' perceptions of the deaf employee's potential for management:

EXAMPLE # 1

I think he has the potential for [becoming a supervisor]. He doesn't have the training in specific [technical] areas in this lab, but he could go and get that. He's certainly got the organizational capacity and the drive for it, and I think he has a good personality for interacting with people. It would just take a laboratory director that had confidence and the right kinds of interaction with him to allow that to happen.

EXAMPLE # 2

Well, I doubt . . . [that he could become a supervisor], but only because of his being stubborn. Unless he was going to solve that problem. I mean, it really showed itself. It was pretty vivid. They'll promote almost anyone here into supervision, but I mean, they do want people who can get along and not argue at every drop of a hat. And also, you know, he'd have . . . a lot of competition here because there's only so many positions and everybody wants them. And he'd be competing with people who don't have the kind of handicap that he's got. I think really he would have had to try a little bit harder than other people, but I think he could have done it.

EXAMPLE # 3

I'd say, generally speaking, his communication skills are great enough that he should be able to do it [supervise others]. Again, everything kind of grows with time . . . He could not be limited because of a hearing loss . . . it didn't limit me. I didn't have a documented hearing loss at the time, but I have one now . . . [Later in interview] With [his] capabilities and his willingness to learn things, there really isn't anything that would stop him [going] all the way through, particularly [in] a company such as mine because we give everyone opportunity for performance—how well you perform. If he shows that he performs well, it [the deafness] should not be a drawback. In fact, it can't be a drawback if looked at legally. It just cannot be, especially a company this size. So it's up to the individual— set your sights high . . . I know you have to be realistic [but] I just can't say that I can find a place to draw the line on someone like that. It's all individual.

Fourth, each of the conditions for promotion described in this chapter reflects skills and qualities which are inherent to either (a) the deaf employee, (b) the work environment, or (c) a combination of (a) and (b). The first two conditions (technical and related qualities of the employee) reflect characteristics, qualities, or abilities of the deaf employee. The third (communication skills, restraints, and accommodations) reflects an interaction between the characteristics and skills of the deaf employee and the specific conditions of the work environment. The fourth (attitudes of others) reflects conditions external to the deaf employee. Interventions which have as a goal the advancement of deaf people within the workplace should be conceived and implemented within a framework that targets *both* deaf and hearing employees, and environmental as well as individual conditions. It may be that personal work qualities are acquired through everyday, routine interactions with co-workers, an experience frequently unavailable to deaf people. As a result, deaf people may need additional opportunities for training and experience in these areas if they are to compete for management positions. Similarly, interventions directed at providing employers with information about deafness and technical accommodations for deaf people may be another fruitful vehicle for change.

In conclusion, promotion—especially into supervisory positions—involves the technical and related qualities of the deaf employee, communication characteristics and accommodations of the employee and others within the work setting, and the attitudes of others (including those attitudes embedded in company policy). Deaf persons who want to move into management need to be aware of these conditions and develop those personal skills which are central to advancement. Additionally, strategies that focus on changing the environment to encourage and facilitate the accommodation and/or acceptance of the deaf person should be used whenever possible.

At the same time, there needs to be interest and commitment on the part of the organization regarding promotion of deaf employees. Equal opportunity policies embraced by most companies endorse the idea that all workers should have an equal chance for promotion. However, compliance with company policy is not the only reason to insure that capable deaf employees have opportunities for management. For example, movement of deaf people into supervisory positions may be the single greatest factor in developing positive working relationships between deaf and hearing people in the workplace. When deaf people have power and status within an organization, their perspectives and ideas draw more attention, and hearing people are more motivated to learn and use alternative communication strategies. Successful deaf managers are role models for other deaf employees. Their presence is also a powerful educational tool, since hearing colleagues will learn to respect their ability and authority. In short, there are many compelling reasons for promoting capable deaf employees into management positions, including legal, ethical, and practical considerations as well as long term, positive changes in the attitudes and behaviors of both hearing and deaf employees.

COMMENTARY

GARY: This was an interesting chapter because it covered a lot of things. But one thing that it always comes back to is communication. Supervisors feel employees need to meet all these criteria for promotion, but communication is the main thing. It was nice that some managers admitted that deaf employees can do supervisory jobs. But others said that communication is a problem, and that it is an issue for them related to promotion. I was disappointed about that. Also, they talked about people who are what they called "loners." One of the supervisors said a person who is a loner cannot be a manager, but I don't think they should label people that way. And at the same time, I feel it's also the supervisor's responsibility to educate the person on what it takes to become a manager.

DAVID: Yeah, I agree with Gary. I found that communication is the main issue throughout the book, and in this chapter particularly. Reading this chapter was painful to me, because so much of it mirrored my experience as a deaf employee. You know, I'm sort of limited in terms of communication with hearing people. Supervisors' descriptions of deaf employees in this chapter often reminded me of the characteristics that I had when I was working in the hearing world. For example, although I did sometimes hang around with hearing people, at other times I was more of a loner. Like, if I wasn't familiar with the topic or issue, I would be reluctant to join in the conversation for fear that I would say the wrong thing or appear silly.

GARY: If a hearing person can do the job and get along with people, they have the chance to be promoted. But there's a lot more involved with a deaf employee.

JANICE: Becoming a manager in one of my past jobs required a lot of communicating on the phone, as well as being able to go to meetings or conferences to get information from lectures. That was a barrier for me. I tried to imagine myself doing that, and I realized I really couldn't be part of that. I couldn't have that responsibility because of the communication. So that was a little bit discriminatory.

DAVID: I worked at my old job for five years before I came here. At first, there was little structure in my office. We all worked in one large room and there was one boss who was in charge of all our operations. I didn't have much contact with him. Then later we divided up into smaller departments, each with its own supervisor. Under this system, I had three different supervisors. My first department supervisor understood about deaf people's abilities. But even so, I was surprised when he said to me, "When the time comes, you will be considered for promotion, David. You're a good worker. You're very reliable. You're very productive." When he asked me, "Do you have any problems with communication with your co-workers?" I thought, "Hmm, not really, no." Later, I had another supervisor who was also very sensitive about my needs. But when promotion time came, I was not picked for the supervisor's position. There were only two people in the department who were being considered, me and a hearing employee. I approached the supervisor with an idea. I said, "The hearing person can answer the phone and go to meetings, and I can do the paperwork, scheduling, and planning. We can work together and share the management job." But then they reorganized the department and I was under another supervisor who knew nothing about my needs. I tried to suggest this new idea again, but it wasn't accepted. I don't know why. Maybe for some political reason. So I wasn't promoted. I didn't feel good about that, but there was really nothing I could do about it.

SUSAN: So, did the hearing person become the manager?

DAVID: Yes. Really, I accepted that fact because that's very common for deaf employees.

SUSAN: Janice and Gary, did you ever get considered for promotion in your jobs?

JANICE: Yes. There was a position open for program analyst, and I wanted the job. I asked my boss whether I was qualified, and she said, "Yes, go ahead." So I applied. Then I got the job interview. They asked some questions related to communication with hearing people, but I defended myself. I said that I could communicate; I'm assertive and I can write. I explained that I can't communicate over the phone. In those situations, I'd have to have somebody else to help me speak on the phone, or I could go to that person in their office to discuss the issue, but that was the only thing I couldn't do. I got the job.

SUSAN: What about managing other people? Do you think that was a possibility for you?

JANICE: Yes, I believe that I could have been a supervisor or a project leader. I would have had to prove to them how assertive I am and show them that I don't let hearing people frighten me. I'd have to learn how to break through, find ways to solve communication problems, but I could see myself doing that.

SUSAN: Can you give me an example of what you mean when you say, "not let hearing people frighten you"?

JANICE: Well, what I mean is not let hearing people from top level administration frighten or intimidate me, like VIP's or Directors of Information Systems or whatever. I'd have to be courageous, go up to them, meet them, discuss things by myself.

SUSAN: Is it harder for deaf people to overcome that fear, or is it the same whether you're deaf or hearing?

JANICE: I think deaf people feel a little embarrassed about their communication skills, especially writing, with people who work at those high levels of management. They worry that they don't know how to say something in a professional way, don't know the formal, technical ways of communicating with upper level managers. So I try to find ways to break through that, to build up my confidence in myself. I have to know what I want, and know the technology, so that I can show the manager that I know what I'm talking about. I want him to know that I'm deaf, yes, but I can do it. I want to make a good impression.

SUSAN: Gary, do you have any stories to share? You're smiling.

GARY: Yes. It's a long story, but I'll try to make it short. I was working in sales. Normally, a person who has outstanding performance for three years is in line to become a manager. It doesn't always happen, only when somebody asks for it. Some people achieve, but don't want to be in a management position. Others want to become managers. I was doing very well in my work. Going into my third year I expressed an interest in assuming a management position. I went up to Boston and sat down and talked with the vice president of the company. He was really very vague. He explained that this kind of structure was very different from other kinds of companies. It wasn't the same as IBM or the General Electric Company. In sales, you start as a sales person, then you become a sales manager, then a general manager. Three steps, and that's all. And some people who sell actually make more money than people at the top two levels. So there's a real variety. But I still was interested in becoming a manager. So I approached my general manager with the idea. He was very blunt. He said, "Well, the problem is you can't use the telephone. This work requires a lot of work phoning to and from the home office." Then he said, "You'd make more money doing what you do now than if you became a manager." I said, "But I want to become a manager, to build more confidence, to understand the system." Next, I approached another manager. He thought I was able to do it, because I had the personality to interact with hearing people. So I had three responses: the manager who felt I could do the job, my general manager who said, "No," and the vice president who didn't say much one way or the other. One day I got a letter from the vice president of the company. They were starting a pilot program and had decided to add another managing position. He gave me the opportunity to work in this position. I had two people reporting to me with the understanding that I'd go out and help them with training.

SUSAN: Do you feel confident in your ability to manage other people, both hearing and deaf?

GARY: It depends on the environment. I would not want to become a manager "just anywhere." It's not an easy task.

DAVID: I agree. I wouldn't want to be in that situation. Sometimes I've faced hard decisions to make, and no, I don't think I'd want to become a manager.

GARY: But David, suppose you were working at a company that employed only deaf workers and you had the necessary skills to be a manager. Do you think you'd take the offer to be a supervisor then?

DAVID: Fifty-fifty.

GARY: In that environment you might like it.

DAVID: But I don't think that will happen in the future.

GARY: Well, you never know.

DAVID: One of the reasons I've been hesitant to become a manager is that, while I believe I have some capabilities, I wouldn't want the responsibility of communicating with hearing people, because I'm not really good at that. I can do it in general conversation, but related to a job, I don't know how to manage. Some hearing people have no patience. Some have big egos. I don't know how to manage them. It's a different world. I don't know how they do it. I feel that I don't fit in the hearing world. How can I manage them? I don't think that's a good idea. If there was a management position in a deaf company, like Gary said, well, maybe I wouldn't mind that.

SUSAN: Could you just explain what you meant when you said you "don't fit"?

DAVID: Well, that's tough to explain. It's not that I have a negative feeling or attitude about hearing people, it's just that sometimes when we are conversing all of a sudden I'll notice a change in their expression and I can sense that they are kind of backing away from me, from our conversation. For example, I remember one time I got into a conversation with a co-worker about allergies. He invited a third person, who also was having troubles with allergies, to join us. So the three of us had a conversation, with the first worker (who knew a little sign language) facilitating communication. Anyway, I am something of an expert on the topic of allergies, and I gave a lot of information to the third person. I offered to bring in a book I had at home on this topic and to talk with him more at a later time. But he never came back to me to talk or to ask about the book. I found out later he had gotten the information from another person. I think maybe we were unable to get close because I was never really able to fully express myself well with him or him with me, because of the communication barrier. You know, the worker who facilitated the conversation for us was not very skilled in sign language, so we had to keep our comments pretty simple. I think maybe that put him off.

SUSAN: How about you, Janice? Would you like to be a manager?

JANICE: I could. But my biggest fear is stress. So it would be a good test for me, whether I could cope with that stress. If I could, then I wouldn't mind—I'd love to be a manager. I like to be in charge.

GARY: (Smiling) I can see that!

DAVID: Another reason why I don't want to be a manager is because I don't want to work overtime. You have to work sixty, seventy hours a week if you're a manager. I prefer the forty-hour limit. Go home, have time with the family. That's my type.

SUSAN: Janice, you said something about stress. What do you think would cause stress for you in a manager's role?

JANICE: Well, project deadlines, people. Managers are always faced with many different problems. You have to know how to solve these problems. So I think stress would be a problem. I observed my boss in my old job. Wow! She was under a lot of pressure with deadlines. So I could see what managers go through. The stress is terrific.

SUSAN: Supervisors mentioned both technical skills and personal qualities in discussing criteria for management, but they stressed the latter. What kinds of skills and qualities do you think are most important?

GARY: Personal interaction, like being able to get along with people, being able to handle problems, complaints. Managers must be able to satisfy everyone in the department, balance their work.

JANICE: And have a lot of patience.

GARY: Yes. Be a good listener.

SUSAN: Supervisors said it's real important to understand management culture.

GARY: Yes, and that's a problem for deaf people, because it involves listening. The deaf can't hear what's happening behind the scene. That becomes more of a problem if you're a manager, because you need to know the system, what's important and what isn't important. This all becomes a problem if you're deaf. So I think that understanding management culture and language should not be a criteria for becoming a manager. I feel that should be eliminated, because it would be difficult for people to have the opportunity to become managers if they have to meet that criteria.

JANICE: From my job experience, I've noticed that politics is an important part of management culture. For example, I remember they picked a person who wasn't a fantastic programmer to become the manager in my department. Why? Because he was really close friends with another manager. They were real buddies. You know the old saying, "It's not what you know, but who you know."

SUSAN: If that's true, does that present a disadvantage for deaf people?

JANICE: Yes, because you don't know who people are. The hearing culture isn't part of their culture. How do you do it? That's the problem. When I was graduating from college, my hearing friends were getting jobs with Fortune 500 companies. I'd say, "How'd you get those jobs?" They'd say, "Oh, my aunt's friend offered the job." You have to have some kind of connection. Deaf people don't have connections with the hearing world.

GARY: No, you're wrong.

JANICE: Well, that's my experience. Maybe your experience is different.

GARY: Several of my students have found jobs through their relatives.

JANICE: Yes, but their aunts and friends, mothers and fathers are hearing. You know, I have a lot of people in my family, but they're deaf. So, as a deaf person from a deaf family, I have no connections. Maybe in a hearing family it is different.

SUSAN: Dave, you were going to say something.

DAVID: Oh, just a brief comment. I've noticed that anyone—deaf or hearing—has a good chance of moving up to become a manager if they are good at interacting with other people. They have to be a real "people person."

SUSAN: Some supervisors said that you can't promote deaf people because the job requires too much communication. They wondered how the deaf person would do evaluations or handle all the little conversations, advice, and so forth with hearing workers. Do you think this is a reasonable concern?

GARY: It depends on the kind of work they're doing.

JANICE: Yes. For example, in my job, mostly what I didn't know, the supervisor knew and could tell me. If there was still a problem, we would bring in the consultant. After that, the boss only had to communicate simple things to me, like she might say, "I want this and this and this." Fine. I solve it. I write the program. But they don't look over my shoulder.

SUSAN: What do you think about the idea expressed by some supervisors that, even if a person has a TDD, they couldn't function as a manager because it takes so long to go through the relay service all the time?

JANICE: The relay service in my home state just started in January, 1991. Before that there never even was a relay service. So it's hard to say. Maybe it'll be a good test for the next generation. Now we're just developing and setting up the relay service. I feel there's already been an awful lot of changes in our generation, so it's still hard to say what the future will be like.

DAVID: The state-wide relay service is much better than the local service in Rochester. It was very hard to make calls with the local service, because they were always busy and only had three operators. But they've got a lot of operators for the state service, so communication is much faster. Still, it's not quite the same as communication in the hearing world, which is even faster. But it helps.

GARY: I did some research with hearing people, in which I asked them how they felt about communicating through the TDD, and many felt that the process was a little lengthy. Also, they said there were long pauses (while the operator translated their words into typed message and the deaf person typed back a response), where they weren't sure what was happening. I think if the hearing person is patient, understanding, and sensitive, then it won't be a problem for the deaf person. But if a person wants to work fast, and they work in the fast lane, then it becomes a problem.

JANICE: I forgot to bring up one important issue. In my company, I found a way to use E-mail through the computer. I sent it to my assistant supervisor. She was shocked to get my message. She came to my office and said, "How did you do that?" So I taught her. But in the end, they didn't feel comfortable with E-mail, so they didn't use it. They'd rather come and talk with me directly. So, I was trying to solve one of the communication barriers by sending E-mail, hoping they'd send a message back, but it wasn't successful the way I thought it would be. They just would rather talk with their voices.

GARY: The technology is always one step ahead of us. It's becoming a problem. A year ago E-mail was "the thing." Now they're talking about voice mail, where you leave a message by voice instead of typing it.

JANICE: That will put deaf people at a disadvantage.

SUSAN: Supervisors said the attitude of hearing people is a factor in whether a deaf person can become a manager. For example, they said some hearing people are unwilling to accept a deaf person as a manager, and this would create problems. What is your reaction to that?

GARY: It depends on the person themselves and their personality. I had two people under me, and it was fine.

SUSAN: David, you said before that one of the reasons you didn't want to become a manager was because you weren't sure whether the hearing people would be patient, or how they would handle communication problems. Could you talk a little bit more about that?

DAVID: Well, I don't know what hearing people would think about being under me, but I get a feeling that they'd be a little upset. Can you imagine a person who's considered a minority, managing the majority group? There might be a little feeling there of discomfort. I think there would be.

SUSAN: Well, that's an interesting point, because a few supervisors compared the experience of deaf people with those of a woman managing men or a black person managing white people. Do you think there are similarities?

JANICE: I feel that communication is a big factor between deaf and hearing. There's not the same problem with black and hearing or Hispanic and hearing, because they already know English. They already know how to listen, how to respond to questions. It's easy to communicate. With deaf people, communication takes a lot more time. But, as long as the deaf manager has a wonderful personality and is an easygoing person, hearing workers shouldn't have any problems or feelings against them. My father is deaf. He owns a business and has many hearing clients. He's never had any complaints. My mother is a senior data operator. She has maybe eight or nine hearing people under her, and she's deaf. She's doing well.

SUSAN: Interesting. One supervisor observed that for a deaf person to become a manager, they have to be better than hearing people. Do you think that's true?

GARY: Yes, probably.

JANICE: Yes. It's just part of our culture. Hearing people have always looked down on us, so we have to prove that we can be as good, or better. It's just always been that way. It's a part of our lives.

DAVID: It's hard to answer that question, because the hearing world is so big. The deaf world is so small.

SUSAN: Imagine there are two people competing for the same promotion. They've both got the same skills and background. One of them's deaf, and one of them's hearing. Who do you think should be picked for the job?

JANICE: The best person, of course.

GARY: Depends on their personality and their ability to interact with people. That's really the question.

DAVID: Depends on the place. If that place has never hired a deaf worker before, maybe they'll go for the hearing person. If they have some experience with deaf employees, then maybe they'd consider promoting the deaf person.

SUSAN: In the discussion part of this chapter, the point is made that if you want a deaf person to become a manager, sometimes you need to change the deaf person. In other cases, you need to change the work environment, or the attitudes of co-workers. What do you think is most important?

GARY: I think it depends on the deaf person. If they want to become a manager, and they're motivated, they'll do it. But you can't just feed it to them. They have to decide if they want to do it or not, period.

DAVID: Yeah, that's right.

JANICE: Yes. I agree.

SUSAN: What would you say to a supervisor who is considering a deaf person for a management position? What should they think about as they make that decision?

GARY: I think that the supervisor needs to look at the deaf person as being equal to other people on the job. What I mean is they shouldn't let the deafness become a problem . . . If the supervisor sees that several people have potential to become supervisors, then he should be honest with each one, but he shouldn't count someone out because they're deaf. If the person has the potential and the motivation and the desire, don't eliminate them outright. If communication becomes an issue, the supervisor should work with the deaf person to help them overcome the barriers. Maybe they can sit down and act out or role play difficult situations, to come up with solutions. This way the deaf person can prepare for the future. But again, that's not something you can feed to someone. The person has to be motivated.

JANICE: I think the deaf person can become a manager, as long as they have good support from other employees, who respect their needs. If they just throw the dirty work to them, then it won't be possible for the deaf person to become a manager.

DAVID: My opinion is that deaf people have the ability to become managers, but the supervisor has to be open minded to the possibility. When it comes to the communication issue, the supervisor has to be very sensitive and considerate and provide the supports which will enable the person to communicate with hearing co-workers. If there are two people—one hearing, one deaf—applying for the same job, they shouldn't disqualify the deaf person based on communication. When a person is qualified except for communication, you need to weigh that and add whatever is necessary to support their communication. If you can meet their communication needs, then go for it. The deaf person can succeed.

RESOURCE LIST

Library Resources

Books and articles listed in this section should be available at local public or college/university libraries or through the interlibrary loan services at these libraries. Purchase prices listed may vary and are indicated only to give the reader a general idea of cost; contact the publisher directly for current cost and shipping/handling charges.

Boyd, B. "The National Leadership Training Program in the Area of Deafness: Its Development and Impact." *American Rehabilitation, 13*(3), 2–5, 29, 1987.

> This article discusses the development and impact of the National Leadership Training Program, an educational model addressing the needs of administrators and future leaders. Many of the deaf graduates of NLTP have since earned doctorate degrees and are employed in administrative capacities in education, rehabilitation, and business.

Career Information Registry of Hearing Impaired Persons in Professional, Technical and Managerial Occupations. Washington, DC: National Information Center on Deafness, Gallaudet University, 1987.

> This registry gives information about hearing-impaired individuals who hold professional, technical and managerial positions. The database was established to promote awareness and understanding of the career achievements of individuals with hearing loss. The individuals listed are willing to provide information about hearing-impaired people working in their career fields.

Careers & the Disabled. (Available by subscription from Equal Opportunity Publications, Inc., 44 Broadway, Greenlawn, NY 11740; Phone 516-261-8899 [Voice]; Cost: contact publisher for current cost)

> This career magazine for people with disabilities focuses on issues relevant to disabled professionals and presents articles which deal with working and advancing in the mainstream.

Crammatte, A.B. *Deaf Persons in Professional Employment.* Springfield, IL: Charles C Thomas, 1968.

> Although more than twenty years old, Crammatte's study remains a benchmark in the area of employment of deaf people. He covers communication problems, entry into careers of deaf people, the occupations and economic positions of people who are deaf, on-the-job problems, occupational mobility, and attitudes of and about adult deaf persons.

Crammatte, A.B. *Meeting the Challenge: Hearing-Impaired Professionals in the Workplace.* Washington, DC: Gallaudet University Press, 1987. (Available from Gallaudet University Press, Box 90, 800 Florida Avenue NE, Washington, DC 20002-3695; Phone 800-451-1073 [V/TDD]; Order no. 2757; ISBN 0-930323-24-6; Cost: $24.95)

> This study contrasts the growth and change in the status of deaf professionals from 1960 to 1982, a period of great advances and wider opportunities in employment for hearing-impaired people. Crammatte includes data from more than 1700 professionals with all ranges of hearing impairment and analyzes whether they have benefitted from the improved employment environment.

"Deaf Professionals on the Rise." *Gallaudet Today, 21*(3), 1991. (Available from *Gallaudet Today,* Gallaudet University, 800 Florida Avenue, NE, Washington, DC 20002-3695. Phone 202-651-5671 [V/TDD]; Cost: $3)

> Articles in this issue discuss the Management Institute at Gallaudet University, use of fax machines to assist in communication, suggestions for deaf professionals when giving presentations, and the effect of the Americans with Disabilities Act on the lives on deaf people.

Fritz, G.S. *Career Mobility and the Hearing-Impaired Employee.* Ph.D. Dissertation, Gallaudet University, 1986. (Available from University Microfilms International, 300 North Zeeb Road, Ann Arbor, MI 48106; Phone 800-521-3042 [V/TDD]; Cost: $28.50 for microfiche, $49.50 for paper copy, $59.50 for hard copy)

> Fritz's dissertation examines the attitudes of supervisors in technical/professional fields regarding career paths judged most probable for hearing and deaf employees and employee skills and characteristics needed by hearing and deaf employees to experience upward career mobility.

Welsh, W. *Career Mobility: A Review of Selected Literature.* Rochester, NY: Office of Postsecondary Career Studies and Institutional Research, National Technical Institute for the Deaf, Rochester Institute of Technology, 1987. (Available from Office of Postsecondary Career Studies and Institutional Research, National Technical Institute for the Deaf, Rochester Institute of Technology, P.O. Box 9887, Rochester, NY 14623-0887; Phone 716-475-6704 [V/TDD]; Cost: free)

> Welsh discusses the various meanings of career mobility, or the movement of an individual's career, by examining the literature pertaining to career mobility. He includes a discussion of the philosophical roots of mobility, the various dimensions of career mobility, and some of its determinants, in order to provide a focus for future research into career mobility.

Contacts

Career Center
Gallaudet University
800 Florida Avenue NE
Washington, DC 20002-3695
202-651-5270 (TDD and Voice)

> The Career Center, available to students and alumni of Gallaudet University, provides career planning and job-seeking services and helps prepare graduates for upward mobility in their field, as well as for career changes.

Foundation for Science and the Handicapped
236 Grand Street
Morgantown, WV 26505
304-293-5201

> Affiliated with the American Association for the Advancement of Science, FSH offers consultation and advice concerning problems faced by handi-

capped persons in scientific fields. The Foundation provides grants to disabled graduate or professional school students in engineering, science, and health related areas.

Management Institute
Gallaudet University
800 Florida Avenue NE
Washington, DC 20002-3695
202-651-5312 (TDD and Voice)

> The Management Institute provides employers with a full range of contract training programs, consulting, and technical assistance services, as well as extended expertise in deafness. For deaf employees, the Management Institute offers business education and training programs through four programs: the Center for Management and Leadership, the Small Business Development Center, the Contract Training Center, and the Microcomputer Applications in Business program.

National Center on Employment of the Deaf
National Technical Institute for the Deaf
Rochester Institute of Technology
P. O. Box 9887
Rochester, NY 14623-0887
716-475-6834 (TDD and Voice)

> NCED offers a workshop entitled "Climbing the Career Ladder," which goes beyond job-search strategies. It includes a self-analysis of skills, assistance in setting career goals, strategies to move towards those career goals, resume writing, interviewing techniques, and ways to network.

Chapter 6

ROLES AND RESPONSIBILITIES

I think the strongest point was [his] straightforwardness [about his communication needs] . . . There are more people that hear than [people who] don't hear, and when you get involved with a group and you get to the person who cannot hear, they're the ones that almost have to initiate the feelings or . . . break the ice, [deal with] the uneasiness of how to approach their problem . . . From my standpoint, it would have been difficult if [he] hadn't come out with the statements the way he did and come very straightforward. It made all the difference in the world to me. It might not work in every situation, but it certainly worked in mine. That's it. That point alone. Everything else kind of just falls in after that. (Excerpt from interview with hearing supervisor of deaf employee.)

In talking about the experience of working with a deaf person, supervisors offered suggestions about "what works," that is, strategies, conditions, and individual qualities that facilitate the successful assimilation of deaf people into the work setting. Many of these suggestions were raised within earlier chapters. In this chapter, they are organized within categories which represent various roles. These roles have been broken down further into (1) roles adopted by deaf employees and (2) roles adopted by hearing supervisors, each of which are detailed in the following pages.

ROLES ADOPTED BY DEAF EMPLOYEES

Supervisors' descriptions of those qualities they most admired in deaf employees fall into four roles: teacher, mediator, super-employee, and entrepreneur. These roles are not mutually exclusive. In fact, workers who were successful at their job frequently incorporated elements of all four roles.

Teacher

Deaf employees often assumed the role of teacher. They frequently taught hearing supervisors and co-workers about their deafness, including specific information about what they could and could not do in the work environment. They also provided supervisors with strategies for overcoming barriers to communication and integration. For example, one person explained that he could not hear the warning alarm and asked that co-workers be alerted to this and reminded to tap him on the shoulder when the alarm sounded. Many employees told their supervisors about amplifiers and TDDs, which would enable them to use the phone at work. Information about agendas, minutes, and interpreters was offered in an effort to educate supervisors about ways to make meetings and training programs more accessible.

Some employees did not take on the role of teacher; these individuals encountered difficulties. Supervisors often admitted they had no idea of how to communicate with a deaf person, and many were unaware of the range of special equipment, such as TDDs, which are available. Just as they appreciated deaf employees who were able to teach them about the special needs of deaf people, they viewed those who did not offer this assistance less favorably.

In defense of those deaf employees who did not assume the role of teacher, it must be noted that it is often a very difficult undertaking. It is not expected of most employees, and in the case of one's supervisor, adopting such a role runs counter to the prevailing tone of the relationship (i.e., supervisor in leadership role). Moreover, being a successful teacher depends to a large extent on the willingness of those who require education to become students. If supervisors and/or co-workers are unwilling to adopt the student role, the deaf employee/teacher will be fighting an uphill battle.

Supervisor's comments suggest that deaf employees were most active in teaching others about their communication needs regarding the more formal dimensions of their work. There were fewer examples of deaf people teaching hearing supervisors and co-workers about barriers to participation in informal interactions, even though supervisors generally agreed that these kinds of interactions were difficult for many deaf workers. Perhaps the social dimension of work was too sensitive for formal educational tactics. Or maybe deaf employees felt it was unfair to expect them to teach hearing co-workers how to overcome barriers to social interaction. Some, no doubt, preferred to spend their free time alone.

Mediator

While teaching strategies were useful in solving problems related to formal dimensions of work, they were less helpful for dealing with interpersonal relationships and the kinds of informal interactions in which employees routinely engage over coffee, in the hallways, and during lunch. The ability to mediate difficult social situations, i.e., to put hearing people at ease, break the ice, and resolve minor issues before they became major problems, was a quality supervisors highly valued. Deaf employees often adopted the role of mediator in the workplace.

Analysis of supervisors' comments suggests that humor and self-confidence are critical to successful mediation. For example, laughter facilitates social interaction, and several supervisors said the deaf employee used funny signs or jokes to break the ice and reduce stress at awkward moments. Also, it takes confidence to enter and manage situations where communication is difficult. A supervisor observed that when the deaf person in his department meets someone for the first time, "He's confident enough in that he'll . . . say, 'Slow down, I . . . have a hearing problem.' That's good. That saves me a lot of time explaining to other people that this is a problem and [to] watch out, don't say this to [him] because he's not gonna understand what you're saying and don't talk too fast. So he'll take care of it himself." As reflected in this supervisor's comment, deaf employees who are successful mediators are valuable at least in part because they take pressure off their supervisors.

Super-Employee

One of the most powerful themes to emerge from supervisors' descriptions of successful deaf employees was the belief that these workers are somehow better than most deaf—or, for that matter, hearing—workers. Their descriptions portray these "super-employees" as people who work harder, take the initiative for problem solving, teach others about deafness, attend social events in spite of communication barriers, show courage in stressful situations, accept responsibility for getting information, and routinely go beyond normal expectations to compensate for their deafness or to prove themselves to others.

Three qualities were consistently associated with the role of "super-employee." The first quality was hard work. Several supervisors said the deaf person works harder than hearing peers in order to keep up. Others simply found the drive of the deaf person admirable. Sometimes, this quality was reflected in creative problem solving, as in the case of the employee who responded to a lack of telephone access by doing a lot of "running around." His supervisor placed him in the "top ten percent [of employees] in amount of effort and drive devoted to the job."

Initiative was a second quality greatly valued by supervisors, who consistently spoke with admiration of employees who took responsibility for managing their own communication needs and interactions with co-workers. An example:

> SUPERVISOR: He never went anywhere without a pad and pencil. He liked having the translator [interpreter] there for any larger meeting or that kind of thing.
> INTERVIEWER: Would he remind people to try to get the translator?
> SUPERVISOR: Oh, yeah. He even . . . made the initial arrangements. I think [for] a person with an impairment, it would be wonderful if they all had the kind of ego that he has and would go ahead and make the situation work. I think that's respected, particularly if it's done not in an aggressive way but in a supportive way. To me, it just seemed . . . he was doing exactly what he should do. I mean, he was very helpful. Many of us [hearing people] didn't know what to do.

A third quality was the ability to approach a problem or potentially stressful situation directly and to clearly state both the problem and possible solutions. This was valued most highly by supervisors, particularly in combination with an ability to take the initiative in difficult or stressful circumstances. Recall, for example, the story told by a supervisor in *Chapter 3* in which he described with admiration the way the employee put him at ease during their first meeting by openly discussing communication barriers and possible solutions.

Implicit in the role of super-employee is the idea that the deaf person is somehow "exceptional" and that other deaf people could not be expected to perform so well. As one person put it, "I think that [deaf employee], by her very nature, was very helpful in the whole situation. I think you could get other people in the same situation [and] . . . the whole situation wouldn't be nearly as good. We do have another deaf girl working here, and we've had, at another time, another part-time girl that worked here. Neither of which situations were quite as good as [the situation with her]." The supervisor whose employee responded to an inaccessible telephone system by "running around" and making direct contact with colleagues concludes by stating that "with a great deal of vigor . . . he . . . does an excellent job, but I could imagine somebody with less energy . . . not quite coping and not doing as well."

Entrepreneur

The most successful deaf employees were those who incorporated elements of all the roles and qualities valued by supervisors. Some situations required demonstrations of hard work and initiative, while others called for education or mediation. Knowing which role to adopt — and when — is a skill unto itself, requiring of the employee an "entre-preneurial" approach. The term "entrepreneur" is used here in the sense of "one who organizes, manages, and assumes the risks of a business or enterprise" (Webster's Ninth New Collegiate Dictionary). The "enterprise" is employment and successful assimilation in the workplace. It is worth noting the entrepreneurial role includes risk. In the case of a deaf employee, the risks include isolation, failure to keep one's job or move ahead within the company, and the frustration of being unable to gener-ate understanding of or responsiveness to the constraints associated with being deaf in a hearing workplace.

Good judgment and flexibility are essential elements of the entre-preneurial role, since the employee must evaluate each situation and adopt or change strategies accordingly. This includes adaptation within a range of circumstances, including those involving differences in com-munication modes, learning styles, and approaches to the management of work tasks. For example, a supervisor who worked in an organization in which most of the hearing employees knew some sign language said that the deaf employee preferred to use sign without voice. However, she pointed out that if hearing people were having trouble following the signed conversation, the deaf person would voice a few words until his colleagues were able to get back on track.

Of course, in order for employees to demonstrate flexibility, they must have a repertoire of possible strategies, roles, and experiences from which they can draw. Thus, the individual who can use his or her voice as well as write or sign is better able to demonstrate flexibility in commu-nication modes than someone who cannot speak clearly. Similarly, the person who is both a skilled mediator and teacher will be better prepared to deal with barriers to social interaction than someone who is limited to a single approach.

Employees who have a good understanding of the people they work with are in the best position to determine which approach to take. For example, teaching strategies may work well with some co-workers, while others respond better to humor or demonstrations of technical skill. Selecting the correct strategy is an essential first step in any interaction.

Understanding the culture and mission of the workplace is also critical. Working hard and taking the initiative on new projects may be very helpful during periods when the organization is experiencing fiscal pressure. On the other hand, providing information about where to purchase a TDD, no matter how well presented, may be a gross miscalculation at times like these.

Sometimes the entrepreneurial role requires deaf employees to incorporate conflicting characteristics within their repertoire of behaviors at work. For example, supervisors valued directness and the ability on the part of the deaf person to be "up front" about possible limitations associated with their hearing impairment. At the same time, they greatly admired the deaf person who could "fit in," "does not let her handicap get in the way," or "does not make an issue of her impairment." The following quotations offer two variations on this theme:

EXAMPLE # 1
[Deaf people] need . . . a great level of self-confidence just because they may be missing what everybody is saying when they chit-chat and what goes on between people every day. And they need to be able to come out of their shell. Just because they can't hear what's going on doesn't mean they can't participate or be part of the group.
EXAMPLE # 2
One thing is that he is not shy or afraid to say things he's concerned about or that he needs to know about . . . and yet, at the same time [he's] easy going enough that he's not offended if I have forgotten, as his supervisor, to tell him something the first day I find out about it.

In these situations, deaf employee/entrepreneurs may be forced to walk a rather precarious tightrope. On the one hand, they are expected to be straightforward about their deafness and the possible limitations which it might impose on them at work. On the other hand, they must try to behave as if it is not a limiting factor, and they are in fact, "just like everyone else." It is possible for deaf people to walk such a tightrope — indeed, the comments of supervisors suggest that some do so with grace and wit. However, walking the tightrope on a daily basis is probably quite stressful and may take a toll on the productivity, job satisfaction, and even the health of deaf employees.

ROLES ADOPTED BY SUPERVISORS

Supervisors also described strategies and qualities which they felt were critical to working with a deaf person. They, as did the deaf employees, adopted a range of roles, including learner, mediator, advocate, and mentor.

Learner

The success of teaching efforts on the part of deaf employees depended in large measure on the degree to which supervisors were willing and able to adopt the role of "learner." Usually, supervisors were grateful for information and appreciated employees who took the initiative and explained their communication needs. Most supervisors described a range of accommodations which they used as a direct result of information provided by a deaf employee. Interpreters and TDDs were the most commonly mentioned accommodations. Others included the installation of signal lights, learning sign language, remembering to face the deaf person when speaking, and reviewing with deaf workers (separately or in writing) information presented orally during meetings.

However, not all supervisors were equally prepared to adopt the role of learner. Some appreciated the suggestions given to them by deaf employees, but did not follow up because they felt the changes were unwarranted, too costly, or time consuming. One supervisor said he did not pursue the deaf employee's suggestion that he learn sign language because he felt they managed well enough using speech reading and voice. Another rejected requests for an interpreter at meetings on the grounds that it was too costly, adding that he could not justify additional expenses associated with the needs of a single worker. Several supervisors noted that, while they understood the deaf person's need to converse in writing, they felt this was too time consuming and, especially in the case of casual conversations, "not worth the effort."

Underlying each of these reasons for failing to implement suggestions made by deaf employees are fundamental questions of relative power and motivation. Employee/teachers are not in a position to require that supervisors use the information given to them. Motivation must, therefore, come from someplace else. In some organizations, equal opportunity personnel policies provide the necessary motivation. Public laws, such as the Americans With Disabilities Act of 1990, are external sources of motivation. Sometimes supervisors were motivated by their own conscience or by a recognition that low performance or productivity on the part of a deaf employee may reflect poorly on them.

The relationship between employee/teachers and supervisor/learners functions best when viewed as a partnership. Constraints and facilitators such as company policy and federal laws provide a context, but in the end it is up to the people directly involved to establish a working relationship. Deaf employees should be sensitive to the constraints within which supervisors make decisions. Supervisors should be responsive to suggestions made by deaf employees and understand that these requests are inspired by a desire to perform well in the job. Always, the goals should be accessibility, reasonable accommodation, and performance.

Mediator

A second role adopted by supervisors was that of mediator. The term "mediation" is used here in the sense of acting as a go-between to resolve difficulties and improve the fit between the individual and the work environment.

Supervisors described themselves as performing at least three types of mediation. First, they mediated between the employee and the performance of work tasks. Several supervisors recalled changes they made in order to insure the success of deaf employees in their job. For example, one supervisor said that he decided to "take work away from" the deaf employee until he could handle it, gradually adding tasks to his work load over time until he was carrying a full load again. Another supervisor moved the deaf person into a slightly different position within the department:

> Now I moved him into another job, which again was a learning experience for me. I moved him from the job he was at there to a more clerical job to try to take some of the pressure off him, because we *did* have conversations. I said, "How do you feel, between you and me, about a lot of these extra conversations and things?" He said that they did put a lot of pressure on him to do things, he got nervous, and in some cases I could sense that. So I moved him into a job

where he's doing a lot of procurement of information, digging out things off of a computer file.

A second kind of mediation involved information sharing and general communication. The role of mediator is by necessity an outgrowth of the role of learner, since the strategies described by supervisors generally were learned from discussions with deaf employees. For example, most supervisors were responsible for making sure their employees received information related to the performance of work tasks. Mediation activities at this level included arranging for interpreters at meetings, providing deaf employees with TDDs and computers for electronic mail, and reviewing with them on a one-to-one basis information disseminated at meetings. Sometimes the little things were the most likely to be overlooked:

> I think you just have to be very, very much in tune to the fact that some of those little things that we talked about might have gotten by her, because you must take that special effort to be sure she knows about it . . . the simple little things, like separating the [materials] . . . and . . . instead of putting it in this spot, we're now gonna put it in [that] spot, and her not to have had that small . . . little change conveyed to her, that she would be continuing to put them in this spot because she just didn't realize that it had been changed to the other spot. Really quite simple things, because the larger things you really get in your mind that you must be sure [to tell her]. It would be the truly little day-to-day things that would get by.

Sometimes supervisors who adopted a role of mediator became teachers in the process. One supervisor said that "part of the learning curve of working with the handicap . . . was just making people more comfortable and familiar with the problem. So when you bring people around, say new people . . . [from] other areas [of the company], I introduced them, but ahead of time I tell them, 'Look at him when you talk because he does have a problem with hearing, he needs to look at your lips move.' It's worked out; he fits right in."

Supervisors were less likely to see themselves as responsible for mediating the informal dimensions of communication in the workplace, such as information sharing, that occurred through the grapevine or other social networks. However, some believed they should try to facilitate the deaf person's participation in these information networks. One supervisor said that she felt responsible to bring up to date any employee who was excluded from these kinds of communication networks, adding that this was particularly important in the case of deaf employees, since they were even more apt to be left out. Others established office procedures which helped keep deaf employees informed, as in the case of supervisors who used written "buck slips" and memos to disseminate information. Inherent in these practices was the belief that supervisors are responsible for making sure everyone in their group has equal access to all information. Yet, as one supervisor observed, this is not always easy:

> The biggest issue . . . I have to be conscious every day that I do not exclude [him] either intentionally or unintentionally in my whole management style. That I include him as full as I do anybody else, and more often than not, that means going out of my way to contact him personally and say, "Here's what's [happening] . . . That is something that's extra, I think . . . that the employer or supervisor must say, "I've got to see [him] on this and this and this today," as opposed to saying, "[He] needs to know these things, and somehow he'll find them out." As a supervisor, I need to be more specifically task oriented to actually go and do that.

Deaf employees may need assistance in learning the overall structure and goals of the organization, as well as where they fit into the structure. This knowledge includes understanding the relationships between different parts of the organization and how to access organizational resources. Below, a supervisor describes the relevance of such knowledge to the day-to-day performance of the job as well as to long range considerations such as those involving mobility and career development:

> . . . does the hearing-impaired person have an understanding of the way in which the administrative structure affects him in his relationships with other people specifically? . . . [Are there] inter-departmental teams which also link them with other parts of departments, and that becomes a bigger and bigger unit . . . I know that, understand that . . . I don't know where I got it. [Maybe] I learned it at school. I understand that I am part of a small structure in my job which is part of a bigger structure and a bigger structure and a bigger structure, and my relationship within that smaller structure has some boundaries, has some expectations, and then my relationship above that in the bigger group also depends on that smaller unit and so on. All of those boundaries and expectations are, if you wish, cultural . . . Somehow those are sort of passed along to us and we sense them . . . I don't say that [deaf employee], in a situation like that, would or would not know or be able to judge those. I'm not gonna make a judgement. What I'm saying is I can't assume that he already knows how those things happen. Does he know what team he's assigned to? [Should I ask him], "Do you know that you are part of a sub-assembly blue, and do you understand that relates to sub-assembly green in this way?" [Or should I explain to him,] "It's . . . all right for you to walk over to another machine in your area to chat while your machine is running itself . . . but really we discourage your going two departments down" . . . Again, it's sort of a vague feeling, but you can't make an assumption that [he] would necessarily

know. I don't know that a hearing person would know either, but I think that a supervisor has to go out of his way to be sensitive to it.

Third, supervisors described themselves as mediators of relationships between deaf employees and their hearing co-workers. Sometimes, this involved resolving disputes between employees; i.e., the argument over whether the radio should be played, or the situation in which a deaf employee felt co-workers were using her tools. Usually, mediation between employees involved educating both parties, explaining the perspective of each person to the other, and, in cases in which compromises could not be found, rendering a decision. In other cases, mediation was ongoing and more subtle, involving less direct intervention and more modeling on the part of the supervisor. In one case, the supervisor felt it would be wrong to force hearing co-workers to include their deaf colleague in casual conversation, but added that she often joined these conversations herself and then drew the deaf person into the group.

As the examples given illustrate, every supervisor had his or her own style and approach to mediation. What they shared is an awareness of the need for some kind of intervention and the willingness to tackle the job using diverse strategies. Sometimes mediation required flexibility in management styles. As one person put it, "I think that you have to be flexible, to change . . . to try new things . . . There's going to be changes . . . [because the deaf] person is different from everybody else in the office. No matter how much you stress the similarities, the difference is going to show. If you're too rigid, if you can't accommodate [them], there could be problems with supervision."

A dilemma faced by every supervisor who adopted the role of mediator is the question of how to preserve a balance between the philosophy that "everybody is treated the same" and meeting the special needs of a deaf employee:

> One thing I've always tried to do is try to be really clear that I'm not giving [deaf employee] special treatment. You know, I don't want to make her stick out like a sore thumb. And at the same time, I want to make sure that the others understand that she's not getting special treatment. I want them to know that they're being treated the same as she is, and she is treated the same as them. Of course, you do have to do a few special things, but I think that's really taken into consideration. I mean, I have to take more time with [her]. I have to go over my notes with her after the meeting, but I think the hearing people understand that that's because they got the stuff at the meeting, and maybe she didn't. I just feel bad because she's so left out of everything, so I try to make up for that.

In summary, mediation is a challenging role used frequently and in a variety of ways by supervisors. As reflected in the above quotation, one of the most difficult aspects of mediation is maintaining a balance between meeting the special needs of the deaf person while helping them to blend in as an equal member of the group.

Advocate

Some supervisors went beyond the role of mediator to that of advocate in their efforts to work with a deaf employee. The term advocate is used to describe the individual who takes actions that are stronger than those associated with mediation tactics. These actions include defending deaf employees in confrontations with others and fighting or laboring through an unresponsive organizational system in order to get appropriate accommodations, such as TDDs and interpreters.

Becoming an advocate requires additional energy and time, and as a result there were fewer examples of supervisors in this role than there were examples of learner and mediator. However, a surprising number of supervisors did serve as advocates for deaf people in their departments, in one way or another. The supervisor who confronted hearing workers when they teased the deaf person and talked behind her back in the coffee room is one example of the advocate role. Another example is the supervisor who vigorously pursued getting a TDD for the deaf person in her group and complained when there were delays.

Supervisors who became advocates for deaf employees often recalled the positive influence their actions had on others. In the following example a supervisor describes an incident involving another employee's reluctance to work with the deaf person:

> This week somebody came in and . . . he really asked for somebody else by name . . . which I couldn't give him because he is already on loan to somebody else, and I told him that I would give him [deaf employee], and he was a little hesitant on it and he didn't want him on the job. But, hey, that is who I am assigning to the job. That is my job, too, to put on the job who I think is the best qualified, and it is funny, he stopped me in the hall on my way home last night and he says, "Geez, I am glad you talked me into it, he is doing a fantastic job."

In the earlier discussion of mediation, it was noted that supervisor/mediators facilitated communication between deaf and hearing workers by explaining the protocols and strategies which worked best. Supervisor/

advocates went beyond explaining communication strategies to hearing co-workers; they became quite aggressive in their efforts to insure that these strategies were used. For example, in describing his approach to communication difficulties, one supervisor observed, "I will not hold back on things . . . If I see something that they are doing, that they're talking right by [deaf employee] and they're refusing to . . . make sure that he is aware that they are addressing [him], I will walk up to [hearing employees] and say, 'Look . . . when you're talking to him, make sure that you've gotten [his] attention, that he's aware.' I will use the direct approach. I feel that I can do that because that's my nature. If I feel that something is wrong . . . I won't beat around the bush about it."

Mentor

Perhaps the strongest role adopted by supervisors involved mentoring the deaf employee. Central to the mentor role is the focus by supervisors on the employee's abilities rather than disabilities. In the words of one supervisor, "You have to be very open minded in judging [a deaf worker]. Be aware of the person's problem, but judge what they have to offer and don't let their hearing impairment get in the way of particular tasks that you're asking them to do. Be aware of it, but let them explain to you what they can do or can't do . . . Go for the individual's talents and skills, not for what they don't have."

Implicit in this perspective is the belief that people are more alike than different. One supervisor, who admitted an initial fear of deaf people, emphasized the importance of focusing on similarities between people with disabilities and those who are not disabled. As she put it, "You don't want someone like I was when they [deaf employees] first came—afraid. People are afraid of deaf people. People are afraid of people who have cerebral palsy, people are afraid of people who have muscular dystrophy, because they're different. And in actuality, they only have a little handicap. They're not different. They have the same feelings that everybody else has." It is important to note that this supervisor also went to great lengths to learn sign language and get interpreters for meetings. Clearly, then, she understood that deaf people may require accommodations if they are to succeed in their jobs. Rather, her remark is more illustrative of the perspective that deaf people have the same aspirations as hearing people and should be treated with the same consideration.

The perspective that one should focus on abilities rather than disabilities and similarities rather than differences influenced supervisors' management approaches. Supervisor/mentors often took the time to work
with deaf employees on an individual basis, encouraging them to take on
new tasks and challenges, supporting them in career advancement, and
expressing pride and personal satisfaction in their employees' growth.
Sometimes this meant getting beyond initial feelings of discomfort. As
one person observed, "You can't be afraid to say, 'I am here and available
to you on a personal, real person-to-person basis,' just because all those
experiences in communication and all those kinds of things are different
and awkward." In other instances, it meant being willing to work with the
deaf person, even when it was easier to walk away. For example, when
most supervisors might shrug their shoulders and chalk up a deaf
person's behavior to lack of motivation or skill, the supervisor/mentor
would pursue the matter one step further:

> I think it's [important] . . . just recognizing their skills and their weak points
> and always dwelling on the good points and not dwelling on that he [deaf em-
> ployee] has a hearing problem. Because . . . when I first came in, he was always
> saying, "Oh, I can't do this, I can't hear." And I'd say, "Well . . . do you hear
> me talking to you?" And he'd say, "Yeah." And I'd say, "Well, you can hear." I
> try to say, sure, it is a handicap, but we can work around it, whereas a lot of
> people would say, well, he can't do this because he can't hear . . . He can pick
> up the sounds or even look at the person. He is able to communicate, and
> this is what I try to look for or to know that he has a hearing problem or
> handicap, and then work around it and not dwell on that problem . . .

In other instances, supervisor/mentors described their relationship to
the deaf employee as that of colleague and, in some cases, friend. A few
supervisors said they had invited the deaf person to lunch, seen the deaf
person outside the work environment, listened to their personal problems and offered advice, and/or expected the relationship to continue
even if the deaf person was no longer working for them.

DISCUSSION

There is something artificial about clustering the behaviors of deaf
employees and their supervisors into "roles." Yet these categories are
useful because they provide a starting point for discussing the many
possible ways in which supervisors and employees interact and the
results of these interactions. For example, some roles are interdependent.

Employees can only be successful teachers if supervisors and co-workers are willing to become learners. Mediation, on the other hand, is useful if just one person is skilled in the role (although one might imagine that when both are skilled mediators, the results are even better).

It is possible to envision both supervisor and employee roles as following a progression beginning with the relatively simple roles of teacher and learner and ending with the more sophisticated roles of entrepreneur and mentor. This is not to say that one kind of role is prerequisite for another, only that the most far reaching impact usually results from roles which are the most complex and demand the greatest amounts of time, skill, and energy. For example, mentoring is probably a more positive, involved, and strong supervisor role than mediation, and while it is possible for a supervisor who describes him- or herself as a mentor to the deaf employee to be a poor mediator, it is not likely. Similarly, the employee/entrepreneur is quite often a skilled teacher and hard worker, but the employee/teacher may not be skilled in changing roles or understanding when demonstrations of hard work will be more effective than providing information.

Running through discussions of every role is the central and unifying theme of "time," and the influence of time in facilitating accommodations and assimilation in the workplace. Interactions between deaf employees and their hearing colleagues were often described as initially stressful, but improving with time. Familiarity with a deaf person's communication style, voice tone, and inflection improved the longer the person was in the environment. Generally, work performance was seen as improving over time.

Underlying all these experiences is the notion that, over time, the initially *unusual* experience of working with a deaf person became thought of as *normal.* As one person observed, "I don't feel at this point . . . it's different than supervising anybody else, but I think that's come after the six years that I've done this work." Another supervisor, who said the deaf person in her employ had some difficulties at first but later was fully accepted and liked by everyone, was asked how this transformation had come about. She responded, "What brought about the change? I guess it's just working with her. Seeing the [clients] . . . accept her and seeing that she was good [at her job]. The other people in here . . . they probably had never known anyone who was hearing impaired, and it just took them a while to become used to her."

A central question which runs through all the chapters in this book is,

"Who is responsible for the success or failure of deaf employees?" Supervisors' discussions of strategies and qualities which facilitate working with a deaf person suggest that there is no one correct answer to this question. Sometimes they placed responsibility with the deaf employee. For example, most supervisors felt deaf employees could and should accept primary responsibility for teaching others about their deafness and its implications for accommodation and success within the workplace. This belief was grounded in the idea that deaf employees are the "experts" in this matter, have the greatest motivation to facilitate communication, must deal with it all the time, and are presumably more practiced in introducing the topic and managing the stress that often accompanies initial interactions between deaf and hearing people.

Supervisors saw themselves as having primary responsibility for insuring that deaf workers were able to function and perform satisfactorily at their jobs. Sometimes this required them to follow through on recommendations made by deaf employees regarding communication accessibility. In other cases, success depended on re-assigning work tasks or adjusting the work load in order to give an employee the chance to learn a new job. A few supervisors complained about the need to make adjustments in order to accommodate deaf workers, but most saw this as the only fair way to approach the situation. One supervisor captured this second perspective well:

> You can't give up, because you never know what degree of handicap the person has. You might tell me that you have a handicap as we're sitting here and I would not have known it, and so I'm treating you as anyone else. Just because you couldn't do the job in the beginning doesn't mean that you can't do the job. So I need to go back to the drawing board and give you the proper tools and the time to grasp what we're talking about. Maybe it's gonna take you a little bit longer, but it doesn't mean that you can't do the job, so we need to try first. You gotta give everyone a fair shake at doing the job.

Perhaps the most successful situations were those in which supervisors described responsibility as resting with *both* the deaf person and others in the work environment. Their comments support the idea that collaboration is the most productive way to accommodate and assimilate deaf persons into the workplace. For example, sometimes deaf employees were hesitant to approach supervisors with their ideas regarding communication. In these situations, supervisors needed to take the initiative. In thinking about advice he might give to other people who find themselves in the position of managing a deaf worker, one supervisor commented, "Probably one of the introductory things for a director [to do] . . . would be to put such a person at ease in terms of saying, 'Look, I'd really like your help . . . This is new to me, I don't really know how we can best communicate, and I'd really like your help. Tell me anything. Don't just let it go, 'cause we'll just waste time doing that.' "

The essence of collaboration is that each person builds constructively on the response of the other. In this way, a simple gesture on the part of one person can have a profound impact on the work environment. An illustration:

> After discussing it with [him] on how I should approach this, and after he explained to me his problem [in communication with the mechanics, he told me that] he's not worried about discussing [it] with anybody. He said, "Look, I've got a problem with those people here. I wanna be able to communicate. If they understand where I'm coming from, then maybe they'll [do better] . . . " But I know the people can be offended and they'll put up their hands and walk away, so you want it up front as quickly as he came on board . . . It just so happened within a week I had a work center meeting . . . It also gave me an opportunity to formally introduce [him] into the work area and explain his capacities . . . I mentioned that [he] was hearing impaired, and then [he] took it from there and explained what he needed . . . He says, "Is my hearing aid on?" He says, "[Then] I can hear you. If I take this off, I don't hear anything." He says, "So when I'm working at my desk, a lot of times because of noise distractions, I'll turn it off. So if you want my attention . . . wave at me, make sure you get my attention first, and I'll probably go turn on my hearing aid, and I'll look at you and we'll go at it. [If I'm] walking down the hall and you're behind me, and you want to get my attention . . . I may not hear you." So he explained the whole thing up front . . . He put it on the line so that everyone else understood what he was requiring.

This story is important, because it illustrates the power of collaboration between deaf employees and hearing supervisors. The supervisor opened a discussion of the problem and provided an opportunity for the employee to explain his communication needs to his colleagues. The fact that the supervisor turned over part of a regular meeting to this topic gave authority and status to the employee's perspective and indicated to other workers the supervisor's interest in resolving the matter. For his part, the employee let the supervisor know right away that he was prepared to openly and directly discuss his communication needs with co-workers and used the time given him during the meeting to clearly explain what should be done to facilitate communication. Neither the supervisor nor the employee would have been able to achieve this level of involvement on the part of co-workers if they had been acting alone.

In summary, analysis of supervisors' comments suggests that there are a range of positive roles that both they and deaf employees adopt at work. Generally, the most effective roles are those involving an entrepreneurial approach (on the part of the deaf employee) and mentoring (on the part of the supervisor). While employee and supervisor roles do not necessarily have to work in tandem to be effective, they are most effective when used within a collaborative relationship in which the supervisor and employee invest similar levels of commitment, interest, and effort.

COMMENTARY

SUSAN: Supervisors said they usually knew little or nothing about deafness and were completely dependent on the deaf person to inform them about what they should do. Did your supervisors know anything about deafness before they knew you? What did you have to teach them?

JANICE: I always told my supervisors that usually I can lipread them if they talk slowly and clearly, and that if this doesn't work, we would use paper and pen. I would also tell them that when I'm working with three or more hearing people, they have to hire interpreters, because this will solve the communication problems which can arise in these kinds of situations. When they talk with me one-on-one, I explain that I need face-to-face, direct visual contact.

SUSAN: Did you explain those things at the interview, or did you wait until you were hired?

JANICE: I did not use interpreters during my interview. I tended to be more independent in that regard. When I sent my resume, they would call me, and then they would find out that I am deaf. They would know because they couldn't talk to me on the phone. They would have to go through a friend of mine who would be interpreting for me. So they'd say, "Oh, okay, you're deaf. So how can I talk with you?" And my friend would tell that person, "Okay, you can write back and forth with Janice, and she's also a fantastic lip reader, so I don't think there will be any problem." So the supervisor would say, "Oh, okay, fine. I would like to set up an interview with Janice." I would start writing with them the first time I met them, and that would give them an idea of how we would communicate in the future. So, I went without an interpreter at the job interview. I think it was a good way to start.

SUSAN: So you feel if you used an interpreter at the interview, then they would not have had a realistic idea of what was going to be involved for communication later on?

JANICE: Yes, that's right. I'm not saying that I encourage all deaf employees to go to an interview without an interpreter. I think it really depends on individual preference. What's really interesting was that they did offer to get an interpreter. They asked me, "Should we contact an interpreter?" I said, "That's fine, but that will cost you." "Well, how much?" they asked. And I told them, "Well, probably $12 to $18 an hour." So it was up to them to decide whether they could afford to hire an interpreter. I let them know that if they decided not to hire an interpreter, that it would be fine with me, that I would solve the communication problem by writing. It was really up to them, but it wasn't my responsibility to pay for an interpreter. So I educated them about their responsibilities for hiring and paying for an interpreter.

SUSAN: But they decided not to hire an interpreter for the interview, right?

JANICE: At my first job interview, they did not hire an interpreter. At the interview for my second job, they did.

DAVID: I remember before I went to interview at my old job, I called and said, "I prefer to write back and forth." So we set a date, time, and so on, and I went, and we started writing. I brought some information describing my communication preferences. I had that written out. I also brought a brochure about communication between deaf and hearing people. And I explained my special needs as well. I told them, "I prefer to write back and forth, because I'm profoundly deaf." Once we started to warm up to each other, he started asking me technical questions related to my background and so on, and it went on fine. And then, after I was hired, I gave them more information about communication. For example, I gave them information about TTYs and having interpreters for meetings and so on. After that, it was smooth.

SUSAN: Okay. So you didn't tell them about all of your communication needs at the first meeting. You waited, and then you gave them more information as time went on?

DAVID: Yes. Oh, yes. You know, I just didn't want to give them all that information at our first meeting. It would be too much of a burden on them right away, and they might think, "Oh my God, to hire this man we need this, and this, and this, and this." That would be much too much pressure on them.

GARY: Because I can communicate very well one on one, I didn't think of communication as an issue. When I called to set up the appointment for the job interview, I had someone call for me and say, "This person is deaf, and they can lipread very well." That was all.

SUSAN: It's not always easy to be a teacher of other people. Did the people you worked with accept you as their teacher?

JANICE: Oh, yes. When I started working, I talked about how they could learn sign language, and they said, "Oh, would you mind teaching us?" So I set up a sign language class at lunch hour to teach them. You know, I had to act in a couple of roles. I had to be a sign language teacher, to solve the communication problem, plus I had to learn my own job. So I had more responsibilities than a hearing person, when I started my job.

DAVID: I think the deaf person is responsible to educate co-workers about the communication needs of deaf people, and about Deaf culture. I don't want them to get the wrong information or have the wrong idea. You know, hearing people don't know about deafness, and they might get their information from sources other than the deaf person, from friends or whatever. I thought it would be easier and better if they got it from me.

GARY: In past jobs, the only thing I felt responsible for is to explain about my own communication needs. I didn't really explain about Deaf culture and sign language. I communicated much, much, too orally to think about explaining those things. But I'd like to add that I believe now that it's very important for deaf people to accept responsibility for teaching hearing people about communication and Deaf culture, so they can become aware of and sensitive to it. For example, imagine that a hearing person is sitting in an office, and the deaf person is there, too. If the deaf person makes some sort of a noise or is loud, the hearing person might think they're rude, but that's not the way it is in Deaf culture. Deaf people may not know that in hearing culture it is considered rude to make a certain noise or be loud. Hearing people have to learn about Deaf culture and be told about all the differences and misunderstandings that can happen. I mean, one thing that happens really often is people think the best way to communicate with a deaf person is to talk a lot louder. That happened to me.

DAVID: Before I started the job, I said to my hearing co-workers, "If I'm ever not polite to you, or I seem very rude, please let me know. I grew up in a deaf world, and I have no idea what is rude in hearing culture." For example, when I get a plate from the cabinet, I open the door, grab the plate, put the plate down, and *slam* the door shut. Or, when I walk, sometimes I shuffle my feet as opposed to setting them down quietly; that makes a lot of noise, but I'm not aware of it. So I tell people, "If I do anything that could be construed as rude or impolite, please tell me, because I need to respect your culture just as you respect my culture, and I may not be aware that what I'm doing is rude." I want to get along in the hearing culture. Also, I want to know what my hearing co-workers are thinking, rather than going along and not knowing and have them look askance at me.

SUSAN: So, did they ever tell you, "Hey, you're dragging your feet?"

DAVID: Oh, yes. Also, when I'm mad I pound the table. (Of course, when they are mad, they yell and swear.) But I pound the table really loud, and it would make a noise, and everyone would look at me. I remember, one time my wife and I went to a restaurant, and we were sitting there eating our dinner, and I was chewing my food. I was eating my usual way, and we noticed that everyone was looking at us. My wife saw how I was eating, and she said, "Please close your mouth." I said, "Why?" And she said, "Well, 'cause you're making noise, and all the hearing people are staring at you."

GARY: You know that we deaf people make noises all of our lives, and everyone stares at us, but what people don't realize is that often, we don't know why they're staring at us.

SUSAN: Janice, did you ever have any experiences like that?

JANICE: I grew up with deaf parents, but I visited my hearing uncle and cousin. Every weekend we would go visit them, and they would always say, "Janice, stop smacking your lips," and say all these things about my manners. Then, when I went home, I was very confused, because I didn't know what was right and what was wrong. My parents never criticized me for smacking my lips or making too much noise 'cause they couldn't hear what I was doing, and neither could I. You know, I thought my hearing relatives were mean. When I got home I would tell my mother, "Oh, my cousin's mean, she criticizes me all the time." My mother said, "Well, now dear, that's what hearing people do. They can hear what you're doing, and you can't." So that's the way I learned about manners. That started when I was about eight years old. Before that, I didn't know.

DAVID: See, I grew up in a deaf world. I went to a residential school for the deaf, a deaf church, and lived in a deaf community, everything.

JANICE: I had exposure to hearing people.

GARY: You know, what I love to do is chew on ice, "Crunch, crunch."

DAVID: Yes, I have that habit myself, and sometimes I make noise and I ask my hearing colleagues, "Do I make noise or not?" Of course, I can do anything at home. It doesn't matter there.

JANICE: One habit I have is I tend to tap a pen on a table or other surface, "Tap, tap, tap." I just do it. It makes a constant noise, and people often tell me to stop.

GARY: What I do is jiggle my leg or tap my foot on the floor constantly.

SUSAN: Hearing people often have the habits of putting their hand in front of their face or looking around when they're talking. Did you ever get people to the point where they'd remember *not* to do those things when they were talking with you?

JANICE: I always have to remind people about that. I feel it's very rude of them. When I was working, sometimes my co-workers would turn away and not look at me when they were speaking, and I'd say, "I can't read your lips. Can you please look at me?" And they'd say, "Oh, Janice, we don't even notice that you're deaf anymore." You know, after a little while they forgot that I am deaf, and that's why I had to keep reminding them. They didn't mean to look away, but they did.

SUSAN: It's one thing for deaf people to try to teach supervisors about communication needs and deafness, but supervisors don't always do what you ask them to do. Now, the ADA, Americans with Disabilities Act, will put in place some legal requirements regarding accommodations. I'm wondering, could you ever see yourself using the ADA to get necessary accommodations at work? Would you tell an employer, "You have to get me an interpreter because it's the law"? Or, "It's my legal right to have a TTY in my job and have access to the telephone. You better get one, or I might sue you." Do you think deaf people will do that?

JANICE: I think the law can be used to educate grassroots deaf people, who are not familiar with ADA. But we're educated deaf people, and I would say that we wouldn't use that as a tool to get what we need.

GARY: Okay, yes. I understand what you're saying, Janice, but my question is, "Who would tend to say those things to an employer?"

JANICE: Grassroots deaf people.

GARY: No, I don't think so. People have come up to me and said, "Well, I told my boss that ADA says you must do this and this and this." And the boss has said, "Well, what does ADA tell me? What should I be aware of?" So, I think you need to be careful. You need to know the law. The law doesn't say you have to provide interpreters. The law encourages people to make reasonable accommodations. Suppose the company is going through some financial problems. How should that situation be handled? The law says you are encouraged to provide support if you are in good financial standing.

JANICE: I've been in that situation. The second company I worked for had financial problems. They couldn't afford to provide some things for me, and I understood, because I knew it was because of their financial situation. You know, I had to accept their limitations.

GARY: The question is whether it causes undue hardship for the company to provide the support. If it does, maybe they can't be required to provide it. You know, this is not a ten cent thing, getting interpreters and so on. Of course we have to educate people about ADA, but I think we need to do it when the time is right, and use good judgment. We can't always say, "Well, that's the law, and you need to do this." Recently, I have been learning about many companies that want to know what they can do to fulfill the reasonable accommodation statute of the ADA. There are pressures there. It's not because they have to, not because they want to, but because the number of available "traditional" employees is dwindling. The trend now is to hire more multi-handicapped people or people from different cultural, ethnic, and racial backgrounds. In the future, there will be more blacks, Hispanics, and women in the work force. The white male employee will be the minority.

DAVID: It won't work if a deaf person says, "If you don't provide this service to me, I'm going to sue you." I think that just ruins the relationship between the deaf person and their hearing employer. I think you have to educate the employer first, and then you can follow through. And it has to be approached with the right attitude.

SUSAN: One of the themes that emerged from discussions with supervisors was the deaf person as a "super-employee." Supervisors said these people work harder than hearing people. They take the initiative. They teach others. They go to social events even when they have a hard time following conversations, and they always go beyond the expectations. Do you think that this is true?

JANICE: Yes, because of communication barriers, we do more work. You know, we don't hear what's going on. That really helps us to concentrate on our business.

DAVID: My sister-in-law's deaf. She's one of the best examples of a "super-employee." She has no college degree. She works for a government agency, and she's very skilled at bridging the communication gap between hearing and deaf people. At this one place, they have a lot of deaf employees, but there are no leaders to bridge that gap. So over the years, my sister-in-law has become that bridge. She would find out the communication needs of the deaf workers, whether they use speech or writing or American Sign Language. Then she would get the employer to provide interpreters or other accommodations for them, which helped the deaf people to be more productive. She got an award for being that bridge between deaf and hearing workers.

GARY: I think it's a very common thing for deaf employees to be "super-employees." Employers take advantage of those deaf employees, because they often get the job done faster than other people in the department. That can become a problem related to promotion. I mean, if their production equals that of three other people, then the company doesn't want those people to move up. They want them to stay right in that level. That happens to a lot of deaf employees.

DAVID: Yes. I'm one of them. I work really hard, and I do the work of two or three or four technicians. The small company where I worked before depended a lot on sales. So when the sales went down, they would lay off people, and when the sales went up, they would hire those people back. I didn't want to be laid off. I wanted job security. I did as much as two or three technicians. I was never laid off when times were bad for the company.

JANICE: You know, I've noticed that a lot of my hearing co-workers talked, and they didn't do as much work as me. I really don't think that's fair.

SUSAN: What about the roles that supervisors can adopt? How did the roles discussed in the chapter fit with your supervisors in past jobs?

GARY: My supervisor was a mentor. I guess that was really the nature of the business that I was in. When you go into sales, you have to have some sort of mentor, and my supervisor mentored me. He taught me everything he knew about the business, like how to talk to people, how to relate with people, when to jump in on a sale, and when to give up. In the beginning, he went on sales calls with me. That's the way he works with everyone, but my mentor happened to be someone that I related with very well. We communicated very well. There was no hidden agenda between us.

SUSAN: Was he assigned to you, or did you pick him because you felt you could communicate well with him?

GARY: He was assigned. I was really lucky, because I had two great supervisors. They have become great friends of mine since that time.

JANICE: With the exception of my first job, my supervisors were more learners. They didn't know anything about deafness, so I taught them. As far as learning my job went, they would send me to work with a consultant. You know, they would call the consultant, and the consultant would come to work with me. So they rarely worked directly with me. On my first job, it was different. My supervisor there was more of a learner *and* a mentor. I taught her about deafness, and I also learned from her how to do programming.

SUSAN: David, how would you characterize your supervisors?

DAVID: I'd say mostly they were learners, because they weren't really directly involved in my department's work. They didn't know my area very well, either. They didn't know about electronics and so on. I wouldn't consider my supervisors mediators; I don't see how anyone could do that for me, because they don't know about deafness and communication with deaf people.

SUSAN: Did anybody show you the ropes so you could get ahead?

DAVID: Yes. There was this one co-worker, who worked with me. We worked right next to each other. He became my mentor, because he was skilled in sign language. I taught him sign language, so he would know how to communicate with me. But I should add that my supervisor did become involved in the Curriculum Advisory Group at NTID. So, maybe because of me, he became interested in deafness.

SUSAN: I wanted to just finish up by asking you what you think is the most important kind of role for a supervisor to have if they are working with a deaf person.

GARY: Mentor.

JANICE: Mediator. But it's nice if the supervisor is already knowledgeable about deafness.

DAVID: A mentor would be nice. I don't think that anyone can possibly take on the role of being an advocate for the deaf person or mediate between deaf and hearing people, because they don't know what the deaf world is like. They're in the hearing world. How can they be a mediator for me? I don't think that would work.

SUSAN: We're at the end of our last discussion. Is there any final advice you want to give supervisors or deaf employees?

GARY: Yes. When I call to set up appointments for job interviews for my students, some companies ask if they should provide an interpreter, while others say nothing about it. I teach my students, "If you want an interpreter, you've got to set it up yourself." The second point I want to emphasize is that awareness and sensitivity about deaf people has improved over the years. I mean, if we were sitting here talking about this topic fifty years ago, our discussion would be very different. I'm seeing more and more companies becoming aware of deafness. More agencies out there are educating people about deafness. Deaf people are coming out of the closet, and they're showing that they can do the job.

JANICE: I think basically that started from the movement to install a deaf president at Gallaudet University. Before that, no one knew what a deaf person could do.

GARY: I think it's more a recognition on the part of employers that the multi-handicapped, ethnically diverse population is growing, with a corresponding decrease in the white, Anglo-Saxon Protestant, "WASP" group. Because, I'll be honest with you, I've asked people, "Are you familiar with the Gallaudet University movement?" Some said, "No." Some said, "Yes." So I think it's had some impact, but it has not been the major impact.

JANICE: Maybe it's had the greatest impact in the Washington, D.C., area and in satellite companies of D.C. based firms.

GARY: You know I work for NCED. One of our functions is to train employers about how to work with deaf people. We give workshops in different cities. This year the number of people attending our workshops has increased. Many of the participants want to know how to interview deaf employees. But that's only the beginning. What's going to happen down the road is that employers will start to ask us, "What reasonable accommodations can we make for our deaf employees, and how can we retrain them?" Many companies now have what we call an "office for the handicapped."

DAVID: This book is about the deaf person's role in working in America. I think, living in this country, we have so many opportunities out there today for deaf employees. Rather than just working in factory type jobs, we're now getting more and more opportunities. I don't think we should take it for granted, and I want to thank the hearing supervisors for helping to make it possible.

RESOURCE LIST

Library Resources

Books and articles listed in this section should be available at local public or college/university libraries or through the interlibrary loan services at these libraries. Purchase prices listed may vary and are indicated only to give the reader a general idea of cost; contact the publisher directly for current cost and shipping/handling charges.

Bowe, F. *Changing the Rules.* Silver Spring, MD: T. J. Publishers, 1986. (Available from T.J. Publishers, 817 Silver Spring Avenue, (206), Silver Spring, MD 20910; Phone 800-999-1168 [V/TDD]; ISBN 0-932666-31-0 cloth copy, 0-932666-30-2 paper copy; Cost: $15.95 cloth copy, $14.95 paper copy)

> *Changing the Rules* is a personal account of a struggle against a disability — deafness. It is also an insider's account of the civil rights revolution that changed the rules and improved the quality of life for people with disabilities, and it provides a positive approach to accommodation.

Knight, J. "The Employer's Expectations From the Job Applicant." *Worklife: A Publication on Employment and Persons With Disabilities,* 1(3), 13–14, 1988.

> Recent legislation regarding affirmative action policies in business and industry should equalize all qualified individuals being considered for employment. The author discusses what this means to an individual with a disability.

Life and Work in the 21st Century: The Deaf Person of Tomorrow; Proceedings of the 1986 NAD Forum. Silver Spring, MD: National Association of the Deaf, 1986. (Available from the National Association for the Deaf, 814 Thayer Avenue, Silver Spring, MD 20910; Phone 301-587-6282 [V/TDD]; Order no. RS002; Cost: $14.95)

> This work examines new advances in family, community, communication technologies, education, and employment. Employment articles look at strategies for career growth and advancement, a model for deaf employment services (Deaf Self-Help, Inc.), training for church related services, career development approaches, and the National Academy Management Series: Supplementary Skills for Managers of Disabled Employees.

Veatch, D. *How to Get the Job You Really Want.* Silver Spring, MD: National Association of the Deaf, 1982. (Available from National Association of the Deaf, 814 Thayer Avenue, Silver Spring, MD 20910; Phone 301-587-6282 [V/TDD]; Cost: $10)

> Written specifically for hearing-impaired people who are preparing to enter

the job market, seek promotions, or change careers, this workbook covers the job-search process, resume development, employment letters, sources of employment, job application, and employment interviewing.

Pamphlets and Brochures

Bell, R. *Polaroid: A Look at its Hearing Impaired Members.* 1981. (Unpublished manuscript available from Polaroid Corporation, 575 Technology Square, Cambridge, MA 02139; Phone 617-577-4200 [Voice]; Cost: free)

> Bell's survey of hearing-impaired workers at Polaroid indicates the amount of communication necessary on the job, the effects of having TDDs, the use of interpreters, and safety measures.

Media

We Know It Can Be Done [video]. (Available from Captioned Films for the Deaf, Modern Talking Picture Service, Inc., 5000 Park Street North, St. Petersburg, FL 33709-9989; Phone 800-237-4599 [Voice]; Cost $50*)

> Bonnie Tucker, lawyer, and Phil Bravin, IBM manager, explain attitudes and barriers that hindered them in education and employment. They also discuss factors related to their success as deaf professionals.

> *Also available on free loan/review basis, in the United States, if an employer has an account number with Modern Talking Picture Service. Call the 800 phone number to set up a borrowing account.

Contacts

Closing the Gap
P.O. Box 68
Henderson, MN 56044
612-248-3294 (Voice)

> Closing the Gap sponsors an annual conference which has earned an international reputation as a leading source of information on innovative applications of microcomputer technology for disabled people.

Job Accommodation Network
West Virginia University
809 Allen Hall
P.O. Box 6123
Morgantown, WV 26505-6123

800-526-7234 (TDD and Voice)
800-526-4698 (in West Virginia)

Project JAN is a computerized information service which stores accommodation experiences submitted by employers for job placement personnel, employers, and disabled people. Information includes how accommodations were made for disabled persons, what costs were involved, and the availability of assistive devices.

National Center for Law and the Deaf
Ely Center, Room 326
800 Florida Avenue NE
Washington, DC 20002-3695
202-447-0445 (TDD and Voice)

This center provides and develops legal representation, information and services, legal counseling, education, and advocacy for deaf persons. It would be an excellent source of information about compliance with legislation on employment of deaf persons.

National Center on Employment of the Deaf
National Technical Institute for the Deaf
Rochester Institute of Technology
P.O. Box 9887
Rochester, NY 14623-0887
716-475-6219 (TDD and Voice)

NCED was established to promote successful employment of RIT's deaf students and graduates. To facilitate employment opportunities, NCED has developed workshops for human resource personnel, trainers, and supervisors of deaf employees. "Working Together: Deaf and Hearing People" is an interactive program with candid interchange regarding employment of deaf people. Topics include communication, job accommodation, understanding deafness, and sensitivity training and experiences. "Train the Trainer" is a training program designed to train and certify in-house trainers or other appropriate personnel to present the "Working Together" program.

Chapter 7

PUTTING IT ALL TOGETHER

He was the first deaf person I'd ever worked with . . . I guess really all you can do is try to put yourself in their position, try to think how you would react if you were them. (Excerpt from interview with hearing supervisor of deaf employee)

A lot of territory has been covered in the last six chapters. The supervisors have given quite a bit of thought and consideration to the topic of working with a deaf employee, and it is possible to learn both from their successes and from their mistakes. The experiences and opinions of the deaf discussants lend a balance to supervisors' perspectives, sometimes confirming ideas suggested by the latter, at other times shedding a completely new light on the situation. The resource sections are not exhaustive, nor do they provide answers to every question. However, it is likely that they will be a starting point for most of the common questions and concerns regarding interactions between deaf and hearing people in the workplace.

What, then, can be given by way of a conclusion to this book? First, the information derived from interviews with supervisors should be placed within the broader frameworks of scope and depth. Put another way, to what extent should readers generalize from the experiences of twenty supervisors and three deaf professionals to the experiences of all supervisors of deaf employees, and how likely is it that supervisors were being honest in describing their situations? Were they, as a group, biased one way or another towards their deaf employees, and if so, how should this shape the ways in which readers interpret supervisors' comments?

Second, there needs to be some exploration and discussion of those central themes and conclusions which can be drawn from the experiences of the supervisors and deaf discussants. Given the information which was collected and presented, what might supervisors want to consider when working with a deaf person? What might deaf people want to consider as they move into employment situations where they are the only deaf person? Are there guiding principles or ways of approaching problems, should they arise?

In the following pages, each of these topics is addressed. The chapter is concluded with a Resource List which focuses on the areas of general accommodations for deaf employees and the Americans with Disabilities Act.

INTERPRETING THE INFORMATION COLLECTED FROM SUPERVISORS AND DEAF DISCUSSANTS

There are several ways to interpret the data presented in this book. First, it is important to emphasize that these are the impressions and experiences of twenty supervisors, not two hundred or two thousand. Certainly, if there were more supervisors in the study, the findings would be more representative of all supervisors of deaf people across the country.

This brings us to a traditional dilemma in the selection of one kind of research design over another—the question of scope versus depth. It would be possible to survey two hundred or two thousand supervisors about their day-to-day experiences working with deaf employees, but, as noted in the *Preface,* this is unlikely to yield the kinds of data required for analysis of such a topic. Surveys are ideally suited to the collection of quantitative data, such as participation in the labor force, salary, or mobility; they are less effective when gathering sensitive information about interactions between people, the challenges associated with supervising a deaf person, or reflections about what strategies are most successful in overcoming communication barriers. Employers are generally very cautious about describing problems with any employee on paper, especially when the person is in a protected class.[1] Moreover, surveys generally do not permit the interactive questioning which is often required to learn how a person works through a difficult situation over time.

Qualitative research methods, including the open ended, in depth interview strategy used for this project, yield detailed descriptive data. Yet, they are very labor intensive and are therefore generally restricted to a relatively small number of participants or cases. At one and a half to two hours per interview, yielding approximately fifty pages per transcript for analysis, one can easily understand why a sample of two hundred or two thousand would be unrealistic for even the most ambitious qualitative researcher.

The trade-off is, therefore, often one of scope versus depth, with the decision in this case being made in favor of the latter. The reader should interpret this to mean that, while the experiences of the supervisors interviewed for this project cannot be assumed to represent all supervisors, their responses are detailed and probably accurately reflect their opinions and experience in working with a deaf employee.

Given that the group of supervisors interviewed cannot be assumed to represent all supervisors of deaf employees, can we speculate as to how they might be different? Perhaps the most significant factor is that all the deaf employees who were the focus of discussion are graduates of postsecondary educational programs; as a result, they are among the best educated deaf people in the work force. What kinds of issues would have come up if supervisors of employees who did not go beyond a high school degree had been interviewed? One might argue that the central theme of communication would be the same no matter what the education level of the deaf person, or that the experience of postsecondary training produces deaf employees who are more sophisticated and skilled in meeting the challenges of communication in the workplace. On the other hand, there may be greater emphasis on communication in professional jobs than in blue collar work and therefore more pressure on deaf professionals to interact with hearing colleagues. Until studies are done which compare the experiences of deaf people with different educational backgrounds and kinds of jobs, it is best to say that the supervisors in this study reflect the experience of working with deaf college graduates.

Other questions concern whether the experiences of these supervisors are typical of all supervisors working with college educated deaf people. For example, are their experiences likely to be better or worse than most? As a group, are they likely to be less or more aware of issues in deafness, sensitive to deaf people, and willing to make accommodations? Given the specific circumstances of this group of supervisors, it is probably fair to say that their experiences may be somewhat more positive, and their awareness, sensitivity, and willingness to make accommodations somewhat greater than might be found in a more widely representative group.

There are two reasons for assuming a positive bias. First, the supervisors all live and work in the greater Rochester area and surrounding communities. The presence of NTID and the higher than average percentage of deaf people in the Rochester area have probably made this community one of heightened awareness and sensitivity. Second, only those supervisors whose deaf employees gave written permission were contacted for an interview. It is likely that the employees who gave permission felt their relationship with their supervisor was satisfactory; those experiencing serious problems would be much less likely to permit the interview.

All of this suggests that the supervisors interviewed may represent a perspective which is more positive than the norm. The problems they describe are probably the same in kind, but possibly less severe, than those experienced by supervisors of college educated deaf people in general, due, in large part, to heightened awareness and sensitivity on the part of the supervisors and the selection process used. Other supervisors may experience more, or other kinds of, challenges in their experiences with deaf employees.

The deaf discussants are all graduates of postsecondary educational programs who have worked in one or more professional positions. Their role in this book is one of reflection and discourse concerning their own work experiences and the perspectives expressed by supervisors. They were not picked with the goal of developing a representative sample of deaf people. However, care was taken to include people who reflect a range of perspectives as a result of differences related to gender, education, communication, and work experience. For example, one person is female, the other two, male. One person attended a separate school for the deaf prior to college, one attended a mainstream program but went to special classes, and the third was fully mainstreamed. One person in the group does not use his voice at all, while the others do. Their employment experiences include electro-mechanical technology, computer programming, sales, and employment counselling. This variety increases the chances of having greater diversity of perspectives than one might get with a group of people whose characteristics and experiences are more similar. But their experiences cannot be assumed to be typical of all deaf people.

Having said this, what are some of the central ideas that can be drawn from the data? How can the information be used by those who wish to improve the employment experiences of deaf people and those who work with them? In the concluding pages of this chapter, an ecological model of the workplace is developed and used as a vehicle for analyzing and increasing accessibility and accommodation for deaf employees.

THE ECOLOGY OF THE WORKPLACE

In order to understand the employment experiences of deaf employees and those who supervise or work with them, it is necessary to describe both the individual(s) and the environment(s) of the workplace and the ways in which they interact to produce a particular situation or result. For example, the deaf person may be unable to use the telephone without assistive devices. An analysis which takes into account only the characteristics of the deaf person must lead to the conclusion that the person is unable to use the phone *because he or she is deaf* (e.g., the problem is due to a deficiency of the individual). Analysis of the environment, on the other hand, reveals the problem to be *lack of a TDD, electronic mail system, or other assistive or alternative device* (e.g., the problem is due to a deficiency in the environment). Similarly, the deaf person who works in a department which relies heavily on written memoranda may be viewed as well informed and "connected" to office news, while someone who works in a setting which depends more heavily on the office grapevine is perceived as a loner, disconnected, even disinterested.

One way of thinking about variations in ways of interacting, communicating, and general orientation (i.e., visual as opposed to aural) is to consider them *differences,* rather than *deficiencies.* The ways in which people respond to these differences determine whether they will remain differences or become barriers. This is where an analysis of the ecology of the workplace may prove fruitful.

An ecological model of human behavior can be used to illustrate and discuss interaction between individual employees (deaf or hearing) and the environment(s) of the workplace. Briefly, this model is grounded in the idea that in order to understand or explain the behavior of the individual, one must perceive that individual as existing within larger groups, institutions, and social systems, each of which interacts with and therefore influences (and is influenced by) the individual and other systems (Bronfenbrenner, 1979). This "nesting" or location of the individual within one or more systems is perhaps best conceptualized as a series of concentric circles (or other shapes), with the individual represented at the center of the circle(s). Systems can also overlap, in which case the representation would include two or more sets of concentric circles which intersect or touch at some point.

There is no single or "universal" ecological diagram of the workplace, since each diagram reflects the characteristics of the specific individuals and environments in its form and definition. However, in describing the ecology of a work environment, one would include environments internal to the organization (such as departments, divisions, and branches) and environments external to the organization (such as type of industry, the social and political context, and, possibly, factors related to the international economy). Such a diagram is useful not only for understanding the relationship between the individual and the surrounding environment(s), but also for developing a blueprint for accommodation.

BLUEPRINT FOR ACCOMMODATION

The ecological model can be used as a vehicle for analyzing specific situations within the workplace and for developing a plan for change. Application of such a model involves five steps; each step is analyzed separately.

Step One: Describing the Ecology of the Workplace

The first step is to describe the ecology of the workplace and where the deaf person (and those with whom he or she works) fits within it. As noted earlier, there is no universal ecological diagram. For now, let's apply the concept to a computer software company, which we'll call New Age Software[2]. The company employs approximately five hundred people, with a national as well as local clientele. The deaf person (let's call him Mark) works for the Design Team in the Department of Business Applications. The team leader and Mark's supervisor (let's call her Nancy) never met a deaf person until Mark was transferred to her team eight months ago.

Imagine a series of shaded areas of increasing size, in which larger areas enclose the smaller ones (see Figure 1). The area around Mark represents the Design Team. Other individuals, such as Nancy and the rest of the Design Team, are also points within this area. They may be clustered, as in the case of social or working sub-groups, or they may be evenly spaced, but they all work within the area representing the team. The next area is the Department of Business Applications, which also includes smaller clusters representing other teams (Product Evaluation and Quality Control). Next comes the area which represents the Division for Product Development, including clusters indicating the other two departments within this division (Entertainment, Education). The Division for Product Development is surrounded by an area symbolizing New Age Software, with clusters representing the other three divisions within the company (Production, Marketing/Sales, Finance).

There are also environments external to New Age Software which must be considered in an ecological analysis. These environments can be symbolized as a series of concentric circles. For example, New Age Software is just one of many companies in the computer software industry, and beyond that are circles reflecting the larger environments of manufacturing industries and the American workplace. All of these must be understood within the context of American society, including political, legal, economic, and social environments (such as the Americans with Disabilities Act, economic boom or recession, social values and norms). Lastly, there is the international dimension, including the global economy, political structures, and shifting social conditions within different parts of the world.

The model represented by Figure 1 provides frameworks for understanding and analyzing the role of deaf employees within the organization and the ways in which internal as well as external forces shape the experience of both the organization and the individual. For example, economic recession will almost certainly affect the job stability of many employees in the software industry, including Mark. However, if New Age Software feels that product design is critical for their survival in a rocky market, then Mark's job may be much more secure than someone working in production or sales. As Mark and Nancy develop a plan for improved accommodation for Mark, this model will provide a map, or reference point, for locating and analyzing the challenges which they must overcome, as well as Mark's current and future potential within New World Software.

Step Two: Taking Inventory

Once the workplace has been described in these general ecological terms, different layers of the model can be analyzed separately. Within the organization, analysis should include both the characteristics of the individual and of the environment. The purpose of this analysis is to describe those individuals and environments critical to successful accommodation of the deaf employee and to identify relevant barriers, opportunities, and resources.

Figure 1: An Ecological Diagram of New Age Software

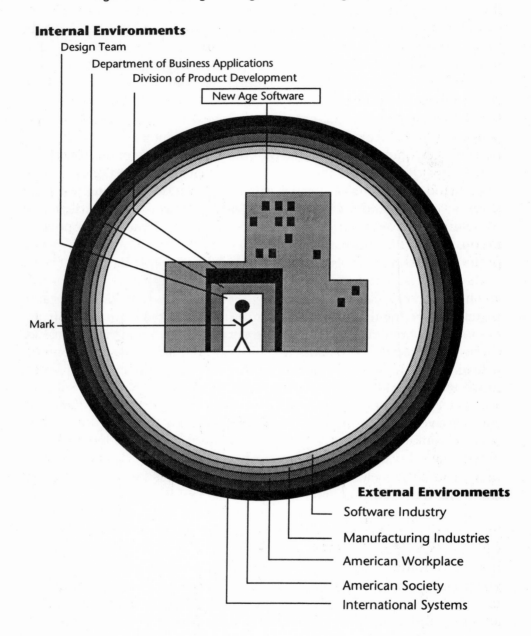

Analysis of individuals in the work setting under study should address the following characteristics: skills (technical, personal/social), communication preferences and abilities (language(s) and mode(s)), attitudes (towards deaf and/or hearing people), personal history (especially as it bears on prior experience with deaf or hearing people), career goals, and personality. These categories can then be used to construct a profile of each individual in the working group, team, or department. It is important to include both the deaf employee and others (co-workers, supervisor, people who work in other areas but have frequent contact with the deaf person) in this analysis.

Analysis of the environments internal to the organization should include the physical settings in which the deaf person works, the relationships between teams and departments, and the fiscal health and general resources of the organization. Company policies would also be important to consider, especially as they address issues relative to special groups or protected classes of employees.

Of critical importance is assessment of management's position towards accommodation and access for employees with disabilities. The workplace is not a democracy, nor is it an environment in which individuals are motivated *primarily* by the principles of fairness or equality. Little or no change will occur without the support, both financial and political, of management. Resource allocation, endorsement for participation in accommodation efforts, and the association of sanctions with failure to comply are just a few examples of ways in which management can facilitate constructive intervention and change.

An inventory of external environments should include a description of the general health of and trends within the industry. It may also take into account the social values of the larger culture, as well as the political climate and overall economy.

At New Age Software, for example, our inventory reveals that Mark has high technical skills and is adept at using humor in breaking the ice with co-workers. Although he uses his voice and has some ability to read lips, he communicates most fluently and comfortably through sign language and written notes. He is very ambitious and hopes to be promoted to team leader some day. His co-workers like him, but tend to avoid him at lunch and break times because of the difficulties and frustrations which often accompany communication with Mark. They acknowledge Mark's technical skill, but feel that differences in communication modes and languages make it difficult for him to assume a leadership role on the team.

Nancy feels much the same way as the co-workers but, in addition, acknowledges frustration at the dilemma regarding Mark's desire for promotion. She knows that unless Mark feels he is making progress towards promotion, he will become increasingly dissatisfied with his job and less inclined to stay at New Age Software. Since he is very talented, this would be a serious loss for the company. Moreover, Nancy has felt pressure in the past from the Personnel Department to make sure Mark does not leave or have a serious cause for grievance with the company.

The physical environment of Mark's department does not facilitate his involvement in collegial interactions. Individual work stations within the Department of Business Applications are separated by seven-foot partitions. While this is intended to provide privacy for employees, it has served to effectively isolate Mark from others on his team. It has become routine practice for people to call out questions and ideas, but in order to include Mark, they must get up and walk to his desk. Most often, this is just too much effort. As a result, Mark has more than once complained to Nancy that he is left out of this informal but critical creative loop.

Although the state in which New Age Software is located has a free state-wide telephone relay service, Mark does not have a TDD at work. As a result, he cannot make or accept calls from other departments or clients. Currently, his job description has been rewritten to exclude phone work and his responsibilities in this area assigned to co-workers. A general recession within the software industry has reduced the overall profits of New Age Software in recent years and therefore the amount of flexible budget within individual departments and teams. Nancy does not feel she can afford to purchase a TDD this year, nor can she hire an interpreter for team or department meetings, as Mark has requested.

The Americans with Disabilities Act (ADA) has been discussed recently at several meetings of upper management. Specifically, managers want to know possible implications of the ADA for New Age Software. Mark is not the only employee who is classified as disabled, and the company recognizes that it must comply with the requirements of this law. Will New Age Software be required to purchase TDDs for Mark and all the other departments with which he has frequent contact? What about interpreters for meetings? The decision is made to ask the company attorney to study the regulations and make recommendations about how New Age Software should respond.

Step Three: Writing a Prescription for Accommodation

After completing the ecological model and taking inventory of the individuals and environments relevant to the situation, the supervisor and deaf employee sit down to review what has been done so far and develop a prescription for accommodation. Each develops a separate "wish list," that is, a description of the ideal work environment and how to achieve it, including modifications in the physical setting, resources necessary, and even changes in company policy or the attitudes and skills of the deaf person and others with whom he or she works. Constraints on implementing changes and achieving environmental goals are put on hold at this point, since the purpose of the activity is to describe the ideal, or best possible, situation. Then the supervisor and employee compare lists and discuss similarities and differences.

Both Nancy and Mark want to buy a TDD for Mark, but Mark has additionally requested a flasher for his desk lamp which can be adapted to let him know when his phone rings. Nancy feels that with one TDD, Mark can contact any department within the company by going through the state relay service. Mark, however, feels that he should be able to call any department within the company directly, arguing that it is time consuming to go through the relay service. He therefore wants TDDs for everyone with whom he might need to have phone contact.

Both want interpreters for meetings, but Nancy feels that in an ideal environment there would be an interpreter present all the time to facilitate any conversation between Mark and others, even those which are casual or unrelated to work tasks. Mark feels it would be better if everyone on his team learned sign language. He says that he is tired of always adapting to them and wants them to make the effort to learn his language. He adds that it would be easier for him to develop friendships with co-workers and join in their casual conversations if they could sign with him. He advises that interpreters be hired only for meetings, inservice training programs, and possibly for critical sessions between him and Nancy. He also feels that co-workers, including Nancy, are generally lacking in information about deafness and could benefit from attending a series of seminars on this topic, offered by a local university.

Nancy wants to move to a new, larger office space, get rid of the partitions, and purchase work stations which can be arranged in ways that facilitate visual contact between people. Mark addresses problems associated with the partitions by asking that co-workers either be forbidden to discuss important creative points except at interpreted meetings, or required to include him in these conversations.

Mark and Nancy then bring these lists to a team meeting, in order to collect feedback from co-workers. They find that team members are generally supportive of most of their ideas. They fully endorse the idea of purchasing TDDs and hiring interpreters. One person suggests using electronic mail as an alternative to phone communication. He points out that, while they have never explored this possibility before, the company's computer system has this capacity. They are skeptical about their ability to learn sign language well enough to include Mark in all conversations. Nonetheless, they are willing to attend sign classes and seminars on deafness, provided they cost nothing and do not cut into their free time (i.e., lunch or breaks). Co-workers are most resistant to a policy which would restrict discussion of ideas to interpreted meetings, arguing that this would seriously interfere with the natural and spontaneous creative thinking which is critical to their work.

Next, Nancy and Mark meet with management at the department, division, and corporate levels to share their ideas and discuss available resources. While she can require changes in the behavior of her staff, Nancy is powerless to purchase new equipment or services or effect changes in the behaviors of employees in other departments, without the cooperation and support of management. Both she and Mark recognize that, in order to develop and implement a workable plan, they must involve management early on.

By now, management has been advised that, as a company with more than twenty-five employees, New Age Software is expected to comply with ADA as of July 26, 1992. While they are not expected to accept lower standards of work performance from an employee with disabilities than they would from a non-disabled employee, they are required to consider and offer alternative means of obtaining necessary information or demonstrating ability. However, the company may be excused from making expensive accommodations if it can be proven that to do so will cause "undue hardship," that is, the action would require significant difficulty or expense. A recently completed market analysis predicts little or no growth in New Age Software sales this year, but some improvement over the next two to five years. Given these circumstances, the executive directors ask Nancy and Mark to develop a plan for insuring Mark's accommodation, but caution them that it may not be possible to implement every suggestion.

Nancy and Mark counter with the proposition that the time is right for taking company-wide action regarding accommodation and access for all employees with disabilities. They suggest that a task force be established to address these issues. Management agrees, and the Accommodation Task Force is established. The task force is given the responsibility of working with disabled employees and their supervisors to insure that reasonable accommodation plans are developed, implemented, and evaluated regularly. Furthermore, the task force is charged with coordinating company-wide initiatives for access and accommodation.

Step Four: Developing a Working Plan

Once feedback has been received from co-workers and management, individualized working plans can be developed. This process involves pooling and analyzing all the ideas and feedback that have been generated and collected. The deaf employee's job description and career goals also go into the "information hopper." The creation of a working plan for accommodation and change involves at least four sequential activities.

First, crucial areas are identified in which barriers to equal access exist or improvements need to be made. It is very important that everyone's perspectives regarding what is critical are considered. This is not a prioritized list. The goal at this point is simply to include all areas which are viewed as critical to successful accommodation of the employee.

Mark and Nancy list six areas which they feel must be addressed: (1) interactive distance communication (i.e., communication usually handled through the telephone), (2) weekly team meetings, (3) monthly department meetings, (4) inservice training, (5) informal communication within the team regarding projects (the creative loop described earlier), and (6) need for increased knowledge and understanding of issues related to deafness on the part of hearing co-workers.

Second, every possible solution or intervention is described, including the most modest and/or inexpensive as well as those which are radical and/or expensive. As an example, Mark and Nancy list five possible solutions to distance communication: (1) continue to reassign phone responsibilities to another team member, (2) use electronic mail, (3) purchase a TDD for Mark and use the state relay service, (4) purchase a

TDD for Mark and five (or 10, 15, etc.) "floaters" to be assigned to those departments which Mark calls most often, or (5) purchase TDDs for every phone at New Age Software.

Third, the areas identified for change are prioritized. Criteria to be considered in prioritizing should include job performance (quality and productivity), job satisfaction, and career development. Often, access to telephones and meetings are listed as most critical. However, depending on the requirements of the job, other areas of activity may prove even more important. For example, both Mark and Nancy agree that being able to participate in informal discussions among team members regarding current projects is more important to Mark's work than having an interpreter for weekly team meetings (where the focus is often simply a review or elaboration of information already covered in inter-office memoranda).

Their prioritized list reads as follows: (1) informal communication within the team regarding projects, (2) interactive distance communication, (3) inservice training, (4) monthly department meetings, (5) weekly team meetings, and (6) increased knowledge and understanding of issues related to deafness on the part of hearing co-workers.

Fourth, specific recommendations for strategies and interventions to be employed within each of the top priority areas are made. This activity requires analysis of both company resources and the impact of change on the productivity of the employee and team. In most cases, such analysis will result in recommendations for both short- and long-term goals. It also results in distinctions between recommendations which can be handled within the department and those which are company wide. Individual employees and their supervisors can work on changes within the department; strategies for company-wide accommodations should be coordinated with the Accommodation Task Force described earlier.

As Nancy and Mark develop their plan, they place the greatest emphasis on strategies that address areas assigned the highest priority levels. Other strategies are incorporated whenever possible, or built into later stages of the plan. For example, interactive distance communication emerged as an area requiring immediate attention. In reviewing their options, they decide that strategies one and five regarding telephone access are both unacceptable. Reassigning Mark's phone work to others does both him and them a disservice. Yet the company cannot afford to purchase five hundred TDDs, nor is it clear that this would be the most efficient use of the limited resources available. They decide to purchase two TDDs; one for Mark and one to be used as a department "floater." This will facilitate Mark's contact with other departments and external clientele. The floater can be used within the company on an "as needed" basis for loan to co-workers with whom Mark is working closely on a project requiring extensive direct contact.

They also decide to convert to electronic mail as an alternative routine form of distance communication. While this does not permit the interactive conversations possible by phone, it does provide quick and relatively direct communication between individuals within the company. Conversion within the Development Team will be immediate, with expansion to the department level over the next six months.

The long range goal is to implement regular use of electronic mail on a company-wide basis over the next two years and will require coordination with the Accommodation Task Force. With input from Mark, Nancy prepares a plan for accomplishing this goal and presents it to the task force. Her plan includes a rationale for the conversion which emphasizes benefits to *all* employees (such as the ability to leave detailed messages and organize mail conversations through the use of the electronic "file" system), timelines, specific strategies, and resources required for implementation.

A second benefit of this decision is the rediscovery of a related computer program called "bulletin board." Mark and Nancy believe this program can be used to share "in person" information within the team which traditionally is communicated orally. While they recognize that old habits die hard, they plan to campaign strongly for use of the board as an alternative for sharing ideas. (Also on this topic, they were unable to get new office space and furniture; but they did take down the old partitions and have added a huge chalkboard to their work area on which everyone can draw or describe new ideas.)

Step Five: Monitoring the Plan

There are two major reasons for monitoring accessibility and accommodation plans. The first is to insure that the plan is followed. As noted in Step Four, most plans have long-term, as well as immediate, goals, as well as team/department-based goals and company-wide goals. Often the long term, company-wide goals are the most ambitious or costly. In order to insure that progress towards these goals is being made, regular updates and review are needed. Often, intermediate steps must be identified and evaluated as measures of progress.

The decision to shift from phone to electronic mail as a means of routine communication at New Age Software provides a good example of an extremely ambitious long range, company-wide goal. Intermediate steps include the extension of this practice to other teams within the Department of Business Applications and later to other departments within the Division for Product Development. These intermediate goals can be broken down even further into specific activities, such as strategies and timelines for the dissemination of information to different departments regarding the use of electronic mail.

The Accommodation Task Force must be heavily involved in developing company-wide accommodation plans and assuring that goals are met. It is critical that the task force have the support of management and be viewed as representing the attitude and philosophy of top level managers towards accommodation and access. Regular reports should be required in which progress towards goals is described and problems aired and resolved.

The second reason for monitoring accommodation and accessibility plans is to insure that they are still reasonable and appropriate in light of changes, both within and external, to the organization. Suppose, for example, that New Age Software experienced an unexpected banner year in sales; this might warrant implementation of a more costly long term strategy ahead of schedule, or even a complete overhaul of the plan. Or, perhaps, all efforts to encourage use of electronic mail have failed; such a development might lead to revisions of the plan, with greater emphasis being placed on allocation of funds to purchase additional TDDs.

It is important that regular meetings be scheduled to review and revise plans and that schedules be followed. Generally, there is a greater need for frequent monitoring during the first months of a plan. The reason is that most accommodation plans require changes in the behavior of people. Often, there is initial resistance to the proposed change. Sometimes, people mean well but find it difficult to change old habits or expectations. Also, there are bound to be glitches in even the best plans. These need to be resolved if the plan is to be effective and the goals achieved.

Again, the Accommodation Task Force plays a pivotal role, since they set the standard for appropriate levels of behavior and commitment to change. If the task force is viewed as powerless, or its members are seen as failing to practice what they require of others, then the signal is sent that recommendations can be ignored and resources used elsewhere.

It is also critical that accommodations at the team level are carefully monitored, since even in these settings there are bound to be challenges to intervention and change. For example, Mark and Nancy decided that interpreters would be hired for in-service training programs, appraisal meetings, and monthly department meetings. Weekly team meetings would be handled through agendas, minutes, and (when necessary) a one-to-one follow up in which Nancy would meet with Mark and review ideas covered at the meeting.

For the first month, weekly meetings went much more smoothly for Mark; he received agendas and minutes regularly and met with Nancy whenever he needed clarification or wanted to follow up on something. But by the second month, Mark noticed that the quality of the minutes was deteriorating, and there was no agenda provided for two meetings. He mentioned this to Nancy, but the problem persisted.

There was a scheduled meeting at the end of the third month to review the accommodation plan. At this time, Mark renewed his concerns with agendas and minutes from recent meetings, documenting those times at which problems occurred. Nancy apologized, explaining that she was finding it very difficult to take notes and run the meeting, adding that it was also time consuming to write up the minutes. She also said that sometimes people would add topics for discussion at the last minute, after the agenda had already been typed.

After discussion, it was decided to rotate responsibility for the minutes among team members. This was not perceived as a hardship, because the responsibility would only fall about once every three months to each of the twelve team members. Guidelines for taking notes and preparing minutes were developed, to insure a higher level of detail and comprehensiveness. A policy was established requiring that all topics for discussion at Thursday team meetings be submitted to Nancy by Wednesday noon. Any topics submitted after that time would be placed on the agenda for the following week, no exceptions.

KEYS FOR SUCCESS

It is very likely that at least some readers are shaking their heads sadly at the story of New Age Software. "What a Pollyana story!" they say.

"That looks great on paper, but it could never happen here." Or, "Another task force? They're doomed already!"

These opinions may well be correct. When offering possible solutions to extremely complex problems, one always runs the risk of appearing naive, simplistic, unrealistic, or just plain out of touch. But one must start somewhere. The scenario of New Age Software is just one example, and Mark and Nancy's experiences cannot be generalized to represent the experiences of others. The ecological model must be adapted according to the environments and individuals in each workplace, taking into account the resources, skills, and creativity of the organization and the people who work there.

Regardless of the specifics of the situation, there are two conditions which are central to the successful development and implementation of a plan for accommodation. First, the entire process revolves around a shared responsibility. The perspectives of both supervisors and deaf employees are critical to the development and execution of an appropriate and realistic plan. Co-workers and upper level managers must also be committed to improving the situation. Everyone must be motivated to make the plan work. Plans developed in isolation or without the support of management are almost certainly doomed to failure.

Second, if there are areas of disagreement, participants must try to achieve resolution through discussion and, where necessary, compromise. Failure to resolve fundamental questions regarding which areas of access are critical, or which strategies to use, will generally result in a non-productive stalemate, or worse, abandonment of the entire enterprise. Only when every effort to reach agreement has failed should employees or supervisors seek external advice or redress. Similarly, co-workers and upper management must be willing to compromise in order to make the plan succeed.

Recall the response of Mark's co-workers to the idea that they learn sign language and attend local seminars about deafness. They were willing, but only if it didn't interfere with their free time. For her part, Nancy didn't mind sending staff to occasional seminars, but was reluctant to let them take time away from routine work in order to attend a weekly sign language class. Upper management was unwilling to pay for either seminars or sign language classes. After much debate, it was decided to allocate funds to sponsor three on-site seminars on issues related to deafness; the initial seminar would occur during the first year and the other two, during the second year of the plan. Mark offered to teach a one-year course in basic sign language, at no cost to New Age Software. The class was scheduled for one hour each week, thirty minutes being taken from the lunch hour and thirty minutes from work time. Both Mark and his colleagues who took the class were officially recognized for their participation through annual appraisals.

Additionally, management established an annual budget for the Accommodation Task Force, as well as smaller line items for individual departments. This money was allocated for the purpose of providing necessary accommodations for Mark and other employees with disabilities. This was a critical step, since it reflected a commitment on the part of New Age Software to its disabled employees and guaranteed a minimum level of funding for accommodation.

CONCLUSION

As stated at the beginning of this book, being a supervisor is not easy. Yet, as the reader has no doubt concluded by now, neither is it easy to be a deaf employee in a "hearing" workplace. Communication differences challenge both deaf and hearing people to be creative, flexible, and patient in their efforts to work together productively and enjoyably. But the talents of deaf colleagues are far too valuable a resource to be ignored; if deaf workers are not accommodated within the workplace and accepted as partners and equals in the American enterprise, everyone loses.

Hopefully, this book offers both deaf and hearing persons some ideas about how to work well together. It is by no means comprehensive, nor is it the final word. However, if, in reading these pages, supervisors find ways to make the workplace more accessible for employees who are deaf, or deaf employees find strategies to advocate for accommodation in their work environments, then this book will have been a success, and well worth the effort.

RESOURCE LIST

Library Resources

Books and articles listed in this section should be available at local public or college/university libraries or through the interlibrary loan services at these libraries. Purchase prices listed may vary and are indicated only to give the reader a general idea of cost; contact the publisher directly for current cost and shipping/handling charges.

Berkay, P.J. "The Establishment of a Deaf Employment Task Force in a Major Corporation." *Journal of the American Deafness and Rehabilitation Association, 24*(3/4): 81–85, 1991.

> The authors propose a model for a Deaf Employment Task Force in a major corporation based on a case study of a similar task force established in a Fortune 500 corporation. The model's components are based on the successes and failures of this case study.

Bowe, F. *Personal Computers and Special Needs.* Silver Spring, MD: National Association of the Deaf, 1984. (Available from National Association of the Deaf, 814 Thayer Avenue, Silver Spring, MD 20910; Phone 301-587-6282 [Voice/TDD]; Order No. F1004; Cost $9.95)

> This book shows how personal computers are changing the lives of disabled people. It discusses how and where to purchase computers, software, and adaptive services.

DuBow, S., et al. *Legal Rights of Hearing Impaired People.* 3rd ed. Washington, DC: Gallaudet University Press, 1986. (Available from Gallaudet University Press, Box 90, 800 Florida Avenue, NE, Washington, DC 20002-3695; Phone 1-800-451-1073 [Voice/TDD]; Order no. 2727; ISBN 0-930323-25-4; Cost: $13.95)

> *Legal Rights* includes the latest Federal and state statutes and administrative procedures that prohibit discrimination against handicapped people. There is a chapter on employment which includes information on Affirmative Action, reasonable accommodations, and enforcement procedures.

Disability Compliance Bulletin. Horsham, PA: LRP Publications. (Available from LRP Publications, 747 Dresher Road, P.O. Box 980, Horsham, PA 19044-0980; Phone 800-341-7874 [Voice]; Fax 215-784-9639; Cost $125/year)

> Updated twice a month, the *Disability Compliance Bulletin* provides up-to-date information on disability law at the Federal and state levels. It also includes articles by experts in the field about the challenging and exciting aspects of the ADA and existing statutes and regulations and provides complete and current case summaries of Federal and state judicial decisions and Federal policy rulings covering the legal aspects of disability rights.

Handbook of Job Analysis for Reasonable Accommodation. (PMS-720-B, Personnel Management Series). Washington, DC: U.S. Office of Personnel Management, 1982. (Available from Superintendent of Documents,

U.S. Government Printing Office, Stop: SSPO, Washington, DC 20402-9328; Phone 202-783-3238 [Voice]; Order no. SN 006-000-01285-0; Cost: $3)

> This booklet focuses on a job analysis process which can be used to plan and select appropriate action(s) necessary to accommodate handicapped individuals in specific jobs and work environments.

Handbook of Selective Placement of Persons with Physical and Mental Handicaps in Federal Civil Service Employment. (OPM Doc. 125-11-3). Washington, DC: Office of Personnel Management, 1981. (Available from the Superintendent of Documents, U.S. Government Printing Office, Stop: SSOP, Washington, DC 20402-9328; Phone 202-783-3238 [Voice]; Order no. 006-000-01278-7; Cost $4.25)

> This handbook outlines concepts and procedures that can and should be used to provide equal employment opportunity for all qualified handicapped applicants and employees.

Managing End User Computing for Users with Disabilities. Washington, DC: General Services Administration, Information Resources Management Service, Clearinghouse on Computer Accommodation, [updated periodically]. (Available from Clearinghouse on Computer Accommodation, Room 2022, KGDO, 18th & F Streets NW, Washington, DC 20405; Phone 202-501-4906 [Voice], 202-501-2010 [TDD]; Cost: free)

> This handbook presents guidance to Federal managers and other personnel who are unfamiliar with the application of computer and related information technology to accommodate users with disabilities and provide for their effective access to information resources.

McCrone, W.P. "A Summary of the Americans with Disabilities Act and Its Specific Implications for Hearing Impaired People." *Journal of the American Deafness and Rehabilitation Association, 23*(3): 60–73, 1990.

> McCrone covers the effects that the Americans with Disabilities Act will have on employment of persons with hearing impairments, public services, accommodations by private businesses, and telecommunications.

Morrissey, P.A. Human Resource Executive's Survival Guide to the Americans with Disabilities Act. Horsham, PA: LRP Publications, [1992]. (Available from LRP Publications, 747 Dresher Road, P.O. Box 980, Horsham, PA 19044-0980; Phone 800-341-7874 [Voice]; Fax 215-784-9639; Cost $135.00)

> This book explains what the ADA requires, helps readers to weigh the extent of their need to accommodate, reveals what prior legal decisions predict, and describes what needs to be done to get and stay in compliance.

Morrissey, P.A. *A Primer for Corporate America on Civil Rights for the Disabled.* Horsham, PA: LRP Publications, 1991. (Available from LRP Publications, 747 Dresher Road, P.O. Box 980, Horsham, PA 19044-0980; Phone 800-341-7874 [Voice]; Fax 215-784-9639; Cost: $12.95)

> The book illustrates the major provisions of the ADA with examples from everyday life, while respecting the meaning of key legal concepts. A full text of the Americans with Disabilities Act of 1990 is included.

NARIC Quarterly: A Newsletter of Disability and Rehabilitation Research and Resources. (Available by subscription from NARIC, Suite 935, Silver Spring, MD 20910-3319; Phone 800-346-2742 [Voice/TDD]; Cost: free)

> This newsletter, as indicated by its title, offers information on disability issues: upcoming meetings, programs, sources of information, services for disabled people, and short research articles.

Steffanic, D.J., with Smith, D.J. (Ed.). *Reasonable Accommodation for Deaf Employees in Federal White Collar Jobs.* Washington, DC: U.S. Office of Personnel Management, Office of Personnel Research and Development, 1991. (Contact the author, D. Steffanic, 1900 E Street NW, Washington, DC 20415, for availability)

> The results of an extensive survey of the Federal government, Steffanic's report presents statistics on where deaf employees are located within the Federal bureaucracy, the kinds of positions they hold, and how they are managing in their positions.

Steffanic, D.J. *Reasonable Accommodations for Deaf Employees in White Collar Jobs.* Washington, DC: U.S. Office of Personnel Management, Office of Personnel Research and Development, 1982. (Available from the National Association of the Deaf, 814 Thayer Avenue, Silver Spring, MD 20910; Phone 301-587-6282 [Voice/TDD]; Order no. RB007; Cost: $4.00 paper copy)

> Steffanic discusses the implications of hearing loss, means of communication among deaf and hearing persons, and makes suggestions for work accommodations and job modifications for deaf employees.

Tucker, B.P., and Goldstein, B.A. *Legal Rights of Persons with Disabilities: An Analysis of Federal Law.* Horsham, PA: LRP Publications, 1991. (Available from LRP Publications, P. O. Box 980, 747 Dresher Road, Horsham, PA 19044-0980; Phone 800-341-7874 [Voice]; ISBN 0-934753-46-6; Cost: $85.00 with binder)

> This hard bound, loose-leaf, very comprehensive work focuses on current forms of discrimination against disabled Americans and the major Federal laws aimed at alleviating such discrimination.

West, J. *The Americans With Disabilities Act: From Policy to Practice.* New York: Milbank Memorial Fund, 1991. (Available from Milbank Memorial Fund, 1 East 75th Street, New York, NY 10021-2693; Phone 212-570-4850 [Voice]; Cost: $8.95)

> This book presents a description and analysis of the ADA's requirements, as well as a synthesis of research and experience that will promote its effective implementation. It is a resource for small and large employers; business and industry; local, state, and federal officials; persons with disabilities; agencies that provide services for persons with disabilities; journalists; researchers; public policy analysts; and those involved in technical assistance.

Pamphlets and Brochures

The Americans with Disabilities Act: Questions and Answers. Washington, DC: U.S. Department of Justice, Civil Rights Division, Office on the Americans with Disabilities Act, 1991. (Available from Office on the Americans with Disabilities Act, Civil Rights Division, U.S. Department of Justice, P.O. Box 66118, Washington, DC 20035-6118; Phone 202-514-0301 [Voice], 202-514-0381 [TDD], 202-514-0383 [TDD])

> In lay terms and in a question/answer format, this booklet covers frequently asked questions about the ADA in terms of employment and public accommodations. Several Federal contacts are listed at the end to answer specific questions.

The Americans with Disabilities Act: An Easy Checklist. 1990. (Available from National Easter Seal Society, 70 East Lake Street, Chicago, IL 60601; Phone 312-726-6200 [Voice], 312-726-4258 [TDD]; Cost: $1.40)

> This booklet was prepared to assist corporations and businesses in evaluating their own policies and procedures for compliance with ADA requirements.

Fact sheets about the Americans with Disabilities Act (ADA) are available in a variety of formats from the Federal government. Paper copies can be obtained from the U.S. Justice Department, Coordinations and Review Section, Civil Rights Division, Box 66118, Washington, DC 20035; Phone 202-514-0301 [voice], 202-514-0381 [TDD]. Audio-cassette copies are available from the Senate Disability Policy Office, Hart Senate Office Building, SH113, Washington, DC 20510; Phone 202-224-6265 [Voice], 202-224-3457 [TDD]. Computer users can access the Justice Department's electronic file and bulletin board via modem by dialing 202-514-6193.

State-Wide Services for Deaf and Hard of Hearing Persons. (Available from National Information Center on Deafness, Gallaudet University, 800

Florida Avenue NE, Washington, DC 20002-3695; Phone 202-651-5051 [Voice], 202-651-5052 [TDD]; Order no. 501; Cost: $1.00)

> This publication lists states that have established commissions and other offices to serve deaf and hard-of-hearing people. These offices provide advocacy, information and referral, interpreting services, statewide planning, and job development.

Media

The Americans with Disabilities Act: New Access to the Workplace [video]. Northbrook, IL: MTI Film & Video, 1991. (Available from MTI Film & Video, 420 Academy Drive, Northbrook, IL 60062; Phone 800-621-2131 [Voice]; Cost $415.00)

> This workshop package includes a video, Leader's Guide, and 10 Participant's Workbooks, and outlines the ADA law, the reasons behind it, and the ways it can help your organization compete. The video portion of the workshop examines the ADA through workplace interviews, dramatic vignettes, and information from on-camera hosts. The Participant's Workbook adds exercises, discussions, and role-plays.

Contacts

Alexander Graham Bell Association for the Deaf
3417 Volta Place, NW
Washington, DC 20007
202-337-5220 (TDD and Voice)

> The A. G. Bell Association for the Deaf promotes the teaching of speech, lipreading, and the use of residual hearing to the deaf. They conduct workshops, offer educational scholarships for oral deaf adults, and publish the journal *Volta Review.*

American Deafness and Rehabilitation Association
P.O. Box 21554
Little Rock, AR 72225
501-663-7074 (TDD and Voice)

> ADARA is a partnership of national organizations, local affiliates, professional sections, and individual members working together to support deafness, social services, and rehabilitation delivery. Contact them for referral to local rehabilitation agencies and to subscribe to their journal and newsletter.

Association for Late-Deafened Adults
P.O. Box 641763
Chicago, IL 60664-1763
312-604-4192 (TDD)

Late-deafened adults are people who grew up in the hearing world and became deaf as adolescents or adults. ALDA provides an outlet where monthly activities give ALDAans a chance to mingle without being uncomfortable about deafness. *ALDA News,* the Association's newsletter, is a forum on issues relevant to people who are deafened later in life.

Better Hearing Institute
Box 1840
Washington, DC 20013
703-642-0580 (TDD and Voice)

The purpose of the Better Hearing Institute is to inform the hearing public and the hearing-impaired public about the nature of hearing loss and the available medical, surgical, rehabilitative, and amplification help.

Equal Employment Opportunity Commission
1801 L Street, NW
Washington, DC 20507
202-663-7026 (TDD)
202-663-4691 (Voice)

The Equal Employment Opportunity Commission is a valuable resource for interpretation of Federal regulations and policy. It also develops and distributes literature on this topic.

National Association of the Deaf
814 Thayer Avenue
Silver Spring, MD 20910
301-587-1789 (TDD)
301-587-1788 (Voice)

The NAD serves to protect the civil rights of deaf citizens in the area of employment. Rehabilitative services include educational opportunities and mental health services.

National Center for Law and the Deaf
800 Florida Avenue at 7th Street, NE
Washington, DC 20002
202-651-5373 (TDD and Voice)

This Center provides and develops legal representation, information and services, legal counseling, education, and advocacy for deaf persons. They also help hearing-impaired students entering law school.

Self Help for Hard of Hearing People
7800 Wisconsin Avenue
Bethesda, MD 20814
301-657-2249 (TDD)
301-657-2248 (Voice)

> SHHH helps to educate members and the public on the nature, cause, and complications of hearing loss and instructs them in its detection, management, and the possible prevention of hearing loss.

State Coordinators of Rehabilitation Services for Deaf Persons

> The scope of services varies from state to state, but in general these programs provide a variety of services, including advocacy, information gathering and dissemination, referral to appropriate agencies, interpreting services, state-wide planning, job placement and development. For a list of these offices, see *State-Wide Services for Deaf and Hard of Hearing Persons* in section on *Pamphlets*.

State Offices/Commissions on Deafness

> Many states have specific offices which provide services to deaf and hard-of-hearing individuals and assist in educating the public and employers about the special needs of hearing-impaired persons. For a list of these offices, see *State-Wide Services for Deaf and Hard of Hearing Persons* in section on *Pamphlets*.

U.S. Justice Department
Coordination and Review Section
Civil Rights Division
Box 66118
Washington, DC 20035
202-514-0381 (TDD)
202-514-0301 (Voice)

> Fact sheets on the Americans with Disabilities Act (ADA) are available from the U.S. Justice Department in a variety of formats. Computer users can also access the Justice Department's electronic file and bulletin board by using a modem and dialing 202-514-6193.

U.S. Senate
Disability Policy Office
Hart Senate Office Building
SH113
Washington, DC 20510
202-224-3457 (TDD)
202-224-6265 (Voice)

The text of the Americans with Disabilities Act (ADA) is available on audio-cassette from the Senate Disability Policy Office.

ENDNOTES

1. The phrase "protected class" is used here in the sense of a group of people who, on the basis of some shared characteristic (i.e., age, gender, minority status, disability) are protected by law from unequal treatment or other discrimination.

2. New Age Software is a fictitious company intended to illustrate concepts of accessibility and accommodation.

BIBLIOGRAPHY

Allen, T. (1987). Understanding the scores: Hearing-impaired students and the Stanford Achievement Test. In A. Schildroth and M. Karchmer (Eds.), *Deaf Children in America.* Washington, DC: Gallaudet University Press.

Allen, T., Rawlings, B., & Schildroth, A. (1989). *Deaf Students and the School-To-Work Transition.* Baltimore, MD: Paul H. Brooks.

Bailey, T. (1990) Changes in the nature and structure of work: implications for skill requirements and skill formation. Berkeley, CA: National Center for Research in Vocational Education, University of California, Berkeley.

Barnartt, S.B. & Christiansen, J.B. (1985). The socioeconomic status of deaf workers: A minority group perspective. *Social Science Journal, 32:* 19–32.

Boatner, E.B., Stuckless, E.R., & Moores, D.F. (1964). *Occupational status of the young deaf adult of New England.* Washington, DC: Vocational Rehabilitation Administration, Department of Health, Education and Welfare.

Bogdan, R. & Biklen, S. (1982). *Qualitative Research for Education: An Introduction to Theory and Methods.* Boston: Allyn and Bacon.

Bogdan, R. & Taylor, S. (1975). *Introduction to Qualitative Research Methods: A Phenomenological Approach to the Social Sciences.* New York: John Wiley.

Bronfenbrenner, U. (1979) *The Ecology of Human Development: Experiments by Nature and Design.* Cambridge, MA: Harvard University Press.

Coates, J.F., Jarratt, J., & Mahaffie, J.B. (1990) *Future Work: Seven Critical Forces Reshaping Work and the Work Force in North America.* San Francisco, CA: Jossey-Bass.

Crammatte, A.B. (1968). *Deaf Persons in Professional Employment.* Springfield, IL: Charles C Thomas.

Crammatte, A.B. (1987). *Meeting the Challenge: Hearing-Impaired Professionals in the Workplace.* Washington, DC: Gallaudet University Press.

Emerton, R.G., Foster, S., & Royer, H. (1987). The impact of changing technology on the employment of a group of older deaf workers. *Journal of the American Deafness and Rehabilitation Association, 21:* 6–18.

Foster, S. (1987). Employment experiences of deaf RIT graduates. *Journal of the American Deafness and Rehabilitation Association. 21:* 1–15.

Gallaudet University Factbook. Office of Institutional Research, Planning and Evaluation at Gallaudet University (1989). Washington, DC.

Johnston, W.B. (1987). *Workforce 2000.* Indianapolis, IN: Hudson Institute.

Kutscher, R. (1987). Overview and implications of the projections to 2000. *Monthly Labor Review,* September, 3–9.

229

Liscio, M.A. (1986). *A Guide to Colleges for Hearing-Impaired Students.* Orlando, FL: Academic Press.

Lunde, R.S. & Bigman, S.K. (1959). *Occupational Conditions Among the Deaf: A Report of a National Survey.* Washington, DC: Gallaudet College.

MacLeod-Gallinger, J. (1991). The status of deaf women: A comparative look at the labor force, educational, and occupational attainments of deaf female secondary graduates. Paper presented at the annual meeting of the American Educational Research Association, Chicago.

National Technical Institute for the Deaf, a college of Rochester Institute of Technology. *FY91 Annual Report (1991),* Rochester, NY.

Padden, C. & Humphries, T. (1988) *Deaf in America: Voices from a Culture.* Cambridge, MA: Harvard University Press.

Rawlings, B.A., Karchmer, M.A., DeCaro, J.J. & Allen, T.E. (1991). *College & Career Programs for Deaf Students.* Washington, DC: Gallaudet University, and Rochester, NY: Rochester Institute of Technology, National Technical Institute for the Deaf.

Rawlings, B.A. & King, S.J. (1987). Postsecondary educational opportunities for deaf children. In A.N. Shildroth and M.A. Karchmer (Eds). *Deaf Children in America,* San Diego, CA: College-Hill Press.

Schein, J.D. & Delk, M.T. (1974). *The Deaf Population of the United States.* Silver Spring, MD: National Association of the Deaf.

Spradley, J. (1979). *The Ethnographic Interview.* New York: Holt, Rinehart and Winston.

Van Cleve, J.V. & Crouch, B.A. (1989). *A Place of Their Own.* Washington, DC: Gallaudet University Press.

Walter, G. (1992). Characteristics of programs serving deaf persons. In S. Foster & G. Walter, (Eds.), *Deaf Students in Postsecondary Education.* London: Routledge, 24–42.

Weinrich, J.E. (1972). Direct economic costs of deafness in the United States. *American Annals of the Deaf, 117:* 446–454.

Welsh, W. & Walter, G. (1988). The effect of postsecondary education on the occupational attainment of deaf adults. *Journal of the American Deafness and Rehabilitation Association, 22:* 14–22.

Welsh, W. & MacLeod-Gallinger, J. (1992). *Effect of college on employment and earnings: Deaf students in postsecondary education.* In S. Foster & G. Walter, (Eds.), *Deaf Students in Postsecondary Education.* London: Routledge, 185–209.

Williams, B.R. & Sussman, A.E. (1971). Social and psychological problems of deaf people. In E.E. Sussman, and G.L. Stewart, (Eds.). *Counseling with Deaf People.* New York: Deafness Research and Training Center, New York University.

Woodward, J. (1972) Implications for sociolinguistics research among the deaf. *Sign Language Studies, 1:* 1–7.

INDEX

A

Advocate role of supervisors, 182–183
  facilitating communications, 183
  influence on other employees, 182–183
  use of term advocate, 182
Alexander Graham Bell Association for the
    Deaf, 224
Allen, T., 17, 18, 19, 229, 230
American Deafness and Rehabilitation
    Association, 224
American Disabilities Act of 1990 (ADA)
  as motivation for supervisors, 178
  interpretation of, 3–4
  mandates of, vii–viii, 3
  use to obtain accommodations at work,
    192–193
American Sign Language (ASL) (*see also*
    Interpreter services)
  importance of, 68–69
  use of, 9
Association for Late-Deafened Adults, 225

B

Background and history of research, 3–20
  autobiographies of discussants, 9–12
  deaf employees interviewed, 8
  description supervisors interviewed, 8
  discussion group, 8–9
  interview approach used, 6–7
  interview study description, 6–8
  method of study, 6–7
  organizations categorized, 7
  purpose of study, 3–6
  selection of supervisor/interviewees, 6
Bailey, T., 19, 229
Barnartt, S. B., 18, 229
Better Hearing Institute, 225

Bigman, S. K., 17, 230
Biklen, S., 6, 7, 229
Boatner, E. B., 17, 229
Bogdan, R., 6, 7, 229
Bronfenbrenner, U., 205, 229
Buddy system, use of, 95–96, 129

C

Career Center, Gallaudet University, 169
Center for Postsecondary Career Studies in
    Deafness, 55–56
Christiansen, J. B., 18, 229
Closing the Gap, 198
Coates, J. F., 19, 229
Communication deaf and hearing people,
    57–106
  at meetings, 61–66
    actions of supervisors, 64–65
    presentations by deaf employee, 65–66
    problems encountered, 64
    use of interpreters, 61–63
  buddy system used, 95–96, 129
  characteristics of participants, 73–80
    as a partnership supervisor and deaf
        person, 79
    commitment, 78–79
    familiarity, 80
    flexibility, 36–38
    interpersonal skills, 77–78
    reactions of supervisors, 75
    willingness and ability to provide
        and/or use information, 73–75
  commentary, 88–97
  complications of, 87
  conditions influencing, 72–86
    characteristics of participants, 73–80
    environmental conditions, 72–73
    purpose of communication, 81–86

231

Communication deaf and hearing people
(*Continued*)
  discussion, 86–87
  environmental conditions influencing,
    72–73
  in the workplace, 57
  informal, at work, 95–96
  one-to-one, 67–72
    gestures, 71
    lipreading and speaking, 67–69
    miscommunication, 68
    reading and writing, 69–70
    sign language, 70–71
  purpose of, 81–86
    informal conversations, 81, 84
    understanding work tasks, 81
    use grapevine to disseminate informa-
      tion, 82–86
  resource list, 97–106
  strategies described, 58–72
  summary, 71–72
  using the telephone, 58–61
    from home to work, 58
    use assistive devices, 59–60
    use of E-mail, 61
    use of TDD, 58
    within the workplace, 58–59
Contact resources, 13, 54–56, 104–106, 140,
  169–170, 198–199, 224–227
Crammatte, A. B., 18, 229
Crouch, B. A., 15, 230

D

Deaf people as employees
  Americans With Disabilities Act, 3–4
  characteristics of as an employee, 110–117
    (*see also* Relationships with hearing
    people at work)
  commentary regarding job interviews of,
    42–51
  compensatory effort for, 40
  communication barriers faced by, 41–42
  factors in employment of
    barriers to advanced positions, 18
    basic skills needed, 19
    demands for communication skills, 19
    educational opportunities, 15

effect on employment circumstances of
    deaf persons, 17–18
  employer-sponsored training, 19–20
  macro level changes in work force, 19–
    20
  need for literacy skills, 19
  summary, 20
fair treatment of mandated, 3
hiring of (*see* Hiring of deaf persons)
history of employment circumstances of,
  15–20
  during W W I, 15
  early learning job by observation, 15
  factory work, 15
  past common vocational training
    occupations, 15
importance personal qualities in evaluation, 40–41
interview study with supervisors (*see*
  Interview study)
problems due inability to hear self, 190–192
relationship education & level economic
  achievement, v
research background (*see* Background and
  history of research)
resource lists, 12–13
responsibility to teach others about deafness, 190
role of supervisors in work place, 3–4
special accommodations for, 40
training for employment (*see* Training)
unintentional exclusion from communications, 81–85, 86–87
Deafness syndrome, 145
DeCaro, J. J., 17, 230
Delk, M. T., 18, 230

E

Ecological model of human behavior, 205–
  217
  basis of, 205
  blueprint for accommodation, 206–217
    describing ecology of workplace,
      206–207
    developing a working plan, 213–215
    diagram illustrating, 208
    monitoring the plan, 215–217
    taking inventory, 207–211

Ecological model of human behavior
  (*Continued*)
    use of, 207
    writing prescription for accommoda-
      tion, 211–213
  conclusion, 219
  describing ecology of workplace, 206–207
  development of a working plan, 213–215
    benefits of, 215
    description possible solutions and
      intervention, 213–214
    identification crucial areas, 213
    identification priority changes, 214–215
  drawing of, 205–206
  keys for success, 217–219
    resolution disagreements, 218–219
    shared responsibility, 218
    use Accommodation Task Force, 219
  monitoring the plan, 215–217
    purposes of, 215
    results of, 217
    role of Accommodation Task Force,
      216–217
  taking inventory, 207–211
    analysis of environments, 209
    analysis of individuals, 209
    assessment of managements position,
      209
    implications of ADA, 210–211
    of external environments, 209
    purpose of, 207
  use of, 205
  writing prescription for accommodation,
    211–213
    compliance with ADA, 212–213
    desire for TDD's and interpreters, etc.,
      211–212
    development description ideal work
      environment, 211
Education of the Handicapped Act, 1973, Section 504, 17
Electronic mail system (*see* E-mail)
E-mail, use of, 61, 164–165, 215
Emerton, R. G., 16, 229
Entrepreneur role of deaf person, 175–177
  difficulties of, 176–177
  elements necessary for, 175–176
  use of terms entrepreneur and enterprise,
    175

Environmental conditions at work
  break patterns established, 109–110
  factors in, 108
  size and physical layout of organization,
    108
  type of work performed, 109
Equal Employment Opportunity Commission,
  225
Evaluations of deaf employee's potential,
  141–170
  accommodation, 150–152
  attitudes of others, 152–154
  barriers to, 158
  commentary, 158–167
  communication skills, 150–151, 158
  constraints, 150–151
  Deafness syndrome, 145
  discussion, 154–157
  emphasis on personal qualities, 155
  experiences of deaf persons with, 159–162
  method of study, 141
  need understand & willingness of promo-
    tion process, 155–156
  overcoming barriers for selection of deaf
    person, 166–167
  personal qualities of employee
    ability to deal with pressure, 144–145
    ambition, 145–147
    assertiveness and self-confidence, 143–
      144
    interpersonal skills, 147–148
    willingness to take risks, 146
  promotion needs target both hearing &
    deaf employees, 156–157
  resource list, 167–170
  responses of supervisors to question, 141–
    142
  special needs and awareness of needs,
    154–155
  technical skills of employee, 142
  understanding management culture, 149
  use of E-mail by deaf person, 164–165
  use of relay service to communicate, 162–
    164
  writing skills, 150
Evaluation of deaf workers, 31–40
  evaluations received on the job, 48
  of personal qualities, 31, 34–40, 40–41
    flexibility, 36–38

Evaluation of deaf workers (*Continued*)
    good judgment, 38
    importance of, 50
    motivation, 36
    willingness to work, 34–36
    working with others, 36–38
  of technical skills, 31–32, 33–34
    changes in, 32
    definition, 31
    importance of, 50
    supervisor's concerns, 33–34
  summary, 39–40
Experiential Programs Off Campus, 54

F

Foster, Susan B., v, ix, 16, 18, 21, 141, 229, 230
Foundation for Science and the Handicapped,
    169–170

G

Gallaudet University
  awareness abilities of deaf persons move-
    ment, 196
  description, 16
Gestures, use for communication, 71

H

Hiring of deaf persons
  characteristics of the deaf job candidate,
    22–23
  factors in, 22
  involvement supervisors in, 21–22
  personal recommendations & connections,
    24–25
  perspective of hiring supervisor towards
    deafness, 25–26
  policy or mission of the organization, 27
  urgency & difficulty filling position, 24
Humphries, T., 56, 230

I

IBM National Support Center for Persons
    With Disabilities, 54
Interpreter services
  at group meetings, 90–92

fear of dependence, 118
fees paid for, 94, 189
presence at job interview, 44
presence at training sessions, 45, 47–49
provision of by company, 93–94
registry of, 104
use at group discussions, 8–9
use at meetings, 61–63
use for job interview, 188–189
Interview study supervisors of deaf workers
  description of, 6–8
  description organizations & persons
    involved, 7–8
  discussion group described, 8–9
    autobiographies discussants, 9–12
  organizations categorized, 7
  purpose of study, 4–5
  resource lists, 12–13
  selection supervisor interviewees, 6

J

Jarratt, J., 19, 229
Job accommodation network, 198–199
Job application
  contacts to make, 54–56
  hiring (*see* Hiring of deaf persons)
  resource list, 51–54
  use of interpreter for, 45–46
  writing "deaf" on application, 42–44
Johnston, W. B., 229

K

Karchmer, M. A., 17, 229, 230
King, S. J., 17, 230
Kutscher, R., 19, 229

L

Learner role of supervisors, 177–178
  accommodations used, 177, 195
  goals of, 178
  rejection of role, 177
  sources of motivation, 178
Library resources, 12, 51–53, 97–100, 133–137,
    167–169, 197, 198, 219–223
Liscio, M. A., 17, 230
Lunde, R. S., 17, 230

M

MacLeod-Gallinger, J., 18, 230
Mahaffie, J. B., 19, 229
Mainstream, Inc., 54–55
Management Institute, Gallaudet University, 170
Media resources, 12, 53–54, 102–104, 138–140, 198, 224
Mediator role of deaf employee, 173
Mediator role of supervisors, 178–182
   dilemma of handling all employees, 181–182
   general communication, 179
   information sharing, 179
   of relationships with co-workers, 181
   performance of work tasks, 179
   teachers, 179–180
   types mediation by supervisor, 178–179
   use of term mediator, 178
Mentor role adopted by supervisors, 183–184
   focus on abilities of deaf employee, 183–184, 194–195
   relationship deaf employee/mentor, 184
Moores, D. F., 17, 229

N

Naisbitt, 19
National Academy of Gallaudet University, 55
National Association of the Deaf, 225
National Center for Law and the Deaf, 199, 225
National Center on Employment of the Deaf (NCED), vii, 55, 170, 199
National Information Center on Deafness, 55, 140
National Institute on Deafness and Other Communication Disorders, 104
National Technical Institute of the Deaf (NTID), 6, 17
National Technical Institute for the Deaf Act, P.L. 89-36, 17
Networking, definition, 24

P

Padden, C., 56, 230
Pamphlets and brochures, 12, 53, 100–102, 137–138, 198, 223–224

Pimentel, Albert T., vi
Postsecondary education for deaf persons
   barriers preventing attendance, 16
   current postsecondary education, 16
   Gallaudet University, 16
   growth in opportunities for deaf persons, 17
   number colleges with services for deaf students, 17
   value of, 18
President's Committee on Employment of People With Disabilities, 140
Public Law 89-36, National Technical Institute for the Deaf Act, 17

R

Rawling, B. A., 17, 18, 229, 230
Reading and writing to communicate, 69–70
Registry of Interpreters for the Deaf, 104
Rehabilitation Act of 1973, Title V, Section 504, 3
Relationships with hearing people at work (*see also* Communication)
   characteristics of hearing co-workers, 113–117
      harassment, 116–117, 131
      insensitivity, 115–117, 130–131
      problems with co-workers, 113–114
      role of personality, 113
   characteristics of the deaf employee, 110–117
      attitude, 112
      interpersonal skills, 112–113
      personality, 110–112
   commentary, 123–133
   discussion, 122–123
   environmental conditions, 108–110 (*see also* Environmental conditions)
   evaluation of by supervisor, 107
   factors contributing to, 108
   length of time within the environment, 120–122
      effect of misunderstandings, 121–122
      positive effect of, 120–1221
   making friends, 123–125
   need deaf employee be open-minded, 133
   need for small groups for conversations, 125–126

Relationships with hearing people at work (*Continued*)
    preference for small company, 127–128
    resource list, 133–140
    role of communication in, 107–108 (*see also* Communication)
    supervisor support and intervention, 117–120
        as a barrier over time, 118–119
        provision positive role model, 117–118
        response to negative co-workers, 119–120
    use of buddy system, 129
Repetitive Motion Injury (RMI), due to signing, 94
Roles and responsibilities, 171–199
    collaboration employee/supervisor for success, 186–187
    commentary, 188–196
    discussion, 184–188
    influence of time on, 185
    interdependence of, 184–185
    resource list, 197–199
    responsibility supervisor for success of deaf employee, 186
    roles adopted by deaf employees, 171–177
        entrepreneur, 175–177
        mediator, 173
        super-employee, 173
        teacher, 171–172
    roles adopted by supervisors, 177–184
        advocate, 182–183
        learner, 177–178
        mediator, 178–182
        mentor, 183–184
    summary of discussion, 188
    working with deaf co-worker as normal with time, 185
Royer, H., 16, 229

S

Schein, J. D., 18, 230
Schildroth, A., 18, 229, 230
Self Help for Hard of Hearing People, 226
Sign language (*see also* Interpreter services)
    teaching co-workers to sign, 92–93
    use at work, 70–71
Spradley, J., 6, 230

Stewart, G. L., 230
Stuckless, E. R., 17, 229
Study conclusions, 201–230
    blueprint for accommodation (*see* Ecological model of human behavior)
    considerations data by supervisors, 201–202
    ecology of the workplace, 205–206
        differences versus deficiencies, 205
        model of human behavior, 205–206
    interpreting information, 202–204
        assumption positive bias, 203–204
        description participants, 204
        scope versus depth, 202–203
        size of sample, 202
        supervisors as typical, 203
        type deaf employees studied, 203
    resource list, 219–230
    use of information, 201
Super-employee role of deaf person
    definition of term, 173
    qualities associated with, 174–175, 193–194
Supervisor
    adapting workplace to deaf worker, 4
    areas where help is needed by, 4
    compensatory effort for deaf workers, 40
    considerations study data by, 201–202
    development relationship deaf worker and, 4
    factors in decision to hire a deaf person, 13–14
    handling communications (*see* Communications)
    involvement in hiring deaf persons, 21–22
        characteristics of deaf job candidate, 22–23
        factors in hiring a deaf person, 22
        personal recommendations and connections, 24–25
        perspective of hiring supervisor towards deafness, 25–26
        policy or mission of the organization, 27
    need for resource knowledge, 5
    perspectives of, 40–56
        commentary, 42–51

Supervisor (*Continued*)
    discussion, 40–42
    on evaluating (*see* Evaluating deaf
        employees)
    on hiring (*see* Hiring of deaf
        employees)
    on training (*see* Training of deaf
        employees)
    resource list, 51–56
    reactions to misinformation given deaf
        worker, 74–75
    role of, 3
    skills and personal qualities of employee,
        22–23
    special accommodations for deaf workers,
        40
    training of deaf persons (*see* Training of
        deaf persons)
    use of information from deaf worker, 75
Sussman, A. E., 18, 230

T

Taylor, S., 229
Teacher role of deaf employee
    regarding communicating, 172
    regarding deafness, 171–172, 188–190
Telecommunication Device for the Deaf
    (TDD)
    awkwardness in use of, 80
    limitations of use, 150
    problem availability of, 72–73
    resource for, 105
    use of, 4, 58, 60–61, 80, 88
Telephone use by deaf
    communication using, 58–61
    compensation for lack of access to, 35
    lack use of and effect on work, 35

placing phone number on job application,
    42–43
relay services, 104–105
resources for services, 105
Telecommunication Device for the Deaf
    (TDD) (*see* Telecommunication
    Device for the Deaf)
use of TDD/TTY by deaf employees, 88
Training of deaf persons for employment,
    27–31
    environmental conditions, 30–31
    lack interpreter during, 45–46
    need for in more than one area, 47
    need interpreters for deaf employees, 47–
        48
    no special accommodations needed, 28
    summary, 31
    use of interpreter for interview, 44
    use of special accommodations, 28–29
TTY (*see* Telecommunication Device for the
    Deaf)

U

U.S. Justice Department, Civil Rights
    Division, 226
U.S. Senate, Disability Policy Office, 226–227

V

Van Cleve, J. V., 15, 230

W

Walter, Gerard, ix, 17, 18, 230
Weinrich, J. E., 18, 230
Welsh, W., 18, 230
Williams, B. R., 18, 230
Woodward, J., 56, 230